CULTURE SHOCK!

Costa Rica

Claire Wallerstein

D0168771

Graphic Arts Center Publishing Company
Portland, Oregon

In the same series

Argentina	Denmark	Japan	South Africa
Australia	Ecuador	Korea	Spain
Austria	Egypt	Laos	Sri Lanka
Belgium	Finland	Malaysia	Sweden
Bolivia	France	Mauritius	Switzerland
Borneo	Germany	Mexico	Syria
Brazil	Greece	Morocco	Taiwan
Britain	Hong Kong	Myanmar	Thailand
California	Hungary	Nepal	Turkey
Canada	India	Netherlands	UAE
Chile	Indonesia	Norway	Ukraine
China	Iran	Pakistan	USA
Costa Rica	Ireland	Philippines	USA—The South
Cuba	Israel	Scotland	Venezuela
Czech Republic	Italy	Singapore	Vietnam

Barcelona At Your Door	New York At Your Door	A Traveler's Medical
Beijing At Your Door	Paris At Your Door	Guide
Chicago At Your Door	Rome At Your Door	A Wife's Guide
Havana At Your Door	San Francisco At Your	Living and Working
Jakarta At Your Door	Door	Abroad
Kuala Lumpur, Malaysia	Tokyo At Your Door	Personal Protection At
At Your Door		Home & Abroad
London At Your Door	A Globe-Trotter's Guide	Working Holidays
Moscow At Your Door	A Parent's Guide	Abroad
Munich At Your Door	A Student's Guide	

Illustrations by TRIGG
Photo credits: David Simson (front cover), Bes Stock (back cover), Claire Wallerstein (127, 128), Frans Baas (68, 114, 120, 124, 126, 142, 147, 152, 217, 220), Instituto Costarricense de Turismo (19, 25, 42, 52, 59, 83).

© 2003 Times Media Private Limited

This book is published by special
arrangement with Times Media Private Limited
Times Centre, 1 New Industrial Road, Singapore 536196
International Standard Book Number 1-55868-692-4
Graphic Arts Center Publishing Company 20-02102707
P.O. Box 10306 • Portland, Oregon 97296-0306 • (503) 226-2402

Printed in Singapore

To Lou and Betty, my parents, whose tales of far-flung lands first gave me a taste for travel, and to Adam for being such a rock.

CONTENTS

Acknowledgments 9
Map 10
Introduction 11

History 16

Columbus 18
Colonial times 20
Independence 23
The coming of coffee 24
William Walker 26

Railways and plantations 27
Social reform and civil war 28
Post 1948 31
Modern politics 33
Dismantling a nanny state 36

The Country 38

Farming and land distribution 40
Provinces and towns 43
Protected areas 48
The environment 56
The green dream under threat 57
Air and water pollution 61
From the frying pan into the fire? 62

The People 64

White Ticos and ideas of color 65
Black Costa Rica 67
Indigenous peoples 72
Guanacestecos or Cholos 79
Guaitil pottery 83

Bombas 84
Nicaraguans 85
Gringos 87
Quakers 88
Heroes and villians 89

Social Customs and Attitudes 97

Family and privacy 97
To 'Quedar Bien' 100
Choteo, class, and snobbery 102
Tico time and broken promises 103
Flirting and romance 104
Infidelity and machismo 106
Women 109
Homosexuality 110
Gossip 112
Natural remedies 112

Pobrecito 114
Piropos 115
Nicknames 117
The pulpería 119
National pride 119
The lottery 120
The rocking chair 121
Dress style and body image 121
Free time 123
Calendar of events/fiestas 128

Social Indicators 133

Religion and witchcraft 133
Crime 138
Culture 141
Education and literacy 146

Press and journalists 150
Soccer 151
Surfing 155

Food and Drink 157

Basic Tico fare 157
Popular dishes 160
Sweet stands 163
Fruits and vegetables 163
Afro-Caribbean food 165

Coffee 165
Other drinks 167
Alcohol 168
Alcoholism 169
Stomach cancer 171

Business Practice and Customs   173

What kind of business *175*
Opportunities from the dismantling of government monopolies *176*
Working as a foreigner in Costa Rica *177*
Types of companies *178*
Legal and other requirements for setting up business *178*
Work Force *179*
Rules for Employers *181*
Doing business ála Tica *182*

The business environment *183*
Bribery and dodgy dealings *186*
Shady characters *188*
Unions *188*
Personal and business security *189*
Intellectual property rights *189*
Translation *190*
Tax incentives *191*
Free trade zones *191*
Stock exchange *191*

Language   192

Pronunciation *194*
Stress *195*
Cognates *196*
Gender *197*
Important points of Grammar *197*
Useful basic Spanish phrases *197*
Voseo *203*
Vos or usted *204*

Tiquismos *205*
Gestures *208*
Conversation topics *210*
Insults *211*
Afro-Carribbean English *211*
Names and surnames *212*
Common abbreviations *213*

Survival Skills 214

Getting there *214*
Visas and residency *214*
Where the streets have
no name... *215*
Getting around *216*
Buying a car or bringing your
car to Costa Rica *221*
Accommodation *222*
Health *224*
Banking and money *226*
Time *228*

Business hours *228*
Power and bills *229*
Mail *229*
Telephones *229*
Television and radio *231*
Internet *231*
Gifts *231*
Shopping *232*
Tipping *232*
Plumbing *232*

Resource Guide *233*
Cultural Quiz *241*
Further Reading *248*
Do's and Don'ts Appendix *253*
Glossary *258*
The Author *260*
Index *261*

ACKNOWLEDGEMENTS

I would particularly like to thank Tía Julieta, María Fernanda, and Tina la Perrita Salchicha for giving me a home in Escazú and, for friendship, wine, and help (in varying degrees), John McCuen, Aisling Mahon, Darren Mora, the staff of the British Embassy in San José, Sergio Chávez and the anthropology students of the Universidad de Costa Rica, Randall Ortega (despite everything), and literally hundreds of other people whose humour, hospitality and tips helped my months in Costa Rica to be so much fun.

For the wonderful pictures, I would especially like to thank Frans Baas and the Instituto Costarricense de Turismo.

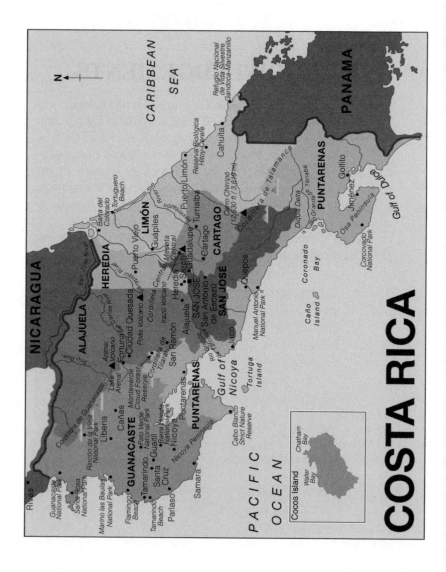

COSTA RICA

INTRODUCTION

Costa Rica was the first country in the Americas, by a few hours at any rate, to declare war on Nazi Germany and Japan after the bombing of Pearl Harbor. Hitler failed to retaliate, however, because—according to a Costa Rican joke—he couldn't find the country on his world map. It was totally obscured by a squashed fly.

The joke may be corny, but it doesn't exaggerate the Lilliputian size of Costa Rica. At 51,000 square kilometers (19,730 square miles), it is about half the size of Ireland, and yet is one of the most visited destinations in Latin America. More than one million tourists flock to this Central American nation every year, more than a third of its total population of 3.8 million (2001 estimate).

Unsurprisingly, scores of travel guides have already been written about the place. Aside from a handful of outdated or Spanish anthropological texts, however, most books limit themselves to either glossy photographs of the country's national parks and wildlife or bus timetables and restaurant reviews. The Ticos (as the Costa Ricans call themselves) are a proud people, and often complain that visitors don't really understand them.

A Costa Rican tour guide told me he regularly has to answer questions such as: "So, how far are we from San Juan?" (the capital of Puerto Rico, a different place entirely) "How big is this island?" and "Have you got any cannibals here?" "They've seen all the Discovery Channel documentaries about our wildlife and endangered species," he complained. "But what about the human species?"

The lack of information for visitors wanting more than a cursory cultural overview could have a lot to do with the fact that Costa Rican culture can seem so bland at first sight. It is almost as if the country only began to carve its own identity with the civil war in 1948, and then gave up soon afterwards when North American cable television and package tourists arrived.

The country was an impoverished backwater during the Spanish Empire and didn't have an advanced pre-Colombian civilization, such as the Mayas or Aztecs, to leave behind any awe-inspiring archaeology or any sense of a shared ancient past. The only place where any real folkloric traditions remain in Costa Rica is the northern province of Guanacaste—which until 1824 was part of Nicaragua. Costa Rica also did not fight the kind of bloody independence battle with Spain that left an indelible stamp on its neighbors. Most of the country today bristles with fast-food restaurants, *gringo* fashions, soap operas, and pop music imported from other Latin American countries.

Scratch the surface, however, and you will find that Costa Rica is actually rather unique precisely because of its special history. Travelers arriving from neighboring countries will immediately notice the physical and social differences from flashy, brash, outgoing Panama, and underdeveloped Nicaragua, plagued by inequality and corruption.

One of Costa Rica's unique characteristics is, well, its lack of large extremes. Historically poor, rural, and lacking in mineral riches, it has a tradition of self-reliance and individualism, an enormous middle class (ostentatious displays of wealth are frowned upon), and a hatred of violence: the army was abolished in 1948, former president Oscar Arias Sánchez won the Nobel Peace Prize in 1987, and the country is the seat of the United Nations' University for Peace.

Costa Rica is also a country of paradoxes. It is socialist yet fiercely anti-Communist, it is a 'green idyll' yet with one of the region's highest rates of deforestation, it is urbanized but with a rural mindset. Paul Theroux, in *The Old Patagonian Express: By Train Through the Americas*, noted how Costa Ricans "go to bed early and rise at dawn; everyone—student, laborer, businessman, estate manager, politician—keeps farmer's hours."

Ticos—who earned their nickname because of their habit of turning words into cute diminutives (making, for example, a *momento* a *momentico* for example)—are also almost unnervingly friendly and polite. Yet they are more reserved and less spontaneous than most other Latinos, and are expert fence sitters who avoid firm stances and confrontation. Theroux—in fact quite a fan of the Ticos—thought they were "the most predictable people in Latin America."

Costa Ricans are hugely proud of everything that makes them different. They traditionally view everything in terms of *nuestra idiosincracia,* painting themselves as the peaceful and cultured 'Swiss of Latin America.' The idiosyncrasy they boast of includes a deeply ingrained sense of equality, a belief in education, and an aversion to parvenus and snobs. Increasingly, however, realistic Ticos admit they are kidding themselves with such blanket self-congratulation and harsher critics would describe them as boring and smug.

Whatever your view, it's clear that major cracks are appearing in the *idiosincracia*, and that Costa Rica is starting to suffer something of a crisis of both culture and identity.

This crisis has various causes. Firstly, the massive inflow of aid money, especially from the United States, once anxious to cultivate a bastion of non-Communism in Central America, has all but dried up since the 1980s, when the region's civil wars came to an end. No longer the proud oasis of stability among war-torn neighbors,

Costa Rica finds itself in an embarrassing struggle to prop up its rambling social security system amid spiraling debts and a declining quality of life.

Like a miniature United States, Costa Rica has historically received refugees with open arms. Large-scale immigration in recent decades, particularly of Nicaraguans (who are now estimated to constitute up to 20% of the population), however, has created competition for jobs and access to the country's overburdened free education and healthcare system. To most outsiders this country is still about as threatening as the Little House on the Prairie, but intolerance and serious crime—until recently almost unheard of—are on the rise.

As a small country, Costa Rica cannot remain untouched by globalization. Ticos are intrinsically conservative and many of them—not just grandparents eulogizing the good old days but very often young adults as well—lament what they see as 'infection' from the outside, and their country's loss of innocence. Newspaper opinion articles almost daily reflect this feeling of assault on traditional values and identity.

One Tico woman told me: "It's as though we've been the guardians of a beautiful treasure which we always took for granted. Suddenly, we can see that the treasure is on the verge of falling from its altar and smashing to the floor but we're helpless to stop it."

Such doom and gloom can seem a little excessive. It's true that Costa Rica is changing rapidly from a coffee and banana republic into an urbanized modern state dependent on high-tech industries and tourism. The winds of change are sweeping in here faster than in many of its neighbors and there is only a nebulous divide between town and country, past and present.

Not far outside the Meseta Central, you will still find working cowboys, indigenous communities, and Afro-Caribbeans speaking an antiquated English dialect. Even within the urban areas, beneath their increasingly slick outer shell, Ticos still live in a world of herbal remedies, magic, and rural traditions. Many city dwellers still grow vegetables on a small plot of land and almost everyone aims for nothing more than to retire to a small house in the country with some coffee plants and chickens.

For me, being in Costa Rica is like constant time travel. One minute you're never too far from the veneer of modernity, another you feel you've slipped back to a more innocent age, when people had time for politeness, generosity, and hanging out in rocking chairs watching the world go by. In my entire time in Costa Rica, the only people who were ever rude to me were other foreigners.

I hope this book will help to shed some light on this occasionally contradictory Costa Rican reality, help you understand how the Ticos see their world, and give you some useful tips on how to live, work, and have fun here.

HISTORY

Costa Rica has been inhabited for at least the past 11,000 years, but its early history remains something of a mystery. Few sites have been excavated, and the records kept by the Spanish conquistadores are far from reliable.

The Ticos' comparative 'whiteness' in relation to other Central Americans—combined with the fact that today there are only around 150,000 indigenous people living in the country—led academics to believe, until quite recently, that only around 27,000 people were living in the country when Columbus arrived.

Recent archaeological digs, however, have revealed structures, burial sites, and artifacts of a complexity and scale too great to have been made by a population of anything less than 500,000 people.

Perhaps the Indian population was almost totally annihilated as a result of warfare, European diseases such as smallpox and flu, to which they had no resistance, and by the mass transportation of slaves to other parts of the Empire—such as the notorious gold mines of Peru, from which few emerged alive. The country's total population would not recover to its pre-Conquest levels until 1930.

Prior to the arrival of the Spaniards, the country seems to have acted as both a bridge and a filter for cultures from north and south, as well as an important trade route. Linguistic research has bolstered the theory that the Chorotegas who settled in the north of the country had moved down from Mesoamerica (today Mexico), while other groups migrated up from South America.

The Chorotegas (the word comes from Choltec which means 'people who fled') are thought to have arrived around A.D. 800 to escape civil strife in their northern homeland. Like the Aztecs, who arose later in Mexico, they worshipped similar anthropomorphic deities, farmed corn, and lived in towns with central plazas—a living arrangement which made them particularly vulnerable to round-ups by the Spaniards. Their sculptures, polychrome ceramics, elaborate three-legged *metate* corn-grinding tables, calendar, paintings, and games also resembled the Aztecs of the north. Skilled craftsmen are also still found in the town of Guaitil.

The groups influenced by the south were nomadic hunters and slash-and-burn farmers who grew root crops, slept in hammocks, chewed coca leaves, and built elaborate irrigation systems. They spoke languages from the Chibcha language group and their most important god was Sibö.

Although there is hardly any gold and no jade in Costa Rica, sophisticated jade and gold working developed using raw materials which came from either war or trade with other cultures.

Gold working reached its peak in the Diquis Delta in the southwestern part of the country, with recurring themes such as frogs (a symbol of fertility), circular breast plates representing the sun, jaguars, crocodiles, and stylized, hook-beaked birds (copies of which are still seen hanging round many male Tico necks on chunky gold chains). The birds are thought to have represented vultures, related to the god of creation and death—Spanish chroniclers noted how the

17

Indians let vultures feed on the bodies of the dead after battle.

Many pre-Colombian people practiced human sacrifice, and tombs show evidence that slaves were sacrificed to accompany their masters into the afterworld. Warrior cults and fertility rites were also important, all of which made the Spanish feel perfectly justified in their 'soul-saving' campaigns, enforced baptisms, and sword-point conversions to Christianity.

The most intriguing remains of this period are hundreds of stone spheres, also from the Diquis Delta. The near perfect spheres, ranging from the size of a grapefruit to more than 2 metres (6.5 feet) in diameter, have not been found anywhere else in the world. Made mostly from sandstone, some of these stones have even been found more than 20 km (12.5 miles) from the quarries where they were carved between A.D. 500 and 1,500. It has been suggested the spheres were used as grave markers, navigation tools, or ancient star charts—but just like Stonehenge and the stone heads of Easter Island, their real purpose remains unknown.

COLUMBUS

Christopher Columbus landed in Costa Rica on his fourth and final voyage to the New World in his quest to find a sea passage to Asia. On September 18, 1502, he dropped anchor at Isla Uvita, just off the shores of Puerto Limón, to repair his storm-damaged fleet.

The area became known as Costa Rica or Rich Coast, allegedly because of the gold gifts given to the Italian explorer and his crew by the locals. The name really could not have been less appropriate as there was actually very little naturally occurring gold in the country.

The Caribbean coast's extreme heat and rainfall, impenetrable jungle and punishing terrain made inland exploration almost impossible. The real conquest of the country would not come for another 20 years when Gil González reached Nicoya after marching up the Pacific coast from Panama.

Roman Catholic Spain, newly freed from six centuries of control

An archaeologist examines one of the mysterious pre-Colombian stone spheres found in the Diquis Delta.

by the Muslim Moors, saw the conquest largely in terms of religious zealotry. González claimed to have 'saved' 32,000 pagan souls in the name of the King of Spain.

After a slow start, the following decades of conquest in Costa Rica would be bloody, typified by fierce indigenous resistance, massacres, and in-fighting among the Spaniards.

By 1562, Juan Vásquez de Coronado, using the successful tactics of Hernán Cortés's earlier campaign in Mexico, finally managed to dominate the fertile Meseta Central (the central highlands where most of the population still lives today) and the Pacific coast by exploiting

19

rivalries between indigenous groups.

As settlement began in earnest, King Philip II granted colonists the right to divide up the indigenous inhabitants under the *encomienda* system, in which families either had to work as slaves for two generations, or pay food tributes to their new masters.

Vásquez de Coronado set up his capital in Cartago. For now, the inaccessible Caribbean coast—swampy, disease-ridden, and the lair of British pirates—remained largely ignored. The pirates, however, also raided the Pacific coast, with Sir Francis Drake himself landing in 1579 on what is now called Bahía Drake, near Golfito.

The English 'privateers,' as they called themselves, were first sent to plunder Spanish possessions by Queen Elizabeth I, and became a thorn in the side of the Spanish Empire in the Caribbean for centuries. They also developed a self-serving alliance with the coastal Miskito Indians of Honduras and Nicaragua, who repeatedly raided Costa Rica's Caribbean cacao plantations, resulting in Costa Rica paying a kind of 'protection money' to the Indians between 1779 and 1841.

COLONIAL TIMES

Costa Rica was the poor relation of all the Spanish colonies, isolated at the southernmost point of the Captaincy General of Guatemala.

The country did not have any gold and little by way of a labor force. Most of the surviving Indians were holed up in the forests, making it impossible to support a plantation economy. Great disease pandemics led to the indigenous population falling to just 999 in 1714, while intermarriage (the original settlers were nearly all male) diluted the indigenous blood line still further, meaning that colonists ended up having to work their own farms.

The settlers soon found that, far from discovering their fortune in the New World, they were facing a struggle just to survive. All but abandoned by Spain, by the early 18th century they were using cacao beans as currency (as the Chorotegas had traditionally done) and fashioning clothes out of goat hair and tree bark.

These humble beginnings would have major repercussions in Costa Rica, which is still famous for its tranquil and largely egalitarian society. In sharp contrast, the hacienda economies of Mexico and Guatemala would result in the much larger indigenous populations being left destitute, landless, and indebted to their masters—leading to massive class distinctions and civil wars in the 20th century. Meanwhile, the lack of precious minerals in Costa Rica also prevented the rivalries, bloodshed, and corruption which marked so many other possessions of the Spanish Crown.

The poverty-stricken population, living in isolated *caseríos* (hamlets) among the broken terrain became self-reliant and individualistic, a characteristic still very evident among Ticos today. Sociologist Professor Price Constantino Láscaris in his book *El Costarricense* said the national character was also shaped by the fact that early settlers came from the Canary Islands, Catalunya, and Galicia. He says such people were traditionally more reserved and distrustful than the outgoing Andalucians who populated neighboring Nicaragua—and where the people today still have a very different personality.

A scattered population also meant taxes were hard to collect. The Bishop of León in Nicaragua also became horrified by both low attendance at Masses among his Costa Rican flock and the number of couples—often close relatives—living in sin. In 1711, he commanded that churches be constructed and towns built around them.

The typical Tico trait of rebelliousness in the face of authority was also well established by this stage, and settlements were slow in growing. Cubujuquí (today Heredia) came into being in 1706, Villa Nueva de la Boca del Monte (San José)—largely settled by smugglers exiled from Cartago—was not founded until 1737, and Villa Hermosa (Alajuela) did not exist until 1782. When the capital, Cartago, was destroyed by the eruption of the Irazú volcano in 1723, it consisted of only 70 adobe and thatch houses, two churches, and two chapels.

Many Costa Rican historians are apt to paint the country's colonial era as a kind of wholesome bucolic idyll. Carlos Monge Alfaro, for example, describes life thus: "Each farm was a small world in which the family was born and raised far from other farms. Their simple life, without ambitions or desires, gave the inhabitants a rude, mistrustful, and very individualistic character. They were without exception peasants who toiled the soil for their food; as a result Costa Rica became a rural democracy. Unlike other Spanish colonies, the country had no social classes or castes, no despotic civil servants who looked down on others, no powerful creoles owning land and slaves and hating the Spaniards, and no oppressed mestizo (people of mixed indigenous and European blood) class resentful of the maltreatment and scorn of the creoles."

While it is clear that everyone was pretty much poor, however, such rose-tinted analysis ignores the fact that there was racial segregation and social distinctions, based on the Spanish class system.

Each Spanish colony was settled by *hidalgos* (noblemen) and *plebeyos* (commoners). There was a hierarchy of *hidalgos*, with the *crème de la crème* getting the first stab at the most lucrative colonies, such as Peru. Only provincial nobles went to Costa Rica.

Only *hidalgos* had the right to positions of power, and their sons stepped into their shoes when they died. Around a dozen families (several of which are still potent forces in the country today) intermarried between 1821 and 1970 to consolidate their power. Three out of four congressmen came from this original dynasty and 75 per cent of Costa Rican presidents were descended from just three families.

With only those with Spanish blood having access to resources, social advancement came to be based on skin color. People tried to marry their children off to whiter-skinned suitors, even if they were poorer, and neighborhoods were segregated along color lines. Spaniards were at the top of the hierarchy, working down through mestizos, Indians, and mulattoes to the bottom of the pile—blacks.

By the end of the colonial period, most of the racial distinctions had gone and everyone had some level of mixed blood. The power of the original noble family names, however, persisted.

INDEPENDENCE

By October 1821, Costa Rica's population had swollen to around 65,000 inhabitants. Most of them were surprised when a messenger bearing the news of Central America's independence from Spain arrived after a three-week journey by mule from Nicaragua.

Unlike the other countries of the Spanish Empire which fought fiercely for their independence, isolated Costa Rica, long forgotten by Spain, was never involved. Today, it is the only country in the continent whose town plazas do not give pride of place to the busts of independence heroes.

On hearing the news, the four largest Meseta towns: Cartago, San José, Heredia, and Alajuela agreed to remain neutral to each other, displaying the kind of Tico aversion to confrontation and decision-making that stay ingrained in the national psyche to this day.

As Nicaragua, Mexico, and Guatemala each sought to control Costa Rica, the four cities started to squabble over which should be the capital. The biggest rift was between the wealthier aristocrats of Heredia and Cartago, who favored joining the new Mexican empire, and the more liberal republicans of San José and Alajuela. After a typically small-scale Tico battle that left just 20 dead, the republicans won and the capital was moved to San José. Further disputes arose in 1824 with Nicaragua, after the inhabitants of Guanacaste narrowly voted to leave the civil war-torn northern neighbor and become part of Costa Rica.

Costa Rica's first president was a schoolteacher, Juan Mora Fernández, and during his term the country was part of the short-lived federal republic of the five Central American states.

THE COMING OF COFFEE

In the early 1830s, the dictator Braulio Carrillo took the step that would define Costa Rica's identity right up until the present day—the introduction of coffee. The young nation desperately needed a cash crop to sustain it and coffee, the fashionable new drink in Europe, seemed the ideal choice. Plants were handed out to the poor and tax breaks and free land offered to anyone who would grow the crop. Coffee-growing spread rapidly in the Meseta Central, which offered the perfect combination of altitude, climate, and fertile volcanic soil.

Things didn't fully take off until an English merchant, William Le Lacheur, docked his empty ship in the Pacific port of Puntarenas in 1843 looking for cargo to take home. Although Le Lacheur couldn't pay up front, some producers entrusted him with their crop on credit. London loved the coffee, Le Lacheur returned in 1845 with the proceeds, and in that year alone 29 ships transported Costa Rican beans to Europe.

As a Spanish colony, Costa Rica had been forbidden to trade with the British, Spain's sworn enemy. Now independent, there was no restriction and Britain, the world's economic power then, would be for decades the biggest purchaser of the country's *grano de oro*, or 'golden bean.'

Roads and bridges were built to transport the lucrative crop, carried by ox carts to the port of Puntarenas—a journey of up to six days—before being laden onto ships for the lengthy journey south around Cape Horn at the southern tip of South America. This journey was considered easier than hacking a route through the steep ravines and impenetrable forests to the Caribbean coast.

Costa Rican coffee (at this time only Arabica was grown) was of very high quality, and the country soon became the richest in the region. With numerous small towns, this wealth was quite evenly spread around and a large middle class developed, still very much evident today. The coffee elite consisted of those—often foreigners—who had

Local workers loading up ripe red coffee 'cherries' which are still a mainstay of the country's economy.

25

the cash and foresight to invest in transport and processing equipment.

Thanks to trading links with Europe, the rich were soon sleeping on Manchester linen and sending their sons to school in England and France. Meanwhile, the old adobe structures were torn down as San José started to sprout coffee-funded, neo-Baroque, European-style buildings, (most importantly the Teatro Nacional—see the Culture section on page 141).

Coffee, however, was also responsible for under-development. This crop was virtually the country's only export from 1840 to 1890, and with all available land being turned over to this monoculture, production of basic food stuffs fell. The country became dependent on imports, leaving it vulnerable to price shocks in the future.

WILLIAM WALKER

Everything was pottering along nicely until the mid-1880s, when invaders from the north brought a major threat to Costa Rica's very survival—a war which still makes Ticos swell with pride today.

The invader was William Walker, a Tennessee gold miner, adventurer, and journalist, who intended to turn Central America into a confederacy of southern American states where slavery would be institutionalized. Supported by a group of US slave owners and industrialists, Walker arrived in Nicaragua in 1855, where he planned to force slaves to dig a canal from the Pacific to the Atlantic.

By March 1856, Walker and his 300 men had invaded Guanacaste in northern Costa Rica. President Juan Rafael Mora quickly called up an army of 9,000 civilians to oust the foreign troops, who were holed up in a large ranch house, La Casona, located in what is today the Santa Rosa National Park. (Unfortunately, illegal loggers burnt down La Casona, a much-prized piece of Tico heritage, in 2001 to protest forest protection measures.)

Walker's troops were forced back to Rivas, in Nicaragua, where Costa Rican drummer boy Juan Santamaría set fire to the wooden building where they were taking cover. The invaders fled after shooting

Santamaría, who became Costa Rica's national hero.

Walker continued to threaten the isthmus until 1860, when he was captured and executed by firing squad in Honduras. Coincidentally, President Mora was executed the same year. Mora had lost favor because of a cholera epidemic brought back by his troops. He was deposed in 1859, and killed after staging a failed coup in 1860.

Without having fought for their independence, the Walker crisis, although comparatively small scale, united Ticos with a sense of national pride and identity they had never experienced before. Patriotism is still extremely strong in Costa Rica today. Even before the army was abolished in 1948, the standing army was small because, Ticos boasted, it would never be difficult to call up a force big enough to protect their country.

RAILWAYS AND PLANTATIONS

In 1871, President Tomás Guardia ordered the construction of a 'jungle railway,' through thick forests and plunging ravines, to the Caribbean coast. This railway was both a means of speeding up coffee exports (it would cut three months off the journey to Europe) and a symbol of national progress and achievement.

Under American-born engineer Minor Keith, the railway started to take shape. The Chinese- and Italians-hired workers rapidly succumbed to diseases such as malaria, dysentery, and yellow fever, that thrived in the hot, swampy conditions. Finally, 11,000 black laborers from Jamaica—who were more accustomed to the climate and genetically resistant to malaria—were contracted. Nevertheless, the 150-km (93-mile) long railway was not completed until 1890, and took more than 5,000 lives to build.

Keith was in part paid with a 99-year lease on 320,000 hectares (470,720 acres) of land in the area—a move that was to have an unimaginable impact on the country. The enterprising engineer planted bananas on the land, and set up the United Fruit Company in 1899. Exports spiraled from 100,000 stems in 1883 to one million

27

in 1890 and 11 million by 1913. Costa Rica was for many years the world's biggest banana producer, today it is second only to Ecuador.

Most of the Jamaican railway builders, waiting to be paid for their labor, ended up working in the plantations—where they often rose to higher positions than the Ticos because they spoke English. Growing union activity and banana diseases, led to plantations moving to the Pacific coast in the early 1930s, where the government stipulated that preference be given to native 'white' workers.

The blacks, prohibited from leaving the Caribbean coast until 1948 when they were finally recognized as citizens, went from being relatively well-off to having to eke out a living growing cacao or fishing.

SOCIAL REFORM AND CIVIL WAR

Although dictatorial presidents, electoral fraud, and monopoly by the elite, which had hitherto been commonplace, did not disappear, things started to change after Guardia's death in 1882. Political life became increasingly secular—civil weddings and divorces were legalized and the death penalty abolished. The Jesuits were expelled, and the country's only university, the Universidad de Santo Tomas was closed down because it was dominated by clerics.

As a result, the sons of rich coffee barons had to be sent to Europe or South America for higher education. This boosted the reform movement further as they came home suffused with ideas of democracy.

Voting at this time was still restricted to literate, male landowners. From 1889 onwards, every president but one was legitimately elected.

A crunch came with World War I as a result of a sharp fall in coffee demand and a rise in debt. The politically powerful coffee elite had deliberately kept taxes indirect and regressive, as they still are today—despite having a sprawling welfare state to sustain. The highest level of personal income tax in Costa Rica is still only 15%, while taxes on goods and services are sky high.

In 1914, President Alfredo González Flores proposed tax reforms that proved even more unpopular than he could have imagined.

González Flores was driven from power by minister of war Federico Tinoco. Tinoco, who ruled with an iron fist, filled the jails with political prisoners and gagged the press.

Costa Ricans were horrified at the removal of liberties they had come to expect. Schoolteachers and children marched through the streets, setting fire to a pro-Tinoco newspaper plant. When the government sent troops against them, public outrage grew still further. By August 1918, General Jorge Volio Jiménez, a former Catholic priest led a coup uprising and Tinoco fled into exile in Europe.

In 1923, Jorge Volio set up the Reformist Party, which espoused extensive agrarian and social reforms. He should have known that his repeated attacks on the ruling elite would be dangerous. Jorge Volio ended up confined in a Belgian psychiatric asylum.

However, his ideas did not disappear with him. By the time of the 1930s depression, social discontent and poverty were growing —exacerbated by a population increase of almost a third between 1930 and 1949. Banana workers on the foreign-owned plantations suffered particularly brutal exploitation (as documented by Carlos Luis Fallas in his novel *Mamita Yunai: El Infierno de las Bananeras*) and led the country's first major strike in 1934. Troops wre sent in to restore order.

With both fascist and communist ideas taking hold in the country, President Rafael Angel Calderón Guardia, a devout Catholic elected in 1940, sought to maintain moderation. He introduced health insurance for urban workers, a Labor Code (reinstating the right to strike—outlawed in 1924) and social guarantees, as well as legislation to allow landless peasants to acquire land titles by cultivating unused plots.

Landowners and businessmen were unsurprisingly wary of Calderón however, and by 1942 he had no choice but to team up with the communist Vanguardia Popular, the party of Jorge Volio's intellectual heir, Manuel Mora. This move meant the unfortunate Calderón lost the support of the country's farmers, who saw communism as a fundamental threat to their way of life, while his Catholic sympathies aroused the suspicions of intellectuals.

As a result, an opposition candidate, newspaper publisher Otilio Ulate, won the 1944 elections. The *calderonista* Congress, however, voted to annul the result, installing a Calderón puppet Teodoro Picado instead. Presidents were constitutionally barred from immediate re-election, but Calderón hoped to make a comeback in 1948.

What Calderón had not bargained for, however, was a group of disaffected young middle-class men, who formed the Social Democratic Party, led by an extraordinary coffee farmer called José 'don Pepe' Figueres Ferrer. Figueres had gained notoriety as the first political exile since the Tinoco years, after he had attacked Calderón on a radio program in 1942. Other political groups—from oligarchs to idealists—joined Figueres's party in the single hope of toppling Calderón, and the, by now staunchly anti-communist, United States lent its support.

One of Figueres's main gripes with communism, according to political scientist Olivier Dabene quoted by the Biesanz family in *The Ticos*, is that it was a "subversive, imported ideology," that couldn't meet the needs of the Tico *idiosincracia*. While Figueres's aims might not have seemed so very different from those of Calderón's, Ticos have always been wary of foreign ideas and influences that don't take Costa Rica's unique characteristics into account.

Figueres and his band of followers declared war on the government, leading to the only large-scale bloody uprising in the entire history of this peace-loving country in 1947. As with the repulsion of William Walker, the sides in the civil war were not exactly evenly matched. Figueres's troops were well armed, partially by the CIA, while Picado had to call in machete-wielding banana workers to help him out.

The fighting lasted six weeks and claimed 2,000 lives before a peace treaty and amnesty were signed. Figueres ruled for 18 months—enough time for him to issue more than 800 decrees which would drastically alter the very fabric of the country, before handing the reins of power back to the legitimately-elected Otilio Ulate. Figueres won a second term in 1951, as well as a third in 1970, during which he would oversee the country's so-called cultural revolution.

Figueres abolished the army, allowing comparatively huge amounts to be spent on health and education. It was also hoped that banning the army would prevent the political instability and coup attempts that had brought many other Latin American countries to their knees.

Since 1948, Costa Rica has relied on the 1947 Rio Reciprocal Assistance Treaty (for protection), in which all American countries agree to support any member under attack. The country also banks on the strength of its vulnerability, which it hopes would lead to a massive international outcry if any aggressor tried to invade.

Some of Tinoco's simpler projects, such as getting shoes for all Ticos had huge effects too. At the time, at least half of all adults went barefoot. Today, the country has a First World life expectancy (up from 40 years in 1927 to 77 years in 1999) and literacy rate.

Other reforms included the barring of former presidents from power for eight years after the end of their term; since the 1970s presidents have been limited to just a single term. Banks were nationalized, women and illiterates given the right to vote, and black Costa Ricans born in the country were finally acknowledged as citizens. A system of autonomous institutions was also set up to manage basic services such as banking and public utilities.

Calderón, who had fled to Nicaragua, attempted two unsuccessful invasions and coups, backed by his friend the Nicaraguan dictator Anastasio Somoza García. Calderón later returned to Costa Rica, where he died after a final failed attempt to win the presidency in 1970.

POST-1948

While civil war changed structures in the country, power remained pretty much in the hands of the same, small coffee elite. However, peace has been the tradition of the past half century. In fact, in 1994, Figueres's son, José María Figueres Olsen took over as president from Calderón's son Rafael Angel Calderón Fournier without a hint of rancor.

Ticos were hugely proud of their status as an oasis of democracy and anti-communism in the civil war-ridden Central America of the 1970s and 1980s. Costa Rica also became—despite its size—an important player on the international stage.

Prosperity boomed and large amounts of international aid flowed in, particularly from the United States after Costa Rica switched its quiet support for the Soviet-funded Sandinista regime in Nicaragua to the US-backed Contras. The northern part of the country was even used as a Contra training ground, in direct violation of its supposed neutrality. At one point, US funds made up more than one-third of the Costa Rican government's operating expenditure, and only Israel received more aid per capita.

Government bureaucracy grew exponentially until the early 1980s, by which time 20% of all workers were employed by the state and the public sector accounted for more than a quarter of the gross national product.

With nearly all growth financed by international lending, the world economic crisis of the early 1980s hit Costa Rica especially hard. Coffee and banana prices slumped, inflation rocketed, and in 1981 the country became the first Third World country to default on its debt payments.

In 1986, the liberal Oscar Arias Sánchez was elected as president. A former political scientist, he started to mediate with his neighbors in the civil wars of Nicaragua, El Salvador, Guatemala, and Honduras, that had between them left 200,000 people dead and two million displaced. Within 18 months, Sánchez came up with a peace plan that called for a ceasefire, the cessation of military aid to the Contras, amnesties for political prisoners and guerrillas, and inter-governmental negotiations for free and fair elections. Although the plan was not fully implemented, the five presidents approved an accord in August in 1987 based on his plan.

Arias was awarded the Nobel Peace Prize in 1987. Arias was so popular that many Ticos wanted to change the constitution to allow him to stand for a second term.

Although national pride was running high, the Arias-brokered peace plan carried a high price for Costa Rica. By 1989, the country's debt had reached US$5 billion—one of the highest per capita in the world and with Central America now at peace, US aid dried up. Creditors refused further help unless Costa Rica slimmed down its overweight bureaucracy through privatization and by encouraging foreign investment and competition.

University of Costa Rica anthropologist Sergio Chávez explained that Ticos have failed to fully accept their decline since the 1980s: "We are a tiny nation, and so we are proud of what we have achieved and all the times when we have been centerstage in world affairs. Unfortunately, times have changed, but we still tend to live in the past. We simply don't want to face up to our current mediocrity."

MODERN POLITICS

Power in Costa Rica swings between the two main political parties. Figueres's Partido de Liberación Nacional (PLN), formed in 1951, and the opposition coalition, the Partido Unidad Social Cristiana (PUSC), formed in 1990. Minority parties haven't done well at the top level because 40% of the vote is needed to win the presidency. Meanwhile, the party in power rarely wins an election—partly, it seems, because of Ticos's deep-seated distrust of authority. In polls, the Legislative Assembly is repeatedly voted the least trusted of all public institutions.

The constitution of 1949, designed to prevent the emergence of dictatorships or overly-strong legislatures that would meddle in elections, provides for weakened powers for both the president and the parliament. While this avoids alienating anyone it also hampers decision-making.

The PLN, in favor of state intervention, has traditionally had

33

a slight edge in the popularity stakes, although in today's times of belt-tightening, the rather more frugal PUSC has been gaining favor. Like the Republicans and Democrats in the United States, there really isn't a great deal to choose between the two, and personality is often more important than policies on polling day.

No president would ever win, however, unless he was suitably *humilde* (humble), a favorite Tico trait. Oscar Arias, during his presidential campaign in 1986, was even sent to a special image clinic in New York, as his advisers were worried about his overly proud manner. Presidents tend to dress simply, and can often be seen out strolling in the street or shopping like regular citizens without any bodyguards. In the early 1980s, president Luis Alberto Monge even had his pocket picked in downtown San José.

Ticos are also proud of the fact that their elections are some of the cleanest and most peaceful in the world. An electoral tribunal, manned by unpaid volunteers, takes over all election-related police and government functions in the run-up to the poll. Election days are rarely marred by violence as travel writer Paul Theroux noted in *The Old Patagonian Express*: "In the rest of Central America, an election could be a harrowing piece of criminality; in Costa Rica the election had been fair and something of a fiesta. 'You should have been here for the election,' a woman told me in San José, as if I had missed a party."

German sociologist Ilse Leitinger, who has worked in the country for more than half a century, said: "Costa Rica must be the only place on the planet where you can see cars leaving polling stations on election day full of smiling people waving the flags of opposing parties out of each window."

The single, four-year term limits imposed by the constitution in order to prevent dictatorship seem to lead to the kind of corruption and favor-currying they were originally designed to prevent. Government ministers are not elected but appointed by the president, while term limits mean expertise gained slowly over the period is effectively useless at the end of each administration.

"Politicians don't need to care about their performance or re-election, so they just concentrate on earning enough *chorizos* (literally sausages but meaning kickbacks/bribes) to line their own pockets and those of their friends," one commentator told me.

Another problem is that, while Costa Rica passes a huge number of often very forward-looking and innovative laws, the framework is rarely in place to actually enforce them. Even if enacted, they are often swathed in labyrinthine regulations that breed their own corruption—and add more fuel to the Ticos' characteristic lack of respect for authority.

The Biesanzes in *The Ticos: Culture and Social Change in Costa Rica* provide an example. Unlicensed *piratas* (cab drivers) operate entirely illegally, yet have so little concern for legal repercussions that they have openly set up an Association of Pirates.

Similarly, while people keep their own homes spotlessly clean, to the extent of placing their garbage in special dog-proof cages on posts to avoid dirtying the road outside their houses, it's a different story on public land. People not only chuck waste willy-nilly out of car windows, but seem to aim it right at the signs warning of a 100,000 colón fine for littering. The most successful means of keeping Ticos tidy seems to be to resort to shaming them with signs saying: "If you throw litter you are a person of very little culture."

Many voters are clearly disillusioned with both the political system and the law, with rural *campesinos* (peasants) particularly disenfranchised. Abstention in the 1998 elections, particularly among first-time voters, was 29%. While this may not be high for the US or UK, it was by far the highest level in Costa Rica in more than four decades.

As authority-suspicious people living in a paternalistic country Ticos do have a few means of making the state more accountable. The Ombudsman's Office, set up in 1993, received 20,000 complaints in 1995, mostly from the poor alleging neglect or mistreatment by public employees or corporations.

They also have the constitutional court, or the Sala Cuarta of the Supreme Court. Challenges against legislation on constitutional grounds in this court are common and often successful, such as the repealing of the seat belt law (see Getting Around section, page 218), although the backlog of cases is massive.

DISMANTLING A NANNY STATE

Costa Rica still has an enormous government (public employees constitute more than 15% of the work force), and a large number of autonomous institutions with their fingers in innumerable pies. More than half of these institutions have been disbanded or privatized as part of the economic structural adjustment pacts of the 1980s, but at one point there were more than 200 of them, many staggeringly inefficient.

The reforms demanded by international lenders have spurred economic growth by forcing a diversification of the economy. The education and welfare spending cutbacks, however, have unsurprisingly brought about a much wider distinction between rich and poor in a country which traditionally liked to bill itself a 'classless democracy.'

Meanwhile, the remaining autonomous institutions—such as the state banks, the CCSS (Caja Costarricense de Seguros Sociales or Social Security Fund) and the ICE (Instituto Costarricense de Electricidad—responsible for both electricity and telecommunications) are still massive, and account for a majority of public sector funds. Supporting them has led to a cycle of increasing internal debt, which has only been moved from one place to another by the central government 'borrowing' from them (by forcing them to buy bonds).

A major headache for the government has been the fact that many Ticos see the autonomous institutions as their 'heritage' and birthright. With so many employed by them, breaking them up is almost impossible. The whole country ground to a halt for a week during riots in 2000 when the government announced plans to privatize the ICE. Tire-burning students, union members, environmentalists, and angry citizens blocked streets around the capital, claiming that selling off the ICE, despite its problems, would result in job losses and higher costs for consumers, with corrupt politicians pocketing the profits.

Their reasoning? Despite its bungling over the purchase of cell phone lines and its notoriously slow service as the country's only Internet provider, the ICE's service is incredibly cheap as almost 80% of electricity is from hydroelectric sources. The company also has the widest distribution network in the region. The ICE is continually providing new connection to unprofitable rural areas, which would otherwise be left in the dark under privatization.

The violence of the ICE riots is particularly important given that, unlike many other Latinos, the Ticos have always been very passive and slow to protest. Don Pepe himself once lambasted his countrymen for being as 'docile as sheep.' Even in the 1947-48 civil war, only a small minority of people took an active part.

Another polemic issue in Costa Rica is tax. Everybody wants to live in the protective shelter of their big government, but no-one wants to pay the taxes to fund it. Personal taxes are low but according to a former minister of the economy quoted by the Biesanzes: "Costa Ricans seem to have created a culture in which cheating the tax collector is an act to be celebrated."

He added that 90% of income taxes and 65% of sales taxes go unpaid—mostly by big businesses. This sum, in 1994, was more than double the fiscal debt. Recent legal changes have introduced punishments such as imprisonment for tax evasion for the first time.

— *Chapter Two* —
THE COUNTRY

For its size, Costa Rica is one of the most physically diverse countries imaginable. Local newspaper advertisements announce houses for sale just 15 minutes outside San José and boast of their 'great climate.' It's not a joke as within the space of just a few miles, the topography, vegetation, and temperature can go from being strongly reminiscent of rolling Devon hills to something more like *Out of Africa*.

One of the country's most distinctive features is its volcanoes, seven of them active, which straddle the meeting place of two tectonic plates along the Pacific Rim of Fire. These also give rise to frequent earth tremors, occasional quakes, and have helped to build the three mountain ranges that run through the country. Costa

Rica's spine is the continental divide, rising to 3,820 meters (12,533 feet) at Mt Chirripó in the Talamanca range, the second highest peak in Central America.

On mountaintops, vegetation is limited to elfin cloud forest and stunted *páramo* (Alpine moorland*)* shrubs. The temperature can drop to freezing, and electric blankets are recommended for a comfortable night's sleep in the highest villages.

At the other extreme, in the northwestern province of Guanacaste, the land is arid and the climate oppressively hot, with temperatures rising above 35° C (95° F). Guanacaste's desiccated and deforested, though beautiful, plains are home to huge cattle ranches, and are dotted with shady Guanacaste trees, shaped like giant mushrooms. The remaining natural forest is deciduous, the trees losing their leaves in the unbearable summer heat.

In between the two extremes lies the Meseta Central, the central highland plateau which is now home to well over half the country's population in the urban sprawl of San José and its surrounding towns. This is *the* traditional coffee-growing area, and the climate is mild thanks to the altitude—San José stands 1,150 meters (3,773 feet) above sea level—and temperatures rarely go above 25° C (77° F).

Both coasts are hot, and are home to steamy banana and African palm plantations (excluding the Guanacaste part of the Pacific coast). While the Pacific side has a distinct dry season, the Caribbean coast is rainy all year round, and blanketed in a profusion of wild greenery.

There's no escaping the fact that Costa Rica (again, except Guanacaste) is a very wet country. During the rainy season (May to November) one can expect at most an hour or so of rain each day in neighboring Nicaragua but in Costa Rica it sometimes seems the clouds will never lift again, and parts of the country receive 750 cm (25 feet) of rain a year. "Costa Rica has two seasons," Ticos joke, "the rainy season—and the even rainier season."

Like Eskimos with their 57 words for snow, Ticos have up to a dozen terms for rain—from drizzly *pelo de gato* (literally 'cat's fur') to a *baldazo* or *aguacero* (downpour), and a *temporal* (heavy rain falling without let-up over several days during the rainy season). Thanks to the large amount of rain, Costa Rica also has more rivers and a higher volume of water for a country its size than any other nation in the world except New Zealand.

Costa Rica's variety of terrain and climate has given rise to mind-boggling biodiversity. Although it only covers 0.03% of the planet's surface, Costa Rica is thought to contain around 5% of the world's plant and animal species—more per square kilometer than any other country in the world. Corcovado National park, in the southwest corner of the country, has been called by National Geographic magazine 'the most biologically intense place on Earth.'

The country is home to 1,500 types of tree, 6,000 species of flowering plant (including more than 1,000 orchids), 10% of the world's butterfly species, and more bird varieties (850) than in the United States and Canada combined.

The country contains 12 'life zones' based on forest type, altitude, and precipitation, which may each contain an even larger range of habitats. Despite everything the tourist literature may say, however, none of these zones is actually a rain forest. Although you will, undoubtedly, get incredibly wet in Costa Rican forests, true rain forests only exist in Asia, Africa, and South America, where enormous forests create their own rain, which falls every day.

The Instituto Nacional de Biodiversidad (INBio) has an excellent website providing details and news stories about Costa Rica's species and environment. The address is http://www.inbio.ac.cr

FARMING AND LAND DISTRIBUTION
The entire history of Costa Rica has been based on agriculture. Ticos' roots with the land remain strong. The city centers are almost 100% commercial, with city dwellers preferring to live on the outskirts, where many still rear chickens or at least have a small vegetable or maize patch. The names of *barrios* in the capital also

reveal their recent rural history, for example, Hatillo (little ranch) and Dos Pinos (two pines). But with more than half of the people living in urban areas, the face of agriculture has changed drastically.

Today, according to the Biesanzes in *The Ticos*, more than half of all Costa Rican landowners own less than 10 hectares (14.7 acres), which adds up to about 5% of the total farming land. Of these, 37% have *minifundios* of less than 2 hectares (3 acres) which are too small to satisfy the basic needs of a family. In 1993, just 2.8% of landowners owned large *latifundios* (usually cattle ranches), which made up 47% of the country's farmland.

In contrast with the past, there are now thousands of *campesinos* with no land, and with no choice but to work as day laborers or peons for larger landowners. Despite ongoing but underfunded government land distribution programs, the numbers of such *campesinos* and the scale of rural poverty is growing all the time. This is a result of both population growth and the fact that nearly all land is now privately owned or in state-protected parks. As a result, many desperate people are flooding to the cities, where their lot rarely improves.

Perhaps most importantly, the role of coffee in the country has changed dramatically. Carolyn Hall says in *El Café y el Desarrollo Histórico-Geográfico de Costa Rica*: "Fifty years ago, to talk of alternatives to coffee was considered heresy or an affront to the fatherland; the 'golden bean' was so venerated in Costa Rica that tearing out a coffee field virtually constituted national agony."

When coffee prices rose after World War II, dozens of countries rushed to plant coffee, the world's second biggest dollar commodity after oil. Supply soon outstripped demand and prices went into a free fall from which they have never really recovered.

Many farmers complain that the cost of producing coffee is more than what they earn from it. Hundreds of fields have been ripped out and today the crop only covers 2% of the land, while San José's rapid growth has permanently cemented over what were once some of the country's most fertile coffee lands.

The crop accounted for only 16% of export earnings in 1995. With ongoing attempts to diversify the economy, many former coffee fields have been planted with higher-earning ornamental plants and ferns.

Bananas are the other major source of income from the land, and now bring in twice as much money as coffee. Costa Rica is the second biggest banana producer in the world after Ecuador.

The difference is that, where the coffee economy was traditionally one of small entrepreneurial family farmers, banana farming requires a lot more land to be profitable. This has led to domination by big, often foreign-owned, firms with local workers (the majority of whom are Nicaraguans) being exploited as peons. Increasingly, many plantations have closed down due to disease, and have been given over to other crops, such as African palm.

The other main farming activity is cattle ranching, which increased to such a point that by 1975, there were as many cattle in the country as people. The clearing of land for cattle farming has drastically changed the landscape. Despite declining beef sales, more than two-thirds of all the country's agricultural land was pasture by 1994.

Cattle on the Guanacaste plains— the archetypal scene of the north.

PROVINCES AND TOWNS

Costa Rica is divided into seven provinces: San José, Heredia, Alajuela, Cartago, Puntarenas, Guanacaste, and Puerto Limón (generally just known as Limón). Almost three-quarters of the population live in the Meseta Central provinces of San José, Heredia, Alajuela, and Cartago, while Limón is the most sparsely populated province. Few of the towns are big, but listed below are some of the most interesting.

Key to Population Size
No asterisk – population under 10,000
* 10,000 to 20,000 people
** 20,000 to 50,000 people
*** 50,000 to 100,000 people
**** 100,000 to 200,000 people
***** 200,000 to 500,000 people

***** **Alajuela**. Located 18 km (11.2 miles) northwest of San José, Alajuela is slightly warmer than the capital. Home to the international airport, and birthplace of the national hero Juan Santamaría, Alajuela is a little less dirty and bustling than San José, but otherwise fairly similar. The Ojo de Agua Springs Complex is a popular weekend spot with Ticos. Alajuela is also a good base from which to explore the butterfly farm at La Guácima, the craft village of Sarchí, and the Poás Volcano.

***** **San José**. The capital city is infuriating and charming at the same time, with congested narrow streets, crowded markets, hustlers and beggars, excellent museums, galleries and theaters, fast food outlets, and cosmopolitan restaurants. Located on the Meseta Central, the city has a cool, pleasant climate. There's only a small amount of colonial architecture, which survives in Barrios Amón and Otoya, but the lavish Teatro Nacional and pre-Colombian gold and jade museums are must-sees. The economic and cultural center of the country, it's

43

almost impossible to go from one point in the country to another without passing through chaotic *Chepe* as the locals call San José.

**** Cartago. In the shadow of Volcán Irazú, the old capital of Cartago is most famous for the Byzantine-style Basílica de Nuestra Senora de Los Angeles, the cathedral that is home to the nation's patron saint, La Negrita. Up to a million pilgrims make a trip here on August 2. Cartago also boasts the ruins of the Iglesia de la Parroquia Church, which collapsed during the earthquake of 1910. The city is also near beautiful Orosí, Lankaster Gardens (famous for its orchids), and the rarely-visited Parque Nacional Tapantí.

**** Heredia. Located 11 km (6.8 miles) north of San José in the heart of coffee-growing country, Heredia is a student town with the most traditional feel of all the big Meseta Central capitals. Heredia has interesting architectural sites, such as the cathedral, built in a squat, earthquake-proof style, and El Fortín, a small fortress just off the Parque Central. Nearby is the colonial town of Barva and the excellent *finca* of Café Britt (Costa Rica's most popular coffee) which runs a fascinating tour about the history of coffee in the country.

*** Puerto Limón. The capital of Limón province, this city has a large black population, plus a Chinese community (the legacy of the railway construction years). Isla Uvita, where Christopher Columbus first set foot on Costa Rican soil, is just offshore. "Was there a dingier backwater in the whole world?" asked Paul Theroux in *The Old Patagonian Express*, going on to say that Limón smelt of "dead barnacles and damp sand, flooded sewers, brine, oil, cockroaches, and tropical vegetation which, when soaked, gives off the hot mouldy vapor you associate with compost heaps in summer." Limón's reputation as dirty and rough is rather unfair, but no-one can deny it has been rather neglected since the banana boats shifted to the nearby, deeper natural harbor at Moín. Limón is famous for its big street carnival celebrating Columbus's arrival in the New World held on October 12.

*** **Puntarenas**. The capital of Puntarenas province was Costa Rica's biggest port before the railway was built to Limón. Goods were brought here by ox cart and then shipped around Cape Horn to Europe—a journey of several months. Ferries run from here to the southern tip of the Nicoya Peninsula, home to popular surfing beach villages such as Montezuma and Malpaís. Puntarenas, built along a tongue of sand in the Gulf of Nicoya, is popular with Tico holiday makers, though the sea water here is polluted.

** **Ciudad Quesada (San Carlos)**. An important farming and ranching center, with a huge cattle fair and auction held each April. Ciudad Quesada is situated on the northwestern slopes of the Cordillera Central, and is famous for its beautifully-tooled leather saddlery.

** **Guápiles**. The transport center for the Río Frío banana-growing region, Guápiles is just over 60 km (37 miles) northeast of San José. Guápiles is a good base from which to visit the Rainforest Aerial Tram in the Braulio Carrillo National Park.

** **Liberia**. The capital of Guanacaste, Liberia is a hot, dusty town in the heart of cattle country with many white-washed colonial houses. Many houses still have *puertas de sol*—an ingenious corner door, which lets light in but keeps heat out. Life centers around the shady Parque Central, although the town gets very busy during the late-August festival celebrating Guanacaste's annexation to Costa Rica. Liberia is a good base for visiting Pacific coast beaches, the traditional pottery-making village of Guaitíl, and the Rincón de la Vieja, Palo Verde, Guanacaste, and Santa Rosa national parks.

** **Nicoya**. The biggest town in the Península de Nicoya, it has a pleasant central park and a white colonial church. Nicoya is a big cattle center located close to beaches, Santa Cruz (Costa Rica's folklore capital), and the traditional pottery-making town of Guaitíl.

** **Turrialba**. The town is a base for white-water rafting on the Río Reventazón River and trips to the Guayabo archaeological site. Also fascinating is the nearby tropical agronomy research center. Centro Agronómico Tropical de Investigación y Enseñanza (CATIE) is one of the top five tropical research centers in the world.

* **Golfito**. Situated on the Golfo Dulce, one of the world's few tropical fjords, Golfito is the most important port in the south. It was the headquarters of United Fruit Company from 1938 to 1985 (when the company finally pulled out of Costa Rica because of banana disease, rising costs, and labor agitation). In the northern part of the town, you can still see the old company houses with their airy verandahs and lush gardens. Surrounded by thickly forested hills, Golfito was used as the setting for *Chico Mendes*, a film about a real life Brazilian rubber trapper working to save the rain forest. Golfito is pretty run-down these days, but it is still popular with Ticos for its duty-free shopping.

* **Quepos**. This is a small, ugly town which made its fortune from bananas and then African palm. Today, tourism is the biggest earner, as Quepos is located very close to the Parque Nacional Manuel Antonio. Quepos is a gay-friendly town and is also big on sportfishing.

Cahuita. A laid-back Caribbean beach village located 40 km (25 miles) south of Limón and adjoining the beautiful marine park: Parque Nacional Cahuita. Like nearby Puerto Viejo, Cahuita is a quiet place, where Rasta colors are out in force, and horses snooze on the beach or wander the streets snatching flowers from gardens. You can snorkel, dive, surf, and fish here.

Fortuna. The base for trips to the active Arenal Volcano, as well as white water rafting and wind surfing on the Lago de Arenal reservoir. Fortuna is a clean, tranquil country town with a nearby waterfall, caves, wildlife refuge, and hot springs.

Jacó. This is a busy central Pacific coast surfing town filled with bars, clubs, and nightlife. Jacó is also a good base from which to visit Parque Nacional Carara. The long beach at Jacó has some of the most consistent waves and rip tides in the country.

Puerto Jiménez. Known as Puerto Hellmenez by local expatriates because of its stifling climate, Jiménez grew largely as a result of logging and gold mining, which gives the place a decidedly dusty, frontier feel. It is also the base for heading into the wilderness of the Osa Peninsula's remote Corcovado National Park.

Puerto Viejo. This town in the banana-growing lands of the northeast has a steamy jungle feel. Historically, goods were shipped down the Sarapiquí River to the San Juan River on the Nicaraguan border, and from there to the Caribbean. Several jungle lodges and the La Selva biological research station, take advantage of the proximity of the tropical wet forest of the Parque Nacional Braulio Carrillo.

San Ramón. Located halfway between San José and Puntarenas, San Ramón is known as the 'city of presidents and poets', as many Ticos in these two occupations were born or lived here. It is a friendly town with a big Saturday farmers' market.

Santa Elena/Monteverde. A straggling community spread out along the unpaved road to the world-famous Monteverde cloud forest reserve. Monteverde has a sizable community of American dairy-farming Quakers, foreign and local artists, a cheese factory making real Cheddar, and the Monteverde Institute, which carries out research into sustainable tourism, agriculture, etc.

Zarcero. At around 1,700 meters (5,577 feet) in the mountains of the Cordillera Central north of San José and near San Ramón, the Zarcero area has an almost Alpine feel. The town is most famous for its bizarre Dalí-esque topiary in front of the church. Local artist Evangelisto Blanco has sculpted dozens of trees into various human and animal shapes, and surreal arches. Look out also for regional food specialities such as *palmito* cheese and peach preserves.

PROTECTED AREAS

Although forest cover declined from 75% in 1950 to 23% in 1990, the country's very broken terrain and (until recently) relatively sparse population, has left many pockets of virgin forest. More than a quarter of the territory is now protected in some form or another by Costa Rica's pioneering system of parks, refuges, and reserves set up since 1969. There are about 136 protected area in Costa Rica.

Tourism is now the country's biggest foreign income earner, and as most tourists come specifically to visit the parks, environmentalists hope official protection, currently often only patchy, will be strengthened. The protected areas are broken down into:

- National Parks (Parques Nacionales)—Twenty-three national parks are equipped for tourism and most frequently visited, surrounded by 'green' buffer zones in which limited farming and hunting is allowed.
- Biological Reserves (Reservas Biológicas)—Nineteen areas of special ecological interest, often conserved for scientific research.
- National Wildlife Refuges (Refugios Nacionales de Vida (or Fauna Silvestre)—Twenty areas preserving special habitats for wildlife.
- Private Reserves (Reservas Privadas)—Six biological reserves and one national wildlife refuge are privately-run reserves. These include Monteverde/Santa Elena and the Cabo Blanco on the Nicoya Peninsula. Other smaller reserves, often owned by foreigners, are also being set up.

There are also about 30 protected areas, 13 Indian reserves, and four wetlands.

Remember that despite the huge number of tourists, some parks are surprisingly remote and are very definitely not theme parks. Always take plenty of sun screen, water, a hat, and insect repellent. Keep your eyes peeled for snakes and peccaries. If peccaries attack, your best option is to climb a tree. On beaches, look out for jellyfish, sharks, and rip tides. Several people drown on Costa Rican beaches each year—usually because they panic. Instead of fighting against the water, wait until the current becomes weaker then swim back to the beach at a 45 degree angle. Swimming back in directly will just lead you straight back into the current. Another warning, don't swim on beaches where turtles nest as these are usually patrolled by sharks waiting to gobble up hatchlings.

These are some of the most popular/important protected areas.

Parque Nacional Rincón de la Vieja. In a landscape of dry and deciduous forest, the main volcano rises to a height of 1,916 meters (6,285 feet). One of Costa Rica's active volcanoes, its last big eruption was in 1992, and the 14,084-hectare (20,717-acre) park offers good hiking and opportunities to see 'gloop-ing' mud pots, steam vents, and sulfurous springs. The park's also famous for its large quantity of the purple *guaria morada* orchid, Costa Rica's national flower.

Parque Nacional Palo Verde. Seasonal wetland that is a major attraction for birders, as many rare water bird species live or migrate here from September to March. The 16,804-hectare (24,718-acre) park, however, is under threat from wide-scale rice farming on its outskirts, which requires the use of large amounts of pesticide.

Parque Nacional Guanacaste. This 47,825-acre (32,512-hectare) park, adjacent to Parque Nacional Santa Rosa, was created out of cattle ranching land in 1989. It provides an added range of life zones to help local wildlife survive year-round in the sometimes severe conditions of dry forest.

Parque Nacional Santa Rosa. This 37,117-hectare (54,599-acre) park, the oldest in the country, is famous for La Casona—the colonial hacienda where the infamous William Walker was hounded out of Costa Rica by the army of President Mora in 1856. The park is also important as it contains the largest remaining area of tropical dry forest in Central America, and beautiful, unspoilt beaches.

Reserva Biológica Carara. Five life zones are found within this 4,700-hectare (6,913-acre) park north of Jacó. This transition zone between the dry environment further north and the Pacific wet forests of the south has abundant wildlife, and this is, aside from Corcovado, Costa Rica's most important refuge for the scarlet macaw.

Parque Nacional Corcovado/ Piedras Blancas. This 55,000 hectare (80,905-acre) park of lowland Pacific tropical forest bristles with tapirs, herds of peccaries, four species of monkeys, and the largest population of scarlet macaws in Central America. If you're very lucky you may see jaguars fishing on the shore. It's still almost pristine, thanks to the fact that getting in and out requires a commando-style 20-km (12.5 mile) trek along beach, through jungle, and across rivers. Watch out as some rivers contain crocodiles and, at high tide, sharks. The park, however, has problems with illegal logging, gold mining, and poaching.

Volcán Poás. Northeast of San Ramón is one of the world's biggest volcanoes, topped by a stunning 1,500-meter (4,921-feet) wide crater, with a sulfurous cauldron filled with steaming turquoise water. Its last major eruption was in 1910. This is Costa Rica's most-visited park and, at just over 5,000 hectares (7,355 acres), one of the smallest and easiest to reach—a road runs right to the top. A second extinct crater holds a lagoon, and a system of paths runs through dwarf cloud-forest at the summit.

Parque Nacional Manuel Antonio. Over-visited and very small, this 683-hectare (1,005-acre) park on the central Pacific coast near Quepos was the setting for Ridley Scott's Columbus movie *1492: Conquest of Paradise*. White sand tropical beaches, steep forested hills, good trails, beautiful Pacific views—and one of the last haunts of the tiny squirrel monkey.

Parque Nacional Tortuguero. The 'Amazon' of Costa Rica on the north Caribbean coast is criss-crossed by waterways and lagoons, and the only means of travel through this strip of luxuriantly wet tropical forest is by boat. Wildlife, such as monkeys and crocodiles, is abundant, and the park's beaches protect the most important nesting grounds of the green turtle in the whole Caribbean, as well as the hawksbill turtle. The park, however, is being steadily encroached upon by banana plantations, which are also causing pollution through the vast amounts of pesticides used.

Parque Nacional Cahuita. This 1,067-hectare (1,570-acre) Caribbean coastal park includes some of Costa Rica's remaining living coral reef.

Parque Nacional Braulio Carrillo. The closest national park to San José, and visible from the steep road that passes through it down to the Caribbean coast. It was made a national park in 1978 as a 'pay-off' compromise for the construction of this road through virgin forest, and includes 45,899 hectares (67,517 acres) of land from just around sea level up to 2,906 metres (9,534 feet) at the top of Volcán Barva. This thick premontane tropical wet forest contains the world-famous Aerial Tram—an ingenious way of viewing the forest canopy.

Parque Nacional Volcán Irazú. The highest active volcano in Costa Rica at 3,432 meters (11,260 feet), last erupted on March 19, 1963, coinciding with the visit of US president John F. Kennedy. The summit is a lunar landscape of ash, pyroclastic material, and four craters. Both oceans are visible from the summit on clear days.

Monumento Nacional Guayabo. About 85 km (53 miles) from San José, this is Costa Rica's national monument and top archaeological site. Originally inhabited around A.D. 300 and constructed with stones brought from some distance away, Guayabo was 'discovered' in the late 19th century. The area has still not been fully excavated, but cobbled streets, aqueducts, and petroglyphs have been found. Guayabo, like some other Central American indigenous sites, was mysteriously abandoned around 1400.

The nightly spectacular at Volcán Arenal.

Parque Nacional Tapantí. A small park measuring 6,080 hectares (8,944 acres) on the northern slopes of the Cordillera de Talamanca. It's also very wet as it contains around 150 rivers and receives up to 7,000 mm (275 inches) of rain per year. The largest moth in North and South America can be found here—*Thysania agripina*.

Parque Nacional Volcán Arenal. A relatively new national park, it contains one of the western hemisphere's most active volcanoes as well as vast biodiversity, being home to about half of all the species of vertebrates in Costa Rica. Arenal, dormant from around 1500, erupted on July 29, 1968, with lava flows killing between 80 to 90 people and 45,000 cattle. Since then the volcano has spewed out ash and lava on an almost daily basis. Near Fortuna, you can relax at night in steaming hot springs with a cocktail, watching the volcano explode above you.

Reservas Monteverde and Santa Elena. The country's second most-visited tourist spot, this world-famous, epiphyte-laden cloud forest is made up of various private reserves, and is home to birds such as the quetzal and the three-wattled bellbird—as well as dozens of species of orchids. The endemic golden toad is sadly extinct (see Environment section of this chapter). There are also plenty of adrenalin-pumping opportunities on various canopy rides, where you whiz through the treetops harnessed onto zip cords. For the less adventurous there are networks of canopy bridges and night tours to spot nocturnal fauna, such as tarantulas, porcupines, and sloths.

Reserva Biológica Lomas Barbudal. Close to the Palo Verde park, this 2,279-hectare (3,352-acre) reserve of tropical dry forest protects many species of endangered trees, such as mahogany and rosewood. It also contains many insect species, including 250 types of bee— about a quarter of all the bees in the world, including the Africanized 'killer' bee.

Parque Nacional Marino las Baulas. Most of the terrestrial area of this park are all six species of mangroves in the country, as well as plenty of crocodiles and water birds. The stars of the show are the huge leatherback turtles (called baula), some up to five meters (16 feet) long, which nest here between October and March.

Refugio Nacional de Fauna Silvestre Ostional. Midway between Sámara and Paraíso, this is an important nesting area for the olive ridley sea turtle (from July to November). The park was set up to protect the nests and turtles from over-poaching by locals. Limited egg harvesting is still allowed—the eggs are popular drinking snacks (*bocas*) in Tico bars.

Parque Nacional Barra Honda. A park which protects more than 40 spectacular subterranean caverns, some over 200 meters (656 feet) deep. The caves, in limestone hills on the Nicoya Peninsula, contain a variety of bizarre rock formations and specially-evolved animals.

Parque Nacional Marino las Ballenas. A 4,500-hectare (6,620-acre) marine park protecting Isla Uvita (an island about 20 minutes by boat from Limón),with its nesting colonies of frigate birds, blue-footed boobies, and other seabirds. The area is excellent for snorkeling and diving, and humpback whales migrate through the area from December to March. Dolphins and turtles are also seen.

Reserva Biológica Isla del Caño. Located 20 km (12 miles) west of Bahía Drake, off the northern part of the Nicoya Peninsula, this reserve includes the 300-hectare (441-acre) island plus 5,800 hectares (6,531 acres) of ocean in southwestern Costa Rica, and is excellent for snorkeling and diving. Some of the pre-Colombian stone spheres have also been found on the island, which is thought to have been a Diquis Indian burial ground. Bizarrely, it also has the distinction of being the place most frequently hit by lightning in the entire region.

Refugio Nacional de Fauna Silvestre Golfito. Originally protected to save the Golfito watershed, this 1,309-hectare (1,925-acre) park also protects rare and ancient plants, such as orchids, tree ferns, and cycads (palm-like trees with leathery leaves).

Parque Internacional La Amistad. The park straddles both Costa Rica and Panama. Declared a UNESCO World Heritage Site in 1983, this is the largest protected area in Costa Rica at 250,000 hectares (367,750 acres) with 340,000 hectares (500,140 acres) of buffer zones, and a further 440,000 hectares (647,240 acres) in Panama. This reserve is an important biological bridge in the isthmus, protecting rare species and diverse environments (nine of the country's 12 life zones are found here), as well as indigenous reserves. More than 500 species of bird have been spotted here, of which 49 are endemic.

Parque Nacional Chirripó. Costa Rica's highest mountain, Cerro Chirripó, stands at 3,820 meters (12,533 feet), and is located in this fairly large park measuring just over 50,000 hectares (73,550 acres). Climbing Chirripó is fascinating for the varied vegetation zones you pass through, as well as the glacial valleys. On clear days you can see both the Pacific and Caribbean oceans from the summit, although the temperature may be around freezing. In the dry season, accommodation in mountain huts is limited and advance bookings of up to three months is recommended.

Reserva Biológica Hitoy-Cerere. The wettest reserve in the parks system is very remote and seldom visited, with dense vegetation, thick mud, and broken terrain that make for hard hiking.

Refugio Nacional de Vida Silvestre Gandoca-Manzanillo. This reserve contains one of Costa Rica's only two living coral reefs, beautiful beaches, and many unusual bird species. Even the giant and extremely rare Harpy eagle (thought to be extinct in the country), was reportedly spotted here recently.

Refugio Nacional de Vida Silvestre Caño Negro. This remote wetland reserve contains a huge variety of waterbirds, including the largest population of olivaceous cormorants in the country.

Refugio Nacional de Fauna Silvestre Barra del Colorado y Toctuquero. This large reserve adjoins Tortuguero. It's harder to get to than Tortuguero, and is most popular with sports fishermen. The area borders Nicaragua, which made it virtually off-limits during the Sandinista-Contra war. This isolation has kept wildlife better protected than in Tortuguero, although illegal logging is rife.

Parque Nacional Isla del Coco. The inspiration for Robert Louis Stevenson's *Treasure Island* and the setting for the opening aerial shots in Steven Spielberg's *Jurassic Park*, this remote Pacific island lies about 532 km (339 miles) southwest of Cabo Blanco. Early sailors, pirates, and whalers used to stock up on fresh water here, and it is also reputedly the site of numerous stashes of buried treasure. The world's largest uninhabited island, it has a unique ecosystem, with around 140 species of endemic plants and animals. Diving here is among the best in the world, with schools of hammerhead sharks seen in their hundreds. It is also a UNESCO world heritage site. However, wild pigs—left behind by would-be settlers who abandoned the island in the early 20th century—are rapidly destroying the environment, along with introduced rats, cats and goats. Trips to the island are extraordinarily expensive.

THE ENVIRONMENT

With more than a million visitors each year, Costa Rica's biggest source of foreign exchange is now tourism, a large part of it eco-tourism. Thanks to its dazzling biodiversity, visitors flock here to see birds and animals already rare or vanished elsewhere in the region, such as tapirs, squirrel monkeys, manatees and sea turtles.

Costa Rica is determined to exploit tourist income still further in the future, so one might imagine that vigorous steps are being taken to preserve its 'golden goose'. However, this country, which paints itself in tourist literature as an ecological paradise, looks very different when you see the piles of garbage along roadsides, trucks spewing plumes of pure soot, and the broken trunks of newly felled trees.

Costa Rica has done much more to protect its wild areas than any of its neighbors and the parks are, for now, still utterly beautiful. It's important to know, however, that there are numerous and growing threats to the very resource base upon which the country's future economy hopes to depend. This is the side of the environmental story you will not read about in the tourist literature.

THE GREEN DREAM UNDER THREAT

At the time the national parks system was being set up in the 1970s (thanks to visionary leadership within the conservation community), Costa Rica had one of the world's highest rates of deforestation. This destruction still continues at a rate of about 60,000 hectares (88,260 acres) per year, six times the size of the showcase Monteverde cloud-forest reserve, to provide new land for cattle farming and banana plantations. Such rapid deforestation, combined with heavy rains and steep mountainsides, is a serious problem. In the 1980s, Costa Rica lost two billion tons of topsoil. Today, about half the country is affected by erosion.

By the 1990s, it was realized that the national parks were increasingly ending up as islands of greenery with development encroaching on all sides, and suffering from problems around their fringes such as pesticide poisoning, logging, over-fishing, sugarcane-burning and dredging, so a system of 11 'buffer zones' was set up.

This seemed like a good solution. In reality, however, the government has only bought about 44% of all the supposedly 'protected' land. With an internal debt of around US$600 million, this situation is unlikely to change anytime soon. In any case, even with buffer zones, many of the protected areas are simply too small to maintain species such as jaguars, which need vast territories in which to survive.

Such habitat fragmentation has already contributed to the extinction of several species such as the Harpy eagle and giant anteater. In fact, 26 animal species and 456 plant species were on the endangered list in 1996. The famous golden toad of Monteverde, found only in a few rain pools in the reserve's elfin cloud forest and nowhere else in the world, was extinct by 1989—probably as a result of climate change, but possibly also through removal of too many animals by over-enthusiastic scientists.

Meanwhile, widely roaming species, although protected in Costa Rica, are often in danger in the absence of international protection. Sea turtles, largely protected (despite egg theft) by conservation projects in Costa Rica, are butchered by fishermen from neighboring Nicaragua as they return to the country to lay their eggs. Jewelry made from their shells ends up being sold illegally, but openly, to tourists on Costa Rican beaches.

Of Costa Rica's territory, more than half is actually ocean as it extends to include Isla del Coco, located 500 km (311 miles) offshore. There are only about 10 areas to protect marine environments. There are only two surviving coral reefs in the country thanks to earthquakes and the clogging effects of erosion run-off, while over-fishing has seen shrimp stocks collapse by more than 50% since the late 1980s. In the Gulf of Nicoya, I found three dead turtles and a dead dolphin

Its eggs laid, a turtle returns to the sea—but will its offspring hatch successfully or be collected as boca *drinking snacks for a Tico bar?*

along a stretch of beach—the victims of encounters with huge drag nets or boat propellers.

To add insult to injury, some protected areas are now no longer protected at all. The government has lifted restrictions on building in some such areas in the Meseta Central, for example, claiming this will allow poor people to build houses. Conservationists are cynical, pointing out that land in the increasingly crowded environs of San José is now at a premium, and potentially worth millions of dollars.

Many innovative projects to help protect the environment, much trumpeted upon inception, have also foundered through lack of official resources. One example was a program to give tax breaks to land owners who set aside forested land, which the hugely overburdened state has been unable to fully fund.

Lack of funds for the national parks system means there are insufficient wardens. Corcovado National Park has only around 10 wardens, which works out to about 1 warden to every 5,500 hectares (8,091 acres). Poachers capture rare species, such as the park's famous scarlet macaws, and visitors can even hear hunters' gunshots. Illegal gold mining also goes on in the park.

Paulino Valverde, a Tico scientist who works at the Sirena biological research station in the park, said: "It's just impossible. I've been here 10 years and the funding has become less and less every year. I don't understand how the government wants eco-tourism to be our future source of income if it's not prepared to put in the money to protect what the tourists are coming to see."

Bruce Moffat, of the Nature Conservancy Council in San José, says corruption is also a problem. "Government staff are paid a pittance and rich landowners can easily entice them into turning a blind eye to activities like illegal logging."

The reality is that not many Ticos have much interest in their environment. Few locals visit the national parks, even though the entry fee is a quarter of the US$6 that foreigners pay. All attempts at recycling garbage have collapsed through lack of interest, and many reasonably well-off Ticos still see hunting and tree-felling as their 'right'—even though the environment can no longer take the strain.

"Unfortunately many Ticos still do not appreciate what we have here," said Ovely Quirós Ríos of the Ministry of the Environment. "A lot of the parks aren't particularly accessible, but that's not really the problem. Most people, if they're going on holiday would just prefer to go to Miami. We hope to slowly raise awareness through education."

AIR AND WATER POLLUTION

Pollution is another unpleasant surprise for many visitors, and is a particular problem in San José. The country has a very innovative legal framework to tackle pollution—but apparently lacks the resources or willpower to enforce it. Although all vehicles have had to be fitted with a catalytic converter since 1995, and must sport an 'Ecomarchamo' sticker certifying that emissions are within certain limits, the clouds of black smoke coming out of many vehicles are testimony to the fact that the rules are flagrantly broken.

The Ecomarchamo program has been riddled by technical problems and corruption, while the import tax on vehicles (more than 50% of the car's cost) means old, polluting vehicles stay on the roads for longer.

Official figures from the government-funded Estado de la Nación report in 2000 show that 75% of air pollution is caused by traffic pollution, which despite the efforts to bring it into check remains more than double the World Health Organization's established safe maximum levels.

Bruce Moffat said: "Recent studies have shown that air pollution could be reduced by 50% if the tariffs on bringing new cars into the country were reduced by 25%. Unfortunately this is unlikely, as the tax is a huge source of income for the government."

What about the water? While Costa Rica prides itself on its hundreds of gushing rivers, the shocking truth is that pollution and mismanaged or unplanned development could leave the country with serious supply problems within just five years. More than 50% of the country's sewage flows untreated into the Gulf of Nicoya, while the waterways running through the capital are so full of detergent that they look more like torrents of whipped cream. The rivers running off the flanks of the Poás Volcano near Alajuela are completely dead, thanks to the extensive farms there growing ornamental plants and ferns, which require large amounts of pesticides.

Banana plantations also use large amounts of pesticides and fertilizers, and the blue plastic bags put over the fruit to speed ripening invariably end up in rivers and waterways. Pesticides used in rice fields in the north are having a serious impact on the nearby Palo Verde National park, a regionally important site for migrating water birds.

According to the Estado de la Nación report, only 20% of solid garbage is managed acceptably, while 47% of municipalities simply dump waste in open air sites.The unresolved issue of dealing with waste is becoming more and more of a headache as cities grow uncontrolled—San José alone has grown by 80% in the past 11 years.

FROM THE FRYING PAN INTO THE FIRE?

In the north, cattle ranching is the major environmental culprit. It has led to wholesale forest cutting since the 1960s to make way for pasture—in turn increasing drought and the degradation of compacted, cattle-trodden soil. Combined with the fact that the industry is non-labor intensive, ranching has directly caused poverty and massive migration away from the area.

In recent years, cattle ranching has declined with the shrinking of international markets, and the region is now setting its sights on sun'n'surf tourism, with huge complexes being built by Mexican and Spanish consortia. The very antithesis of eco-tourism, such developments are already causing social discontent by sucking up precious water to irrigate golf courses, and threatening to turn the northwestern coast into a new Cancún, says Bruce Moffat.

"This kind of development could lose the country its distinctive eco-tourism niche, and have long-term economic consequences. I think the government is basically shooting itself in the foot by promoting these get-rich-quick developments," he said.

Various other plans the government has on the drawing board include opening up some of the national parks for hydroelectric exploitation, in order to boost sales of electricity to neighboring countries such as Nicaragua. One such project under consideration, to build one of the tallest dams in the world, would flood the valley of the Río Grande de Térraba in the south of the country and displace an indigenous population.

Indigenous people feel particularly helpless because, while they have surface rights to the land in their reserves, they do not own underground resources. This means the government could theoretically grant licences for mining under their feet.

Meanwhile, inhabitants of the Caribbean coast were outraged by permission given by the government to a US firm to explore the whole coastline for oil—including the national park of Cahuita, which contains one of the country's only two surviving coral reefs.

Bruce Moffat said: "Most Ticos are quite aware of these issues—but they also have no faith in the government to act honorably. Unfortunately, electoral single term limits here mean that politicians often dedicate their time in office to lining their pockets as comprehensively as possible, with no need to worry about serving their constituents—because they're not going to be re-elected anyway. In this situation, and with up to 25% of the population living in poverty, it is very easy to understand why so many people feel justified in getting involved in relatively high-earning activities like illegal fishing or poaching."

— *Chapter Three* —
THE PEOPLE

Like all Latin American people, Costa Ricans are a mixture of many things. Among the ethnic groups which remain distinct today are the indigenous population, Afro-Caribbeans, and Chinese (originally brought in to build the jungle railway), North American retirees, and an ever-growing number of Nicaraguans.

The population has also been swollen over the years by people fleeing persecution and hardship from all over the world—such as Argentineans, Chileans, Colombians, Russians, Salvadorians, and Cubans. You only need to see the number of cars driving through San José waving a particular country's flag after a football match to realize how many communities there are.

Many immigrant groups, such as Italians, Jews, and Arabs, have long since been assimilated into the dominant culture. Author Samuel

Rovinski says this is a sign of how easily outsiders are accepted into Tico society.

This, however, has not always been the case with everyone. An entry in an 1875 official gazette seeking to limit Chinese immigration to the country claimed: "Their abuse of opium and decided inclination to suicide leads them to have a disrespect for life, which makes them a danger, especially in domestic service." Even today, despite some mixed marriages, the Chinese community still remains quite culturally cohesive and separate.

While all Costa Ricans are Ticos, some are clearly less Tico than others, and in many senses the term only really applies to the huge Spanish *mestizo* majority of the Meseta Central.

The country's population in 2000 stood at over 3.8 million, up from just 400,000 in 1930. This growth was largely due to the fact that—despite its declining birth rate—Costa Rica has the lowest infant mortality rate (11-18 deaths per 1,000 live births, 2001 est.) in Latin America after Cuba, and a First World life expectancy of 76 years. This can also be attributed to the high level of literacy (about 90%), widespread use of contraceptives and family planning, and its high standard of healthcare.

The population is very young, with 31.4% of Ticos under the age of 14, and 64% under 30. Ticos have also become, in recent decades, a very urban people (even though they retain many rural habits). Around half of the population lives in the greater San José area alone, and more than two-thirds in the urban sprawl of the Meseta Central.

'WHITE' TICOS AND IDEAS OF COLOR

It is only a few decades since Costa Rican tourist literature trumpeted the 'whiteness' of the people as an attraction. In his 1943 *Nueva Geografía de Costa Rica,* author J. León said the country was "effectively the white state of the Caribbean... in Heredia, 96.6% of the population are direct descendants from Europe—a little more than in New York."

Compared with other Central Americans the Ticos really do look quite different—particularly when you see the children streaming out of some of San José's more expensive private schools. Blond hair and blue eyes, owing, perhaps, to original Catalan settlers or German forefathers are not so unusual. After all, between 1870 and 1920 immigration accounted for up to 25% of population growth.

The 'whiteness' is, however, a myth. The original Spanish settlers were nearly all men, and took Indian women as wives. Mathematically, this makes virtually all Ticos mestizos, or of mixed blood.

The country is dominated politically, culturally, and in every other way by the 'white' Ticos of the Meseta Central. Ethnic minorities exist largely only in far-flung pockets, and even the road network is arranged so that to get from one part of the country to another you have to go through San José.

With transport historically so difficult (the highway to Limón was only built in the 1970s) it is easy to see why areas outside the coffee-growing highlands seemed foreign for so long. Guanacaste has traditionally been little more than a place to go on trips to the beach, and few people have visited the Caribbean coast.

Now, however, with more and more people abandoning the *campo* in search of work or higher education in the cities, cultural assimilation is increasing, although color is still an issue in Costa Rica (as it is in almost every other country).

"It's only recently that San José has started to get so cosmopolitan, with the influx of refugees, people from the countryside and the Caribbean, and Nicaraguans," said Darren Mora, a Tico whose complexion could not be described as anything darker than *café au lait*. "When I was young, people here used to call me *negro*."

Although colonial society was more egalitarian here than in many other corners of the Empire, it was still organized around the Spanish class system. Only those with Spanish heritage could get into positions of influence, and everybody thus wanted to marry their children off to paler-skinned people, even if they were poorer, in order to climb the social ladder.

University of Costa Rica anthropologist Sergio Chávez said: "It is as if the people who run Costa Rica, sitting up here on the Meseta Central, have always tried to make the country's black and indigenous people invisible, and perpetuate this myth that we are all white, or at least lighter-skinned than other Latin Americans.

"Thankfully, society is more dynamic now, and color is no longer such an impediment to advancement. But you still hear some pretty ignorant remarks, and we still don't really accept our multi-ethnic and cultural nature. We are alienated from our own culture, feel superior to our Central American neighbors, and relate instead to the United States and the paradise of Miami."

BLACK COSTA RICA

Black people in Costa Rica today make up only 3% of the country's population, but despite the poverty and problems they continue to face, they are one of the most vibrant and interesting sections of the country's population.

Most black Costa Ricans arrived as slaves with the Spanish conquistadors in the 16th and 17th centuries to work on large cattle haciendas and cacao farms in the north. While they have long since been assimilated into the population at large, traces of their heritage can still be seen in the features of people from Guanacaste province.

Musical instruments still used in the country, such as the *marimba* (a giant xylophone with gourd resonators) and the *quijongo* (a basic one-stringed double bass) are of African origin. The slaves also left behind some words in Costa Rican Spanish such as *angú* (mashed plantain), *candanga* (the devil), *lapa* (macaw), *mandinga* (coward or faggot), *panga* (type of boat) and *timba* (belly).

Today, by far the biggest black population of Costa Rica lives along the Caribbean coast—which in itself forms part of a much bigger, virtually continuous belt of black, English-speaking people stretching all the way from Belize down to Panama.

In northern Costa Rica, you're rarely far from the haunting sound of the marimba *—originally an African musical invention but now 100% Central American.*

These immigrants first arrived from Colombia, Nicaragua, and Panama, as migrant turtle hunters fishing up and down the coast in the late 18th century. Later, some settled as farmers, planting the coconut groves which today line the coast. They lived almost totally isolated for nearly a century—hunting, trading with the local Talamanca Indians, and supplementing their income by making coconut oil, yucca starch for linen, and salt from sea water.

Things changed in the 1870s when the population was swollen by thousands of workers from Jamaica brought in to complete construction of Minor Keith's (the North American banana magnate) railway from San José to the Caribbean.

After the railway was built, many Jamaicans—waiting months for back pay—worked in Keith's new United Fruit Company banana plantations. The Jamaican communities steadily grew, hiring English-speaking teachers from their homeland, putting on Shakespeare recitals, dancing the quadrille (a 19th century European parlor dance still practiced today), and holding Sunday Schools.

However, there was plenty of hostility between the blacks and the locals who were looking for work. The blacks, still intending to save some money and return to Jamaica, felt superior to the Costa Ricans, dubbing them *pañas* (Spaniards). It was held that the *pañas* were dirty, drunk, had lice, and spat on the floors of their own houses. The children were even warned that if they were bad the *pañas* would chop them up with a machete.

The discrimination was two-way. Although no legislation was actually passed controlling their movement, the blacks were in effect prevented from leaving the Caribbean area. In the late 1930s, President León Cortés even tried to introduce a colored bar in Limón.

Unfortunately, the prejudices only served the interests of the all-powerful United Fruit Company, known as *Mamita Yunai* (Mummy United), preventing the formation of cohesive labor unions to fight for decent conditions.

The situation was therefore ripe for the arrival of Marcus Garvey (see *Heroes and Villains* section of *The People* chapter), who preached racial segregation, and formulated a 'Back to Africa' movement after witnessing the exploitation and misery of black workers in the banana plantations.

Garvey's plans were doomed to failure, however, and when the plantations were largely transferred to the Pacific Coast in the 1930s due to union activity and crop disease, the black workers found themselves trapped and increasingly destitute. Many took to cacao farming, although this would later become unsustainable as a result of pest infestations.

The official discrimination against blacks did not end until after the civil war in 1948, when Jose Figueres Ferrer, president of Costa Rica (from 1948–1949, 1953–1958, and 1970–1974) granted full citizenship to the blacks and gave women the right to vote.

Citizenship, however, has not stopped the communities along the coast from remaining plagued by poverty. The government still invests very little in the province of Limón. For example, while Costa Rica as a whole focused massively on improving health care following the civil war, the communities of the Talamanca coast—despite numerous requests—didn't receive their first doctor until 1977.

For many, the downside of citizenship has been cultural assimilation. Black children, taught by Costa Rican teachers from the Meseta Central, have often been ridiculed for talking in their English dialect, and many youngsters in Caribbean communities now see English as old-fashioned. I have seen older people trying to reason with children chattering away in Spanish, saying: "You should be proud to speak English, it's the language of the world"—and getting nothing but blank looks or giggles.

The old Jamaican placenames have also gone—Old Harbour is now Puerto Viejo and Monkey Point is Punta Mona, while English language Calypso music (developed by slaves as a means of transmitting messages under the noses of their masters) is giving way to salsa. Many people have left the area altogether to look for better opportunities in San José or even abroad.

Little is heard these days of once common African traditions, such as the devil cult *pocomía*. However, the obi-men—men with supernatural powers used to cure illnesses or work spells against, or provide protection from, enemies—still exist. Black writer Quince Duncan says many people have died from easily-curable illnesses because of their firm belief in the obeah.

The Jamaican influence is obvious in many other ways. Sitting outside the brightly colored houses on stilts (which protect against animals and flooding), adults play dominoes. Children carry school books African-style, on their heads, and some of the older men still get together for cricket matches on the beach. Festivals involve the traditional English May Pole Dance, and local cuisine is much more Kingston than San José (see *Food and drink* chapter).

On Sundays, as elsewhere in Costa Rica, people get dressed up for church—although in the Caribbean it's more likely to be Baptist, Adventist, or Jehovah's Witness (although some people have converted to Catholicism to make life easier). The variety of groups, according to Quince Duncan, is a relic from the old days of slavery, and was encouraged by the British to prevent social cohesion among the slaves.

Many other old traditions still persist, such as Set Up and Nine Nights. When someone dies, the body is prepared, or 'set up' for viewing. Friends and family are summoned, and stay up all night drinking, talking, and playing dominoes and cards. After burial the following day, people return every night for nine nights to show respect for the dead and keep the mourning family company. The demands of modern life—such as getting to work on time—make such traditions harder to keep, but they still exist.

People also tell stories of Anansi the spider, passed down by oral tradition and almost identical to those still told to children in West Africa today. Slightly tailored to fit modern times, they are like an African version of Aesop's Fables, where the morally ambiguous spider pits his quick wits against brute force.

While there are plenty of people wandering around sporting dreadlocks, listening to reggae, and smoking *ganja*, Rastafarianism—unlike in Jamaica—is little more than a fashion statement, and you definitely won't find people who follow true Rastafarian religious principles such as washing with the akee fruit instead of soap and never eating a fish more than 30 cm (12 inches) long.

Not everything is reggae and sunshine though. Outspoken Puerto Viejo resident Edwin Patterson said: "We are still suffering. Limón is the poorest province in the land, despite the fact that it brings in more wealth for the state than pretty much anywhere else. We pay taxes to the government, but for them it's as if we don't exist."

Mr. Patterson supports controversial black academic Rigoberto Stewart, who has called for autonomy for the province, and helped found the separatist Partido Auténtico Limonense. The party has long since disappeared as it couldn't win a seat in government, but in the 1980s the province buzzed with revolutionary talk of armed uprising.

"We should be independent of Costa Rica," said Mr. Patterson. "I certainly don't feel Costa Rican, and nor do many others—I'm an African. Unfortunately, the problem is that our black population is disenfranchised and divided."

Opportunities for black people are limited. While a few have risen to fairly prominent political positions under the umbrella of one of the two big parties, many members of their community see them as sell-outs, who have agreed to toe the party line and so cannot possibly represent them.

Growing unemployment and drug problems—Mr. Patterson says around 90% of the young black population uses or deals drugs either to earn a living or through sheer disillusionment—are creating pressure that he feels will only be released by violence.

Not everyone is as extreme as Mr. Patterson, however. Many mixed race couples can be seen strolling through the center of Limón, and the pace of life in the Caribbean coastal villages is so relaxed it's very hard to imagine anyone having the energy to riot.

INDIGENOUS PEOPLES

One of the most intriguing and unique archaeological aspects of the country is its profusion of almost perfect rock spheres carved by indigenous Costa Ricans hundreds of years ago and scattered across the Diquis Delta. No-one has any idea as to their purpose, and now it seems unlikely that we ever will—because nearly every sphere has been uprooted and hauled off to decorate government buildings and private gardens the length and breadth of the country, sometimes even painted in gaudy colors.

This plundering is indicative of the country's attitude to its indigenous past—and the general lack of understanding or interest in the Indians who inhabit it today. This is perhaps best illustrated by President Rafael Angel Calderón, who on a state visit to Spain in 1992, explained that Costa Rica had 'no Indians'.

Katya Cordero, a mother-of-two in her mid-30s, recalls her primary schoolteacher's reaction to an essay in which she had written that Columbus had not 'discovered' the Americas.

"I remember how upset I was," she said. "All I wrote was that Columbus could not have discovered the place as there were already people living here. The essay came back with a red line through it and a failing mark."

Although the Indian population today numbers just 60,000, a little over 1% of the population, there were probably up to 500,000 people living in the country when Columbus arrived.

Cindy, a university student, added: "It's obvious from looking at any Tico's skin that we all have indigenous blood—but in school, there is much more focus on our Spanish than our indigenous heritage.

"A lot of people speak about the *indios* as if they were a different species. It makes me sick the way we patronize them as *nuestros indígenas* (our indigenous people), and have put them in *reservas* as if they were museum pieces or animals in a zoo. In Panama and Nicaragua the indigenous people at least live in autonomous areas and can make their own decisions."

Until 1991, the Guaymí and Cabécar peoples did not even have *cédulas* (the identity cards which each citizen needs to do anything from opening a bank account or writing a letter to a newspaper to leaving the country). They were only given the documents— and thus officially recognized as Costa Rican citizens—after taking over roads in San José and occupying the capital's cathedral.

Within the past few decades, however, much greater official efforts have been made to recognize indigenous people's needs. A National Commission on Indigenous Affairs (CONAI) was set up in 1973, and an Indigenous Law passed in 1977. Since 1976, 21 indigenous reserves have been created.

This, however, may have been too little too late. While communities such as the Bribris and Guaymíes remain relatively culturally intact, their distance from San José means they are often 'out of sight, out of mind'. They score very low on health and literacy indices relative to the national average.

In 1995, the 124 schools in the country's indigenous reserves met only two-thirds of demand, with 40% of teachers not even graduates. Despite the government's promises of bilingual education, nearly all material used in schools is in Spanish and Meseta Central-focused.

Few Indians actually own any land now, having been tricked or cheated into selling it, or driven off by poachers and settlers. One reserve, China Kicha, even ceased to exist after being over-run by white settlers.

In the north and center of the country particularly, reserves are so small they are like pinpricks on the map. The Huetar Indians, once fierce warriors who dominated the whole of the Meseta Central, are now confined to less than 5,000 people living in two small reserves.

The incursions have had a major impact on the indigenous people's physical and cultural survival. They have been unable to fight back against hunters, miners, and bigger interests, such as the United Fruit Company (suspected to have orchestrated the poisoning of the last Bribri *cacique* (chief) Antonio Saldaña, who in the 1930s fought against the conversion of his lands into banana plantations).

Meanwhile, deforestation means that in many areas indigenous people are now unable to hunt for food, find medicinal plants or build traditional houses. They are left with no option but to work for a pittance on Tico farms or as drug traffickers. Many are on the verge of genetic extinction through inter-marriage. Languages, art, religions, and cultural practices have almost disappeared.

As elsewhere in the continent, evangelical churches have sprung up all over the indigenous reserves, encouraging indigenous people to renounce their pagan traditions. By 1905, the Bible Society had even published the Gospel of St. John translated into Bribri.

Carlos Pérez, a Huetar Indian from the Quitirrisí reserve near San José, said: "We have lost our own religion, but we deal with this now by trying to think of Jesus in our terms. To us, he was like an indigenous healer—he healed with his hands, mud, and saliva, just as our ancestors did."

Unlike the Huetares, the Bribri's retain their religion, and a creation myth that describes how they were made by the god Sibö from ears of corn. White people, however, came from Plékeköl, the king of the leaf-cutter ants.

In *Taking Care of Sibö's Gifts*, Gloria Mayorga explains: "Just look at the leaf-cutter ants, how they all work together cleaning and clearing all land around their nests. Where the leaf-cutter ants live, all the vegetation is gone, because they cut every last leaf to take them back to their big nests. That's how the white man is. He works very hard, but he destroys nature. He chops down all the trees to make his big cities, and where he lives all the vegetation is gone, there are no trees, no rivers, no animals. There is nothing there... he destroys everything in his path."

With so much lost, many indigenous people are now determined that what remains of their culture must survive. Projects such as iguana farms, organic fruit farming, traditional craft workshops, and eco-tour guiding have been set up to help ensure an income. Indigenous people are also becoming more self-confident in denouncing hunters and loggers, are running their own reforestation programs and making efforts to document and recuperate their culture.

Carlos Pérez said: "The birth rate among Ticos is low now, but we Indians still have six or seven children. I really hope that in 20 years or so our population will have grown to a size where we will finally have a political voice in our own country."

Unfortunately, however, many indigenous communities are very divided and greedy community leaders have misappropriated a lot of foreign aid money. The budget for CONAI, which actually achieves very little, is also in continual decline.

Alcoholism has also wrought havoc among people who traditionally drank *chicha* (a fermented drink of corn or other crops) only on ceremonial occasions. Carlos Pérez's grandfather, like many others, became hooked on drink, and gave a Tico a large tract of land —later turned into a profitable coffee *finca*—in exchange for a bottle of rum and a kilogram of meat. While it is illegal to sell alcohol anywhere within an indigenous reserve, it is easily available at the *pulperías* (small stores) which have sprung up all around the reserves.

Oscar Mena, 74, the only remaining Quitirrisí Huetar with knowledge of traditional healing, said: "The younger people especially are fascinated by outside cultures. Many leave the reserve and are almost ashamed to acknowledge their heritage.

"We need more work opportunities here so that people don't leave and become corrupted. But I think that by the time people come to really appreciate what we had, I will be dead, and all my knowledge will be gone with me."

The Bribris

The Bribris live on both sides of the Talamanca mountains. Theirs is the second biggest indigenous group, made up of 8,000 people. Pirates, banana companies, the railway, miners, and hunters have continually invaded their land since the conquest. The people still preserve their customs, but these are disintegrating. Their crafts include hammocks and *chácaras*, 'string' bags made from *pita* leaf fiber, baskets, and drums made from tree trunks and iguana (or other animal) skin. Similar drums are made by the Malekus and Ngabës.

The Cabécares

Numbering 10,000 people, the Cabécares make up the country's biggest indigenous group and live on an 80,000 hectare reserve in Alto Chirripó. Due to this remote location not much is known about them. They still preserve their language and rituals to some extent, although the younger people are losing interest.

Like the Bribris, they are from the South American Chibcha family, believe in Sibö , and have matrilineal clans. The Bribri *awá*, or shaman, is the *jawá* of the Cabécares.

The Brunjkas or Borucas

Around 2,000 individuals live on the reserves in Boruca and Rey

Curré on both sides of the Interamericana highway. They are famous for their textiles (woven blankets and bags) and masks—used in the famous *Fiesta de los Diablitos* (see sections in the *Social Customs and Attitudes* chapter). Their language is, however, rapidly being lost.

The Teribes

Their reserve is south-east of the bridge over the Río General. Although 1,500 people live there, only 40% are indigenous, and only 25% of the land is in their hands.

A warlike tribe, the Teribe were brought to Costa Rica from Panama by the Spanish in the 18th century in an attempt to pacify them. In Panama, they had killed many colonists and refused to submit. They were forcibly settled in the town of San Francisco de Térraba, built by the Franciscans, but 48 years later the Teribes burnt it down. Their language, Naso, has already been lost, but they are now undertaking exchanges with the larger Terraba nation in Changuinola, Panama, in an effort to save their culture.

The Guaymíes or Ngabës

This is the biggest indigenous group in the Central American isthmus, with 100,000 individuals in Panama alone. However, there are only 3,000 of them in Costa Rica, divided among four reserves (Coto Brus, Abrojo Montezuma, Conte Burica, and Osa) in the Zona Sur.

This group has preserved its traditions more than any other, and its women are the only ones to still wear their traditional dress. They still speak their two languages, Ngäbe and Buglé (Guaymí was the name given them by the conquistadors). Traditionally, they worship the god Ngobö, but now are either Christian, or follow the Mama Chí religion, which blends pagan and Christian elements.

The Huetares

The original inhabitants of the Valle Central are now reduced to a few thousand people in two tiny reserves in Zapatón and Quitirrisí.

77

They are some of the richest of the country's indigenous people, thanks to their proximity to the capital, and their speed to lobby for their rights. Their language and culture, however, is virtually extinct.

The Chorotegas

Most live in Matambá near Nicoya. They have lost their language, although their traditional art of pottery-making is preserved in Guaitil (see following section on Guanacastecos). Originally Mesoamericans, also found in Nicaragua, they are believed to have been pushed south by conflicts in their Mexican homeland around A.D. 800.

The Malekus or Guatusos

Their tiny northern reserves are in Palenques El Sol, Margarita, and Tonjibe, areas easily accessible by road. Inter-marriage with whites means that there are now only 500 Malekus left. They live in one-family concrete and zinc houses built by the government, and—as most of their lands are actually in the hands of ranch owners—they have to work as *peones* for a low salary. Incredibly, the Maleku language still exists to some extent, as does their art work—although deforestation has made it very difficult for them to find the wood they need for this.

- You could easily live for years in Costa Rica and never see an indigenous person. If you have genuine interest in their culture and the problems they face, one of the best ways to meet these 'invisible' people is to spend some time alongside them on a reserve. Some groups have embraced low-level eco-tourism projects to help boost their income.
- To spend a few days with the Bribris along the Yorkín River on the Panamanian border (one of the groups which still maintains a traditional lifestyle), contact Aisling French at the Galería Namu, Avd 7, Cs 5 & 7, San José, tel: (506) 256 3412 or email: aislingmahon@hotmail.com (Galería Namu is also the only

art store in the country dealing exclusively in Costa Rican indigenous and modern art.)

- The non-profit Asociación Talamanqueña de Ecoturismo (ATEC) in Puerto Viejo can also organize visits. Tel/fax: (506) 750 0191, email:atecmail@sol.racsa.co.cr. For more information on indigenous issues in general, contact CONAI on (506) 257 6465.

GUANACASTECOS OR CHOLOS

Chorotega Indians originally inhabited the large northern province of Guanacaste. The name of the province comes from *cuahuitlnacaztli* in Náhuatl, the language they shared with the Aztecs, meaning 'the place next to trees with ears,' referring to the large ear-shaped pods of the area's giant Guanacaste trees.

Guanacaste is renowned for being the only part of the country with really vibrant culture. Pretty much everything described as Costa Rican folklore is in fact from Guanacaste—including the country's national dance, the 'Punto Guanacasteco' (allegedly invented by a bored musician jailed for drunkenness), national tree, and national costume. Guanacaste is the only part of the country where colonial architecture can still be seen intact and traditional ox carts are in use.

In fact, however, Guanacaste only became part of Costa Rica in 1824. Previously the southernmost province of Nicaragua, its inhabitants narrowly voted to leave that country because of the on-going civil war between the liberal capital, León, and the powerful conservative trading town of Granada following independence from Spain in 1821. Nicaragua did not accept the loss of Guanacaste until 1858, when a border limit treaty was finally signed.

The people of Guanacaste (known by Meseta Central Ticos as *cholos*) clearly have a richer ethnic mix than most other areas of the country. Their Chorotega Indian heritage is very evident, as is the black blood from African, and mulatto slaves brought with the original Spanish settlers. Many still live in colonial houses with central patios and are expert horsemen.

79

Despite the dash of color it has given the country, however, Eduardo, a Guanacasteco in his early 30s, says the region has been regarded with almost as much suspicion as Nicaragua.

"Just a few years ago when I studied in Heredia, people still called us *Nicas regalados* (gift Nicaraguans)," he said. "I felt like a foreigner in my own country. I think Ticos have started to travel and get to know their country much better now, though. They can also see that this area is going to become more and more important as tourism grows—and they're going to be coming to look for work here rather than the other way around."

The tourism Eduardo refers to includes some massive tourist developments on the coast, such as the controversial Papagayo Project in Bahía Culebra, once called off on environmental grounds and now re-slated for completion in 2010. It will be a massive complex of hotels, apartments, entertainment parks, and shopping zones, which will double the number of hotel rooms available in Costa Rica, and will be the biggest tourist development anywhere in Central America—even bigger than Cancún in Mexico.

"It's going to totally change Guanacaste," Eduardo said. "We need the work, but we're also a very traditional people, and I think this could have drastic effects on our culture and environment. This development is right next to a national park, and we've already had problems with other hotels, which have used vast amounts of water for their golf courses. Guanacaste is almost a desert as it is."

Tourism would seem to be the only option for Guanacaste. Cattle ranching requires very little labor, and in any case many ranches are now uneconomic and closing down. As a result, only 52% of the province's workforce has a steady job, and the unemployment rate (35.5%) is the highest in the country.

Guanacasteco Traditions

The following poem, *Sabaneros and bullfights,* was dedicated to the once ubiquitous *sabaneros* (cowboys) who would ride straight-backed and inscrutable across the vast Guanacaste plains with a cow horn (*cacho*) of firewater (*guaro*) hanging by their side.

> *Sabanero, Sabanero*
> *Duerme ya tu sueño entero*
> *Sin trajín ni despertar*
> *Mas tu esfuerzo decidido*
> *Como tu está en el olvido*
> *Y hoy te vengo a rescatar*

> Sabanero, Sabanero
> Dreaming your deep sleep
> Without anything to waken you
> Your decided determination
> Like you, is forgotten
> And today I'm coming to rescue you
> > Rodolfo Salazar Solórzano,
> > *Sabaneros and bullfights*

Sabaneros, who could break in a wild horse in a matter or hours, lead a poor and lonely life. They lived for big fiestas, drinking sprees, and the periodic round-ups of cattle herds for branding and sale, in which they would prove their machismo by 'riding' the biggest and angriest bulls. This was the origin of Costa Rica's brand of bull-fighting—in which the bull gets to walk away (almost) unscathed.

Unfortunately, the 'real' sabaneros, also known as *pamperos* or *bramaderos*, have died out. Cattle these days are often transported in trucks, the plains have been fenced off, and parasite dips and injections for cattle have made the roving cowboys almost superfluous.

In Guanacaste, horsemanship is still much prized and the spirit of the sabanero is romanticized in local folklore and myth. You'll see some children almost too small to walk riding horses, while older kids practise their cowboy skills by lassoing tree stumps.

Traditional bullfights are still also a crucial component of local festivals. While *corridas de toros*, in which young men get a testosterone rush by taunting a small cow in a ring, can be seen at festivals all over the country, bulls are only ridden in Guanacaste.

Calderón, a former bull-rider, or *montador*, told me: "Bull-riding became like an addiction for me. It's impossible to explain the adrenalin rush you get when that huge animal is leaping around under you, and you're just desperately hanging on—and then the crazy scramble to get away from under the hooves once you fall off. It meant I was always a huge success with the ladies, but unfortunately I had to stop after I got gored through my knee."

Many *montadores*, mostly males who do it professionally, have died or been permanently disabled. Some women, called *chigüinas,* also ride the bulls, these animals weigh in at up to 770 kg (1,700 lbs). Female participation, however, is generally frowned upon.

Today's bulls are no longer the wild creatures of the days when they roamed the plains unchecked, and so have a *verijera* or *mecate* tied tightly around their groin to enrage them into serious bucking.

The bulls have innocuous names like Pineapple Juice or Holy Spirit, and wait in holding pens while the *mecate* is fixed and the rider gets on. Montadores either ride bareback or on a leather *albarda* (saddle)—sometimes two at the same time, facing each other.

A *cimarrona* (untamed) band plays crashing, discordant music as the spectators wait for the bull to come leaping out of the booth. Montadores are lucky if they manage to stay on top of the bull for a whole minute. Once they have fallen off, the real fun (for the young machos in the crowd) begins.

While the bull snorts and paws the ground, the boys leap into the ring to wave red capes at it and poke it with electric cattle prods. Those that think themselves really tough will dart past it, touching its head or pulling its tail. If the bull chases you, the best option is to get to the bars around the ring and climb up them as quickly as possible!

Once the bull is tired, horsemen come into the ring to lasso it and haul it out— although this may not be necessary, as these days most animals have caught on, and wait by the exit gate, desperate to get out.

GUAITIL POTTERY

In the small villages of Guaitil and San Vicente on the Nicoya Peninsula, more than 90% of the inhabitants make their living from pottery-making. Children learn to make ceramics exactly like those used by their indigenous Chorotega ancestors, which are now on display in the country's museums (although the traditional designs— outlawed by the Spanish as pagan—are only now being re-discovered).

These once-controversial designs feature animal forms and the deities that the Chorotegas once shared with the Aztecs, such as Quetzalcóatl, the feathered serpent; Tezcatlipoca, the smoking mirror; and Tlaloc, the god of rain and fertility.

Firing pottery the traditional way in Guaitil.

83

The whole pot-making process takes days, requiring special clay, sand and natural red, black and white *curiol* dyes, carried in from miles away. The clay is pounded in a massive wooden *pilón*—a kind of mortar and pestle, dried several times in the sun, and fired in wood-burning dome-shaped kilns at high temperatures.

A special jade-type stone called a *guaca* (often found in the graves of Chorotegas) is still used to bring up a gleaming shine on the finished ceramics. Nowadays, some people resort to using shampoo and plastic brushes.

Unfortunately, the supply of crucial dark clay on public land is now running out, and the potters are trying to negotiate with local landowners to secure a new supply.

BOMBAS

A peculiarly Guanacasteco fiesta custom, these short, humorous rhymes are recited as interruptions during traditional dances. The idea is to shout *'bomba!'* to stop the music, before saying your rhyme. (Unfortunately much is lost in translation...)

> *Ayer pasé por tu casa*
> *Y en la puerta un burro había*
> *Y pensando que eras vos*
> *Le dije: Adiós, vida mía!*

> Yesterday I went past your house
> And in the doorway there was a donkey
> Thinking it was you
> I called out: 'Hello, my love!'

> *El zapatito me aprieta*
> *La media me da calor*
> *El muchacho de enfrente*
> *Me tiene loca de amor*

My shoe is too tight
My sock is too hot
I've got a crazy crush on
The boy in front of me.

NICARAGUANS

"Nicaragua and Costa Rica are like the fans of two opposing football teams," a diplomat told me. "They can't survive without each other, but they never have a good word to say about each other either."

These neighboring countries have had all manner of territorial disputes and border spats. Nicaragua even attempted to invade Costa Rica in 1955, when the Nicaraguan dictator Anastasio Somoza tried to help defeated Costa Rican ex-president Dr Rafael Angel Calderón Guardia make a comeback. As a result, the Ticos strongly supported the Sandinistas, which toppled Somoza—but soon swapped their support to the US-backed Contras after deciding they didn't really want a communist neighbor. This gives just a small insight into the background to a very dynamic relationship, in which many Ticos paint themselves as sober pacifists and their *Nica* neighbors as inherently violent.

Nicaraguans are the butt of Tico jokes, much as the Irish are for the English or the Canadians for the Americans. Nica-busting also gives the Ticos an excuse to avoid looking at their own faults. For example, many Tico jokes about the Nicas focus on domestic violence—conveniently overlooking the fact that domestic violence is rife in Costa Rica too.

Depending on whom you believe, up to one million Nicaraguans have come to Costa Rica in the past two decades, driven by poverty, conflict, natural disasters, and chronic unemployment. The official figures are 300,000 (which is still almost 10% of the population), and this number doesn't include the huge numbers of illegal *indocumentados* who easily slip over the border.

What is certain is that Costa Rica has become to Nicaragua what the United States is to Mexico. The staunchly anti-Communist Ticos worry at every mention of a return to power of the Sandinista regime or severe droughts in Nicaragua, which could spark another huge wave of immigration.

Although some Ticos gripe that the Nicas are stealing their jobs, in reality the hard-working Nicaraguans provide the workforce for jobs which most comparatively highly-educated Ticos now refuse to do—as domestic help, security guards, and on construction sites. San José's Parque de la Merced, now more usually known as the Parque de los Nicas, is full every weekend with Nicaraguans who gather there to meet friends and reminisce about home.

"If we didn't have the Nicas to help at harvest time, our sugarcane and coffee would probably rot in the fields," Tomás, a taxi driver grudgingly admitted. "But they're different from us—they're violent people. I feel sorry for them with all they've been through, but they've brought a lot of crime to the country."

Many Ticos complain that their social security payments go towards supporting Nicas who now have equal access to health and other services. "There are so many of them now that we're going to have to start calling this country Costa Nica," grumbled Tomás.

Henry Briceño Barrios, a Nicaraguan working for over a year in Costa Rica, said: "It's true that a few crooks and thieves have come over here, but we're all tarred with the same brush. Most of us just want to work and save some money and go home.

"We would never stay here if it weren't for the terrible conditions we left behind. A lot of Ticos treat us like we're lesser mortals, and make fun of our accent. If we have no documents, employers pay us way below the minimum wage. Many of us aren't educated, and we don't know the law here or our rights so they take advantage of us.

"Our embassy had to complain at international level after the police were rounding up *indocumentados,* stealing their wages and deporting them, without even giving them time to collect their belongings or say goodbye to their families."

GRINGOS

It's estimated that up to 80,000 North Americans, mostly retirees, make their home in Costa Rica—tens of thousands more than the country's entire indigenous population.

It's impossible to know the exact figure as many live in the country as 'perpetual tourists,' but what is certain is that the number has grown steadily since the 1960s, thanks to the relatively low cost of living, good climate, political stability, and tax breaks. There are now more *gringos* in Costa Rica than in any other country in Central America.

Unlike in many Latin countries (especially Mexico), being called *gringo* is not a term of abuse in Costa Rica. (Originally used among Spanish Americans, the Spanish word *gringo*, which means gibberish, is a contemptuous name for an Englishman or an Anglo-American.)

Not having suffered the kind of US occupations or military interventions of much of the rest of Central America, it is hard to find many Ticos with a bad word to say about Americans. Most locals welcome the influx of American and other foreign firms, that help to diversify the economy.

"I've lived here for 10 years," one American told me, "and this is the only Latin country where my being an American has not once caused any problem. I've never even felt that anyone resents me."

A number of shady American characters, wheelers and dealers, however, have sought refuge in Costa Rica's ever-welcoming bosom and secretive banking laws (see, for example, Robert Vesco in the *Heroes and Villains* section at the end of this chapter). There is also a fair crop of Vietnam veterans who could not adjust to life in the United States and who can be found slowly drinking themselves to death in Costa Rican girlie bars.

This has dented the *gringo* image somewhat, and people do complain about the steady Americanization of youth culture, fashion and music. Ticos even have a verb, *agringarse*, for people who take on American styles and habits. Others also lament the changing face of Costa Rica, claiming that gringos have bought up large tracts of the best land, or altered particular neighborhoods. A prime example is Escazú, in San José, now commonly called *Gringolandia*, where prices have been pushed up to such an extent that none but the richest Ticos can afford to live there.

Many gringos live quite closed off from Tico society in wealthy, razor wire-ringed, gated communities, and some—even after decades of living in the country—still struggle to speak Spanish.

A glance at the What's On pages in the English language *Tico Times* gives an idea of the size and organization of the American community. More like a flyer from a Californian New Age social group, it offers clubs in such very un-Tico areas as shamanic healing, dowsing, kite-flying, communicating with dolphins, and judo for pregnant women.

QUAKERS

One of the smallest, but most interesting, social groups in Costa Rica is made up of the descendants of a group of dairy-farming Quakers from Alabama, USA.

Having been imprisoned in the early 1950s for refusing, on moral grounds, to obey the military draft for the Korean War, they decided, once freed, to start a new life in a more peaceful place. Costa Rica seemed the perfect choice, and they slowly carved the mountain community of Monteverde out of the surrounding cloud forest and set up the cheese factory, which would one day come to make the best cheese in the country.

Their foresight in preserving some of the forest to protect their watershed led to the arrival of biologists who were intrigued by the area's endemic species. Later, intrepid tourists also started to arrive, and as dairy farming became less and less profitable, more and more areas were allowed to revert back to forest. Monteverde is now the second most visited tourist spot in the country, and contains more plant species in 26 square kilometers (10 square miles) than the USA and Canada combined.

Several thousand people now live where 50 years ago there was hardly anyone but a few Tico farmers and illegal hooch distillers. The atrocious road leading to Monteverde still acts as a kind of filter. There are now controversial plans afoot to pave the road, however, which, according to Quaker Joe Stuckey, could mean "one of the final barriers to isolation will fall."

Only around 50 practicing Quakers remain. Several families have left, disillusioned with how their quiet retreat has turned into a tourist attraction, and others have married into Tico families.

Those that remain are fairly wary of outside contact. They retain the Friends Meeting House where silent group worship is held, and their children still receive English-language education based on Quaker principles at the village school.

HEROES AND VILLAINS

Ticos are very proud of the achievements of their compatriots, and are really appreciative if a foreigner knows anything about them. The following list (including some non-Ticos who have had a major impact on the country) provides a brief rundown of some of the most famous goodies and baddies in Costa Rica, past and present.

Claudia Poll Ahrens: Costa Rica's Olympic medal-winning swimmer. Born in Managua, Nicaragua, she grew up in Costa Rica and is a Tico citizen. Won her first Olympic gold medal in 1996 in Atlanta, and has established many new national, Latin American, international, and world records. In June 2000, Claudia tested positive for an illegal, performance-enhancing steriod and was suspended from competition for four years. She claims innocence.

Laureano Alban: A poet chosen by the Spanish government to write an official poem *El Viaje Interminable* to mark the 500th anniversary of Christopher Columbus's discovery of the New World. The poem presents Columbus's journey as a metaphor for the human confrontation of the unknown.

Padre Mínor Calvo: A Catholic priest, famous for his crusades against homosexuality, who was plunged into controversy after police surprised him in his car with a young male passenger late one night in a notorious gay cruising area of San José. The scandal grew as details of this event—along with the alleged financial management of the Catholic station Radio María which he ran—were repeatedly broadcast by journalist Parmenio Medina (see below). Supposedly sent to Italy by his superiors in the Church after the closure of Radio María, Calvo was found to be hiding out on a farm in Cartago following Medina's brutal and mysterious murder.

Pancho Carrasco: Costa Rica's first heroine. In 1856, she enlisted as a cook in President Juan Rafael Mora's army fighting the American freebooter William Walker. Unusually for a woman of her time, Pancho was literate, and served as the president's secretary. In the famous Battle of Rivas she fired at an enemy soldier, forcing him to abandon his cannon and flee, and was carried victoriously on her companions' shoulders. She later worked with sick and dying soldiers, and after the war received a medal for heroism. At her funeral in 1891, she received the military honors of a general.

Jorge Jiménez Deredia: Famous Tico sculptor selected to produce a sculpture of St. Marcelino de Champagnat, founder of the Marist brothers, to mark 150 years of diplomatic relations between Costa Rica and the Vatican. The 4.5-meter (15-feet) tall marble sculpture is situated in the left transept of St. Peter's Basilica, and was blessed by the Pope in September 2000.

Dr Franklin R. Chang-Díaz: Costa Rica's very own astronaut. One of 19 people chosen from 4,000 hopefuls and the first Latin American to be accepted by NASA (although this required him to become an American citizen). He has made numerous space flights and headed investigations into subjects as varied as Chagas disease and anti-matter. Most famously, his work on a plasma rocket is hoped to get the voyage time to Mars down to seven months.

Jorge Debravo: Brilliant young poet born into an extremely poor family who went without shoes throughout his childhood. He spent all the money he earned harvesting corn on a dictionary, and a teacher helped him win a scholarship to get through primary school. His first poems were published in a local newspaper shortly afterwards. Debravo died in a car accident in 1967 at the age of 29.

Fabián Dobles: Wrote about 20 books of poetry, novels and short stories, most famous of which were his 25 tales of Costa Rican life in *Historias de Tata Mundo*. Dobles often wrote using the *campesino* language of the countryside and peasants, and won the Magón National Culture Prize in 1986.

Quince Duncan: The country's top black writer. A prolific writer of academic works, essays, and novels about the Afro-Caribbean experience in Costa Rica.

Editus: A popular Tico musical trio whose eclectic music combines violin, guitar, Afro-Caribbean percussion, and sounds from the rain forest. They accompanied Panamanian salsa legend Rubén Blades on his European tour, and produced a record with him, *Tiempo*, that won a 1999 Grammy award.

Geovanny Escalante: Saxophone player from the famous Tico band Marfil, who broke Kenny G's world record for holding a single saxophone note in 1998. After three months of training in the gym, the 24-year-old held the note for 90 minutes and 45 seconds, nearly double Kenny G's timing.

Carlos Luis 'Calufa' Fallas: Grew up desperately poor and started to work on a banana plantation at the age of 16. As well as being a notorious womanizer, he went on to become a Communist Party leader who led the first big strike of banana workers against the United Fruit Company in 1934. Most of his literary works were gritty pieces focusing on the tough conditions suffered by the poor. The most famous of his works, *Mamita Yunai*, was a 'denunciation of the abuses' suffered by the country's mainly black banana workers. He won the prestigious Magón National Culture Prize in 1965 and died the following year.

José 'Don Pepe' Figueres Ferrer: Coffee farmer who led the

91

civil war of 1948 and became the architect of the present Costa Rican state and constitution. A virulent anti-communist, Don Pepe served as president three times, and was responsible for abolishing the army, nationalizing the banks, giving the vote to women and blacks, and overseeing the country's 1970s cultural revolution. He died in 1990.

Carlos Gagini: An intellectual, anti-imperialist, and linguist, he was a proponent of the international language Esperanto and compiled a dictionary of the Costa Rican indigenous Térraba language. In the 1910s, he wrote *La Caída del Aguila*, or the fall of Aguila, a spookily prescient novel about a world war involving an alliance between Germany and Japan. In the Jules Verne tradition, the book also featured a submarine base under the Isla del Coco. He died in 1925.

Dr. Marcus Mosiah Garvey: Founder of the black Back to Africa movement, whose slogan was 'Up you mighty race, you can accomplish what you will'. Born in Jamaica, Garvey developed many of his ideas after working in a Costa Rican banana plantation and seeing the misery and exploitation suffered by his fellow workers. In 1919, he set up the Black Star Line to buy ships to return several million of his followers to the homeland, and the following year proclaimed himself provisional president of Africa. This move was supported by many white supremacists, such as the Ku Klux Klan. He suffered a series of economic disasters, however, and in 1922 was arrested for having tried to fund the Black Star Line by selling 'shares' in ships he had not yet bought to disaffected black people all over the USA and Caribbean. He was jailed, later deported to Jamaica, and died in 1940 in obscurity in London. Older black Costa Ricans remember Garvey's visits to the country, and the Black Star Line Club still operates in Limón as a social center.

Joaquín Gutiérrez: The 'man of the century' in national literature, according to the newspaper La Nación, Gutiérrez wrote novels, travel books, and translated both Shakespeare and Mao Tse Tung into Spanish. He wrote his most famous prize-winning novel *Cocorí* in a week, was national chess champion at 25, and twice a vice presidential candidate. A communist like his friends, Calufa and Fabián Dobles, he traveled in the Soviet Union, China, and Vietnam. He spent 25 years in Chile, and the Chilean Nobel Prize-winning poet Pablo Neruda was one of his biggest fans. A bronze bust of him can be seen in the Teatro Nacional, along with those of many other great figures from the Costa Rican arts. He is the first Latin American sculptor whose work is included in St. Peter's Basilica, Rome. He died in 2000.

Max Jiménez: Probably Costa Rica's best known artist. Also a sculptor and writer, Jiménez was strongly influenced by black art in Cuba, and is known for his colorful and monumental paintings of misshapen figures. He died in 1947.

Parmenio Medina: Colombian investigative journalist who lived for almost 30 years in Costa Rica. His irreverent radio show *La Patada* (The Kick) mercilessly sniffed out wrong-doing and dodgy dealings. He was shot in a professional hit-style killing in 2001, which was the first of its kind in the country and left peace-loving Ticos dumbfounded. The murder came after he had spent months lambasting the alleged financial management of the Catholic Church radio station Radio María run by charismatic priest Padre Mínor Calvo.

Carmen Naranjo: In the vein of many Latin American literary figures, Naranjo has combined her writing work with a career in the civil service. She was the administrative manager of the CCSS, first female Minister of Culture, and ambassador to Israel, as well as a board member of Editorial Costa Rica, a University of Costa Rica professor, director of the National Museum, and an expert advisor for UNICEF and the Organization of American States. Her works attack the meaninglessness of urban life in abstract, experimental style. She won the Premio Magón, Costa Rica's top culture prize in 1986.

Dr. Clodomiro 'Clorito' Picado: Famous scientist who Ticos claim discovered the properties of penicillin before Alexander Fleming. He had published a paper in 1927 on how *penicillium sp* inhibited the growth of streptococus bacteria in his patients. As a young man, he studied zoology and biology at the Sorbonne in Paris, and later became director of the San Juan de Dios Hospital in San José. He published 115 works, studied poisonous snakes (developing many pioneering anti-venins), bacterial infections of beans, fermentation of coffee, the benefits of iodine, and the morphology of the guava fly before he died in 1944.

Teodürico Quirós: An architect and painter, who won the coveted Premio Magón. In his paintings he specialized in Tico themes such as farms, churches, and pulperías. He died in 1977.

Sor María Romero: Nicaraguan-born nun, made an honorary Costa Rican citizen, famous for her work with the poor, apparently miraculous cures, and supposed clairvoyance. She died in 1977 and is in the process of beatification by the Vatican.

José León Sánchez: Huetar Indian wrongfully convicted at the age of 20 of stealing religious art from the Basílica of Los Angeles in Cartago and killing a guard. He was sentenced to 45 years on the notorious prison island of San Lucas in the Gulf of Nicoya. Although Costa Rica was the first Latin American country to abolish the death penalty in 1871, life on San Lucas was almost worse than death and few survived more than five years. The prisoners, who wore leg irons and chains, were regularly lashed with steel-tipped bullwhips, caged in inhuman conditions, and drowned if they tried to escape. Sánchez survived being machine-gunned, a suicide attempt, and torture by having toothpicks forced into his ears. He spent 20 years on the island, during which time he was known only as number 1713. Sánchez taught himself to read and write on San Lucas and became the jail's letter writer. He is now touted for potential Nobel Prize nomination, having written such books as *La Isla de los Hombres Solos* (The Island of Single Men), which recounts with horrifying clarity conditions of life on the island. Sánchez, who was not declared innocent until July 24, 1998, now lives in Mexico, where he has written several works about the Aztecs. He is a vocal campaigner against miscarriages of justice and the death penalty.

Oscar Arias Sánchez: President in the 1980s who was so popular that many people wanted to change the constitution to allow him to govern for a second term. Arias was responsible for drawing up a peace plan for the war-torn neighboring countries of Central America which, although only partially implemented, won him the Nobel Peace Prize in 1987.

Juan Santamaría: A Costa Rican national hero, Santamaría was a young soldier who bravely torched the wooden fort where the US filibuster William Walker and his men were hiding out during their failed invasion of Central America in 1855, despite being shot repeatedly.

Rigoberto Stewart: Controversial black Costa Rican intellectual and president of Associación Limón Real, which claims to create a free and autonomous region in Costa Rica, coupled with absolute economic freedom and other individual liberties. Limón has traditionally been ignored by politicians in San José and is one of Costa Rica's most discriminated against and exploited areas.

Robert Vesco: Disgraced US financier indicted for his involvement in the Watergate scandal, he fled the United States in 1972 after being accused of defrauding US$224 million and being linked with the illegal drugs trade. He was offered shelter by President José Figueres Ferrer and lived for several years in Costa Rica (as well as the Bahamas, Antigua, and Nicaragua), where his wealth gave him massive power. None of these countries agreed to extradition requests and he continued to increase his huge wealth through arms sales to Libya. In the early 1980s, he was accepted in Cuba for 'humanitarian reasons,' but was later condemned there for defrauding investors with his mystery drug TX, a supposed cure for AIDS and cancer. He was finally jailed after being extradited to the United States in 1995.

Paulo 'Chope' Wanchope: Costa Rica's most famous footballer. Has played in the UK for various teams including Manchester City, but ran into trouble with the British clubs for his temper tantrums and supposed sense of self-importance. At home, Chope is a hero and

Costa Rican newspapers chart the fate of whichever club the striker is playing for on an almost daily basis. He played in the Costa Rican team at the 2002 World Cup, scoring twice against Brazil.

Ronnie Zamora: Tico sentenced to a life jail term in the US in 1977 at the age of 15 for shooting an old lady during a robbery. He and his friends sold her belongings and went to Disneyland with the proceeds. Zamora was tried as an adult and, famously, his trial was the first ever to be televised in the US. His lawyer raised an insanity defense, brought about by "television intoxication", 'brainwashed' by violent TV programs. The case stunned peaceable Costa Rica, and people continue to be divided over Zamora, who is now trying to secure parole.

Francisco Zúñiga: Famous Tico sculptor, originally trained by his father, who was a sculptor of wooden religious images. He moved to Mexico in 1936, saying he felt limited and under-appreciated in his homeland. He continued working even after he became blind in 1990 and died in 1998 of cancer, aged 86, apparently as a result of prolonged contact with sculpting materials. He won numerous prizes, and his biggest works were the 1954 reliefs on the Secretaría de Comunicaciones y Transportes in Mexico City. He also collaborated on the Monumento de la Revolución. His style was simple and austere, and he specialized in pre-Hispanic and rural themes.

Manuel 'Melico' Salazar Zúñiga: Costa Rican opera singer who came to be known as 'El Gran Tenor de América.' At the age of 20, he went to train in Italy and performed there as well as in the United States, Europe, Canada, and all over Latin America. At 40, he returned to Costa Rica to set up a national school of song. He was a member of the Metropolitan Opera Company in New York where he was given 'all the Italian roles', and performed his favorite opera, *Aida*, 10 times. He died in 1940.

— *Chapter Four*—
SOCIAL CUSTOMS AND ATTITUDES

FAMILY AND PRIVACY

It is impossible to exaggerate the importance of family in Costa Rica. I lived with one family for three months, and in all that time—although someone popped around to the house virtually every day— only twice was the visitor a non-relative. Nor was this a family of social freaks.

Historically, Ticos lived in isolated mountain hamlets, where they had to rely above all on their relatives for working the farm, emotional support, and socializing—to the extent that the family is described in the constitution as the "natural basis of Costa Rican society."

If you become extremely good friends with a Tico, they will probably describe you as being *como un hermano* (like a brother). Meanwhile, Mother's Day is probably one of the most extravagant holidays in the country, and Father's Day is also seriously celebrated.

On the Day of the Dead graveyards are full of people bringing flowers to relatives' graves and cleaning headstones.

Until very recently, most people lived in the village where they grew up, and even now family members rarely live far apart from each other. A plot of family land is often divided up so that offspring can build their houses right next to their parents.

The irony, however, is that Costa Rica today has a fairly high rate of divorce. This has led to a situation in many families where, for example, one child lives with the mother, another with the father, and a third with a grandparent.

Even when family members do not actually live in the same house, they get together on weekends and holidays for *reuniones* and talk on the telephone to each other constantly. They are not embarrassed to let their relatives know exactly how much they mean to them. One girl I traveled with, who was going to see her mother later that same day, finished a phone call: *'Chao Mamita, la quiero muchísimo, que Dios me la cuide... le mando un beso Madrecita,'* (Goodbye Mummy, I love you very much. I'm asking God to take care of you... I'm sending you a kiss Mummykins.)

This may seem over-the-top to say the least to non-Latinos, but this constant love-bombing ensures that Ticos do not feel unloved or awkward with intimacy. Coming from a rather typically inexpressive English family, I was hugely impressed by Tico children, who do not screw up their faces in disgust when asked to kiss grandma, and will happily chat away quite maturely with all generations of family members. Sisters and brothers generally get on with each other a lot better than their counterparts in the United Kingdom or United States.

Such confidence among children is probably due to the fact that they come in for a huge amount of pampering. It's suggested that this is a remnant of the extremely tough early days of Costa Rica, when youngsters were unlikely to survive until the age of five. In order for them to enjoy the little life they might have, they were, and still are *chineados* or spoilt. In some rural areas, you still see babies with red ribbons tied around their wrist, supposed to ward off evil and illness, and during the rainy season every baby in the land is swaddled in a massive furry rug or quilt—even though the temperature is usually still considerably hotter than a British summer.

Although the country's birth rate, especially in urban areas, has declined sharply in line with the infant mortality rate (from 7.3 children per woman in 1960 to about three today), Ticos love babies. If you haven't had children by your mid-20s you will be considered strange, and you should fully expect to be roped in as an impromptu babysitter.

Most people live in the family nest much longer than in the United States or United Kingdom, often even after they are married. Students, given the size of the country, obviously don't leave home to study in a distant city, and most young Ticos cannot afford their own home. Ticos rarely rent and house ownership is more than 70%.

Grandparents often also live with their children and older people are well respected, being known as *ciudadanos de oro* (golden citizens). One woman told me: "The fact that we live with our families for so long means that we really get to know our parents as adults. They become like real people to us rather than just parents, and we start to really appreciate everything they have sacrificed for us. That's why, unlike in your culture, it makes it very hard for us to put them in an old people's home."

With home having such a sacred quality for Ticos, it is not surprising that they are often reluctant to allow any but the most intimate of friends into the bosom of their family. This may also have something to do with having to share their house with many family members and the fear of outsiders finding out how modest their living conditions actually are. Middle-class highlanders are definitely more formal and reserved in this sense than those in the countryside, but in general most Ticos would prefer to socialize away from home.

That's not to say you won't be invited to a Tico home, but quite often these invitations are meaningless—intended as a gesture of friendship, but never really serious. Because of this, Ticos invited to someone's house often fail to turn up.

Nicaraguans, who are generally perceived as more open and relaxed than their southern neighbors, joke: "A Tico is quick to invite you to his home—but it's tough to make him give you the address."

Juan Carlos, a model, said: "You can't just say to a Tico: 'Pop round to my house any time you like.' That, to a Tico, sounds like you're being nice, but—because of the way we feel about our homes—he would never act on it. You'd have to confirm a specific day and time, probably several times, before a Tico thought you really meant it."

Another man in his 30s added: "When I was growing up, everyone in my family had locks on the inside of their bedroom doors—I never even thought that was strange. I've also got friends I've known all my life, but I've never been in their houses.

"The way I see it is that this is a small country, so the boundaries of privacy are very important to us. The home is a sacred haven pretty much for family only, but even there we need our own space."

Television seems to have had an effect too. Most Ticos are hopelessly addicted to television, particularly *telenovelas* (soap operas). In many middle-class homes, instead of everyone sitting down to watch a program together, there is a set in every individual's room.

TO 'QUEDAR BIEN'

Within a very short time of being in Costa Rica, you will start to feel as though you are a pawn in someone else's game of 'Six Degrees of Separation.' Even in San José, you will bump into the same people again and again—and if you are meeting someone for the first time you will no doubt discover that they either know, or quite probably are related to, several other people you have already met.

This is not surprising in a small country with only a few million people. Imagine how much worse it must have been in the early 20th century, say, when people hardly ever left their own small community and everyone literally did know everyone else. In this situation, communal in-fighting would have spelled disaster, so Ticos developed a coping mechanism: being nice.

Ticos are internationally renowned for being some of the nicest and most generous people you can meet. Their overuse of *con mucho gusto* is almost as bad as the British obsession with 'please' and 'thank you.' Ticos want to *quedar bien* (pronounced Kay-DAR bee-EN)with everyone, which means something like 'not rocking the boat, staying on good terms, saving face, and appearing amicable.'

If you want to *quedar bien*, the basic rule is never to be rude or to openly refute what others say. It also means never groveling; it is a solution which allows everyone to walk away with their pride intact.

Most importantly, you must not shout at, humiliate, or criticize anyone, especially in public. Ticos are so proud and easily offended that the criminal code lays down a prison term of up to 50 days for a person who offends another's 'dignity or honor,' especially in public.

All of this is, in essence, what gives the Ticos their peaceable reputation, but it also results in what some outsiders regard as hypocritical behavior .

Ticos don't like to admit they are wrong, and you will not *quedar bien* with anyone by trying to push the point—as I found out in a particularly stressful incident after someone wiped four hours' worth of work off my computer. I was the one who ended up apparently at fault for having made an unseemly fuss in public.

In order to *quedar bien*, many Ticos say 'yes' when they mean 'no', simply to avoid conflict or offence. The result for outsiders can, unsurprisingly, be infuriating. Long-term civil servant and award-winning author, Carmen Naranjo, even went as far as to publish a list of all the phrases Ticos (especially civil servants) use in order to be non-committal.

Similarly, many people don't like to appear foolish or unhelpful by admitting they don't know something, so you should always ask factual questions rather than ones with yes or no answers. When asking directions, it's always best to check with two or three people just to make sure their answers coincide.

In *The Ticos* by the Biesanz family, playwright Melvin Méndez explains: "People in other countries can be categorical. Not Ticos. We beat around the bush to avoid saying: 'No,' a syllable which seems almost rude to us, and rather than hurt someone, we say one thing and do another."

Tico's need to *quedar bien* means that problems must be solved by bargaining and consensus, even within the government. On the plus side, conflict is avoided—but sometimes at the expense of real decision-making.

CHOTEO, CLASS, AND SNOBBERY

If there's anything Ticos hate, it's people who show off or get ideas above their station, and *choteo* is a kind of good-natured mockery that nips any such arrogance firmly in the bud. In Costa Rica pride always comes before a fall.

Choteo rarely extends beyond friendly irony (after all, you still want to *quedar bien* with your victim), but at times can descend to violent attacks, often behind the person's back. Many say *choteo* stems from small-minded envy of those who do well. Ticos are intrinsically conservative and resistant to change; the added prospect of *choteo* can make them fearful of attempting anything outstanding or imaginative.

The flipside of the *choteo* coin, however, is its power to *igualar* (to make everyone the same) that is evident in the general lack of snobbery in Costa Rica. While the popular myth of a classless society is clearly not true, the country's special history, plus decades of social spending by the government, means that there is a massive middle class. While there is obviously a social elite, there are none of the obscene class differences between very rich and very poor seen in most other Latin countries. Ticos say that in their society people have *roce*, meaning that all the classes mix.

Rich people aren't ostentatious—you don't see any stretch limos or lavish parties here. San José does have a big country club, but many of the members are foreigners. "Really rich Ticos wouldn't join," explained Darren Mora, a book shop owner. "They see it as a place full of brash, tasteless Americans. In fact, the richer classes traditionally encourage their children to socialize with members of lower classes in order to instill them with a sense of equality."

The president is a regular mortal who usually does not even have bodyguards. "I've met all of the last eight presidents just walking in the street," said Darren. "There's nothing surprising about that."

Ticos value people who are *humilde* (humble) and don't feel that they are any less worthy than someone who is financially better off. The company janitor will feel comfortable striking up a conversation with the CEO, although they wouldn't be likely to socialize.

There is, however, some class-based snobbery. The middle-class like to *aparentar* with nice clothes and possessions—which are often beyond their means and have to be bought on installment plans. Many of them until recently *campesinos* themselves, they might look down on both the rural poor (*maiceros*) and *comehuevos* (literally 'egg eaters')—the Costa Rican equivalent of American 'white trash.' *Comehuevos* tend to camp at favorite beaches during holidays, where the sand is often black and volcanic, becoming burning hot in the sun. The *comehuevos*, who can't afford restaurant food, bury eggs in the sand to cook them. They are also seen as loud drunks who leave litter behind. At the other end of the scale, the pampered offspring of rich families are known as *fresas* (strawberries).

TICO TIME AND BROKEN PROMISES

While the Spanish have the Mañana Syndrome, the Costa Ricans have Tico Time. Until around 100 years ago, the fastest you could travel across Costa Rica's treacherous mountain roads was at the speed of your nimblest mule. It took almost a week to reach Puntarenas from San José. As hurrying was senseless in this environment, people unsurprisingly, developed a very elastic sense of time.

Tico Time means arriving late (around 15 to 30 minutes for official appointments)—and up to several hours late for meeting friends.

Once you have waited in a few lines in Costa Rican government offices, you will soon learn that *ahorita* (right now) in fact means 'maybe never.' The less emphatic, and sadly much less common, *ahora* (now) is actually more immediate.

Increasingly, contact with foreigners has led many Ticos to recognize their lateness as rude, though usually only in the work environment.

"I invited a group of people to dinner recently," said Ray, an American living in San José. "All the Ticos turned up late, some of them four hours late. Incredibly, they were peeved with me for having served dinner before they got there. Others didn't turn up at all, and didn't even call. When I saw one of the no-shows later, they were completely bewildered that I saw their behavior as a lack of respect."

"We're really *incumplidos* (unreliable)" my friend Natalia del Valle happily admitted. "We make an arrangement with someone, and at that moment we're genuinely enthused about the idea, but later we forget, or something else comes up.

"We're not used to making arrangements way in advance, and we never think that the other person is taking it very seriously either. The best way to make sure we do something is to call us right then and there and say: 'Hey, are you busy? Let's go for lunch!'"

In 1853, Moritz Wagner and Karl Scherzer, two Germans traveling through Costa Rica, reported on exactly this unhappy kind of culture clash. Coming from one of the most notoriously punctual nations on Earth, you can almost hear the tone of indignant betrayal in their voices: "One cannot trust the promises and contracts of a Costa Rican. This is the most characteristic trait of his nature. Punctuality and conscientious keeping of one's word are extremely rare."

Little has changed, and today, some foreigners at the ends of their tethers end up only maintaining friendships with people they can trust to show up on time.

FLIRTING AND ROMANCE

"It's harder to find a faithful man in Costa Rica than a Piña Colada in the Sahara," I was told by an earnest young Tico I had met only an hour earlier. He grabbed my hand across the table and looked deep into my eyes, adding: "But I want you to know that I'm really different."

As if this didn't sound fishy enough, it didn't take long to verify with friends that he was, in fact, an incorrigible womanizer .

"I'm a Latino," he explained, unabashed, when confronted with the truth. "I have my pride and a reputation to maintain. I'll say anything it takes to get a woman out on a date. Being serious and sincere with a woman like you usually works like a charm."

Ticos love to *dar pelota* (flirt) and clearly do not do so surreptitiously. If you're a woman, men will use any opportunity to smile, blow kisses, or strike up a conversation with you, and their heads continually swivel, owl-like and slack-jawed, at passing female pedestrians. The waiter at one restaurant I ate at bombarded me with hopeful little notes telling me, for example: "Meeting people like you makes me happy to be alive." Some restaurants and public places even have signs banning *escenas amorosas* (amorous scenes).

"I was quite shocked at first," said Adrian Hepworth, a British photographer living in Costa Rica. "In my country, if you fancy someone you do your best to ignore them and appear really cool. There's none of that here—if someone likes you they'll make it really obvious. They'll stare and smile at you for ages, or just come up and tell you right out."

Ticos are also very traditional, however. Heaven help the man who expects his date to pick up her half of the tab, or the woman who fails to pamper her boyfriend as if he were a small child. You will also become heavily involved with your opposite number's family at a much earlier stage than in an American or European relationship.

"Before you know it, you will spend every weekend either going to your partner's parents' place, or having them to yours," said a German, who had been dating a Tica for six months. "The first time I met my girlfriend's family, they threw a huge party with 80 family members who had come to check me out! They're wonderful people

though, so I don't mind, and it's fun to be part of a close family after growing up in such a different society."

INFIDELITY AND MACHISMO

"All the men here think I'm stupid and pathetic," complained my Dutch friend Frans Baas, who was working in a small Tico town. The outrageous behavior that had earned him such harsh criticism was not taking up embroidery, hating football, or refusing to drink *guaro*, but staying faithful to his girlfriend from home and—even worse—limiting himself to just the one girlfriend.

Frans's Tico friends were continually trying to set him up with local women so he could be suitably *macho*—a characteristic which itself is said to have come to Costa Rica via the Spanish from the Arabs.

Machismo almost demands that men be unfaithful—leading to Costa Rica's profusion of 'love motels,' which offer special short-stay rates for men and their *queridas*, or mistresses. These are also used by younger people, who usually live with their families until they are married.

Many men have children with different women and marriage is becoming less and less popular, with couples instead being involved in loose *uniones libres*. There were historically always a certain number of these in the *campo* because of lack of access to churches. Around 51% of children are born to single mothers. The figure in the UK is 44%, but the difference is that many more UK couples actually live together. In response to growing pressure, the government has passed a law allowing women to force their (ex-) lovers to take DNA paternity tests, to enable them to claim child support.

Infidelity, unsurprisingly, breeds jealousy, and although Ticas tend to forgive their men's infidelity, some foreign women living in Costa Rica find it hard to make female friends, as Ticas sometimes view them as a threat. Unfortunately, machismo can also make it hard to find a truly platonic friendship with a man.

One foreign man, who has lived, worked, and dated all over Latin America, said: "I find Ticas generally less passionate, open and spontaneous than any other Latinas. They'll be calling you *'mi amor'* within minutes, but it often seems quite insincere.

"I think this is because they come from a culture in which male infidelity is virtually condoned, and this has made many of them quite mercenary about getting hold of a man who will at least provide them with a comfortable lifestyle while they put up with his affairs. They are not ashamed to admit this."

Consequently, for many Ticas, comparatively wealthy foreign men are an irresistible honey pot.

In any Internet café in San José you are virtually guaranteed to find several young women searching the web on sites such as http:www.spanisheyescostarica.com and http:www.MyTica.com, looking for gringo boyfriends. Such sites post scores of new women each day, and promise wife-hunting Americans that they can meet up to 600 hopefuls during a special six-day reconnaissance trip. In addition, they claim, bringing home a Tica poses fewer immigration difficulties than a wife from Russia or Thailand.

Saray Ramírez, who has had both a Spanish and a Swiss husband, says it is not a question of money. "Ticos are very loving and romantic, but you can't trust them," she says. "Foreigners seem to be much colder, but at least they're more sincere. They don't tell you they love you unless they really mean it, and they're also more progressive and open-minded."

Many Ticas are definitely being corrupted by the growth in tourism, and many male holidaymakers come for one thing alone—prostitution, which is legal and widespread. Worryingly, cases of child prostitution and pornography are also on the rise, partly as a result of large-scale crackdowns in other hot spots such as Southeast Asia.

However, Bruce Harris, director of the Casa Alianza organization, which fights child abuse across the whole region, says the majority of demand comes from local pedophiles. According to him, up to 3,000 children are being prostituted in San José alone (more than anywhere else in Central America), and nearly 300 complaints have been lodged with the special prosecutor. So far, however, there have been very few prosecutions. According to UNICEF, up to 80% of these children have been previously sexually abused at home.

Milena Grillo, director of the child advocacy group Paniamor, explained: "We've been too distracted by the popular claims that Costa Rica is a peaceful democracy with no army. This prompts a collective unconscious perception that violence is non-existent. How can society fight a problem it's not willing to recognize?"

The government is legally bound to hand over funds to the Patronato Nacional de la Infancia (PANI), the country's child welfare organization each year to help address the problem. It has, however, defaulted on the payments in recent years, as it has in its funding to almost every other state-funded welfare and environmental body, claiming that there simply isn't enough money to go around. Casa Alianza has resorted to legal action to try to force payment.

Mr. Harris said: "In the past, the government has swept the situation under the carpet, and attacked us rather than admitting there was a problem, but hopefully things will now change. The first step in getting to the root of this child abuse must be prevention, education, and tackling *machismo* and violence in the home, as well as training and equipping the people who are going to go after the abusers. It's going to be tough though, in a culture where children can still be married at the age of 14, and where—until the late 1990s—a rapist of an underage girl could not be prosecuted if he offered to marry the victim."

It is also hard to wonder whether the country's legitimate sex industry is not adding to the problem. Various sex cinemas in San José advertise their films in the national newspapers—with names such as *Adolescentes en Celo* (Teenagers on Heat) and *Cuando las Colegiales se Confiesan* (When Schoolgirls Confess).

WOMEN

Today, Costa Rica has a higher percentage of female politicians (including several former vice presidents) than either the United States or Britain. The majority of university students are female too.

Things, however, have not always been this way. Women only got the vote in 1948, and until 1974, they could only divorce adulterous husbands for 'open and scandalous concubinage.' Interestingly, no such requirement existed for men.

Machismo may be on the decline, but it's far from dead, and while violence in public is minimal, domestic violence is widespread. Women have traditionally been too ashamed or afraid to denounce abusers, and the scale of the problem is only now becoming clear. At least two women are killed each month by violent partners and the women's support group Cefemina receives up to 100 calls on its domestic violence hotline every day.

A female response to machismo has been *marianismo*, in which women take a kind of long-suffering pride in their strength in dealing with their situation. In fact, many women are now effectively the family breadwinner.

109

Xinia Vindas of Cefemina said: "Most men think of nothing but work, sleep, football, and other women. They expect us to accept their infidelity, because, they say, Tico men are just naturally *muy calientes* (very passionate) and can't help it. Usually we can't leave them even if we want to, because getting financial support for ourselves and our children is like getting blood out of a stone."

Many women's rights advocates also feel the traditionally powerful Catholic Church has been an added fly in the ointment of women's progress. It has historically done its utmost to prevent sex education in schools, which is at least partly to blame for the country's huge number of teenage pregnancies. More than half of all young people use no contraception at all, abortion is illegal, and it's not at all unusual to meet 50-year-old great grandparents.

HOMOSEXUALITY

While Costa Rica is seen as something of a gay Mecca in Central America as there is no explicit official repression of homosexuality, *machista* attitudes still prevail.

In a 2001 survey in the *Tico Times*, Costa Ricans were asked whom they disapproved of most in their society. While Nicaraguans came in with 13%, well over 30% of respondents pointed the finger at *playos* (homosexuals).

Rick Stern, a psychologist and gay rights activist, who has lived in Costa Rica for 13 years, said there has been no official repression in the country since the Supreme Court ruled in the late 1990s that the police had acted illegally in raiding a gay nightclub. Such raids had been common in the 1970s and 1980s, when police would even shave the heads of those they arrested.

"There's still a lot of intolerance among society itself, the family and the Church though," said Mr. Stern, "and this means a lot of people, especially in traditional rural areas, remain firmly in the closet."

Many Ticos perceived as being too openly gay have been kicked out of their families and, as in many Latin countries, Costa Rica has traditionally had a large number of 'bisexual marriages,' with gay husbands trying to conform to social norms for appearances' sake.

Anti-gay hysteria reached a peak in 1998, when charismatic priest Padre Mínor Calvo, the country's self-proclaimed 'Guardian of Morality' incited the beach community of Quepos to stop the planned visit of a group of gay tourists. He called gay people examples of debauchery and decay, and tried to link homosexuality with child sex tourism. His crusade led to street protests and a bomb threat against Triángulo Rosa, a gay support group. In a bizarre twist, three years later Calvo was caught by police late one night in a notorious San José gay cruising district, La Sabana, with a young man in his car. The priest insisted he was giving the boy a driving lesson.

Conservatism in Costa Rican society, along with legal prostitution, has also led to a phenomenon which surprises many first-time visitors passing through the area of El Registro by taxi at night—the transvestite prostitute patch. Up to 200 *travestís*, many of whom make disturbingly convincing women, ply their trade on the streets.

"It's the only thing they can do," said Rick Stern. "Latin culture means that young men who want to dress up as women and are not prepared to hide it cannot get any kind of regular job, so they usually start in prostitution as teenagers."

He added that attitudes are changing, and being gay in San José is probably better than being gay in a similarly sized city in the United States—and definitely better than elsewhere in Central America. Despite their *machismo,* Ticos loathe public violence, meaning open abuse or attacks in the streets are almost non-existent. San José has many gay bars and saunas, as well as a newspaper *Gayness*, which is available in bookstores around the university area.

"We Ticos are quite naïve, and very good at turning a blind eye to uncomfortable realities we don't want to see," Juan Carlos, a gay model, told me. "You can be gay as long as you don't force people to confront it by being too indiscreet. The worst you're likely to experience is some frowning and muttering."

GOSSIP

Gossip, or *chismes,* is a major part of life in Costa Rica, and the old Spanish saying *pueblo pequeño, infierno grande* (small town, big hell) is still more apt than ever. People really worry about *el que dirán?* (what will people say?).

A hugely popular radio show featuring the ever-nosey character Doña Vina, highlighted the issue and spawned a whole new verb, *vinear,* meaning to gossip (a nosey person is *muy vina*), and Samuel Rovinski's play *Las Fisgonas de Paso Ancho* (*The Busybodies of Paso Ancho*) is obligatory reading in schools.

People from Cartago are particularly renowned as gossips, and are sometimes called *begoñas,* supposedly because they plant begonias in their window boxes as something to hide behind as they spy on their neighbors.

Ticos will happily talk for ages, and in great detail, about the most seemingly insignificant goings-on in the lives of friends, neighbors and television stars—particularly if any whiff of scandal is involved.

My Dutch friend, Frans, who went to work in the small town of Puerto Viejo de Sarapiquí, told me of his arrival there.

"The first night, I only met the family I was staying with and didn't leave the house. The next morning I went for a walk around the town and people were going past waving at me and shouting: 'Hello Frans!' I couldn't believe it was possible that word had got around that fast."

Fabrizio Gómez, an actor, said: "People think it's wonderful that we have no army in our country. But why would we need one when we're so good at spying on each other's every move?"

Perhaps it's unsurprising then, that many Ticos have very few friends with whom they would trust their most intimate thoughts or worries, instead relying on family for emotional support.

NATURAL REMEDIES

One of the most fascinating aspects of getting to know Ticos is the strong link they still have with the herbal remedies of their rural forebears, many of which were taught to the first Spanish settlers by their indigenous neighbors.

Despite having one of the best free healthcare systems in the world, many Ticos still swear by natural cures. If you even mention feeling on anything less than tiptop, chances are you will receive suggestions to boil up a tea of special leaves or bark, or to take a bath in cleansing herbs.

If you have earache, you may be told to find a lactating mother willing to squirt some breast milk in your ear, while preparations from the multi-purpose *guarumo* tree are suggested for both boosting fertility and inducing abortion, as well as ensuring an easy birth for farm animals. A traditional remedy for asthma is the *escarabajo del asma*, a small beetle boiled in milk or eaten alive, which is reputed to open up the airways of the lungs.

"We might have a good system now, but you have to remember that until a few decades ago it was almost impossible for someone living in the countryside to get to a doctor," explained Don Daniel, a teacher.

Proud San José market stall holder Billy Acuña has a herbal remedy for whatever might ail you, as well as magic potions to spice up your love life.

Luis 'Billy' Acuña Araya, whose family has run one of the dozen-or-so medicinal herb stalls in San José Central Market for several generations, said: "Our products are getting more and more popular all the time. People prefer pure, natural products, because they're starting to realize that many conventional drugs can harm their liver or kidneys. Lots of people come to me after drugs from the doctor didn't work, or because they can't afford stuff from the pharmacy."

Billy's stall sells everything from aloe vera and rosemary to shark oil and sea urchins. He claims his preparations can cure anything from baldness and constipation to diabetes and cancer. Individual purchases cost less than a dollar, while a specially-prepared *receta*, costs about US$5.

Many people go a lot further than simple herbal health cures, and swear by magic and witchcraft too (see Religion and Witchcraft section of Social Indicators chapter).

POBRECITO

A deeply Tico trait is to feel sorry for the *pobrecito* (poor little thing)— something which could go a long way to explaining their ready acceptance of thousands of refugees from Cuba, Russia, El Salvador, Colombia, Argentina, and Chile over the past couple of decades; and the fact that street begging has become a lucrative profession.

Even when it comes to the much-maligned Nicaraguans, Ticos are wont to qualify their criticisms with: "They can't help it, the *pobrecitos*, they've had such a hard time in their country."

People who have done something wrong will often come up with outlandish excuses, often medical, to try to invoke the *pobrecito* reflex of employers or judges. Unsurprisingly, children learn how to exploit this at a young age, and are allowed to get away with murder.

PIROPOS
Piropos are an old Spanish tradition from the good old days when people would take a *paseo* around the town park every evening, with the single young men walking in the opposite direction from the single young women.

As the 'piroper' knew the 'piropee,' the idea was to come up with the most clever or flowery limerick-like piropo possible in order to impress the object of your affection. One among dozens which became almost commonplace was:

Del cielo cayó un pañuelo
bordado en sedina negra
decile a tu mamacita
que si quiere ser mi suegra.

From the sky fell a handkerchief
Embriodered in black silk
Go and ask your mummy
If she'd like to be my mother-in-law.

With the growth of cities, migration, and greater anonymity, however, the *piropo* went into something of a decline, and often took on more of a clever-dick, often insulting air. The infuriating thing about today's *piropos* is that they're usually muttered as you go past someone, by which time it's too late to come back with a clever retort. Two you are most likely to still hear are: *'Dónde fue el choque?'* (Where was the crash?) and *'Tantas curvas y yo sin frenos!'* (So many curves, and me without brakes!).

Sociologists have compiled various lists of other piropos which are still in use, however, such as:

"Qué vestido más lindo, lástima la percha!"—Nice dress, shame about the hanger.

"Tanta carne y yo en ayunas!"—So much meat, and me on a diet!

"Por usted sería capaz de buscar trabajo"—For you I could go out and find a job.

"Parece la carreta lá Sarchí... solo pintura!"—You look like a Sarchí cart (the traditional Tico brightly-colored ox-drawn coffee cart)... nothing but paint!

"Qué dichoso su doctor!"—What a lucky man your doctor is.

"Quisiera ser bizco, para verla dos veces"—I wish I was cross-eyed so I could see you twice.

Especially clever plays on words (but which lose all cleverness in English) are:

"Amor... a mortadela huele tu boca"—My love... your mouth smells of mortadela.

"Adiós... a Dios le pido que cambie tu cara" —Hello... I pray to God that he changes your face.

These *piropos* don't have to be just from men to women, although unsurprisingly they usually are, and more often than not you'll just get the kind of construction worker/truck driver monosyllables you would expect at home. For some men, it seems that articulating even one word is just a bit too tricky, so they have to make do with hissing (poor lambs). At times it seems that you have stepped into a snake pit. Some men even have wolf whistle car horns.

"Of course I don't really like it," one beautiful young Tica told me. "But it's just part of the background noise, and I ignore it like everyone else. The thing that really surprised me was when I went to the United States and no-one whistled or hooted at me—I started to think there was something wrong with me."

NICKNAMES

Ticos delight in nicknames, and Alajuela in particular is famous for them. "Basically, as soon as you set foot in the town you're going to have a nickname—whether you realize it or not," said Daniel, a middle-aged teacher who grew up there.

The Alajuelenses, also famed for their love of practical jokes, even have a nickname for their town's statue of national hero Juan Santamaría, who is called *El Erizo* (The Hedgehog) because of his frizzy hair. The people of Alajuela and their football team are now known throughout the country as *Los Erizos*, or *Los Manudos* because they were traditionally known for their big, rough hands.

Heredianos, and their football team, are called *Florenses*, as their women are supposed to be the most beautiful 'flowers' in the country.

In race-conscious Costa Rica, a lot of nicknames have to do with skin color. Daniel, whose skin could hardly be described as darker than sallow, grew up being known as *Tijo* (a type of black bird).

Many times, a whole family will take on a nickname because of the attribute of just one member. "If someone walks like a bird, or is really slow, the whole family may end up being called the *Gallinas* (Chickens) or the *Tortugas* (Tortoises)," said Daniel.

Other nicknames are more ingenious. One man whose parents came from Río Frío (Cold River) and the spa town of Aguas Calientes (Hot Water) was called *Tibio* (Lukewarm).

On a two-day visit to Puerto Viejo de Sarapiquí, I was introduced to a man with some indigenous blood called *Cacique* (Chief), a rather chubby man called *Comeburras* (Packed Lunch Guzzler), and stopped

to buy ice cream at a *pulpería* owned by a man with narrow eyes called *El Chino* (the Chinaman).

Often, however, people might be totally oblivious of their nicknames. One Tico friend, who is short with rather goggly eyes, is referred to by everyone, even his good friends, as *Sapito* (Little Toad)—although they would never tell him that. On the other hand, a waiter in San José's Vishnu restaurant who is so concerned with his appearance that he even gets his eyebrows trimmed is loudly hailed as *Cejas* (Eyebrows).

While in other cultures Tico nicknames might sound racist, sexist or otherwise politically incorrect, for Ticos they are usually nothing more than a mark of camaraderie. Among Ticos, who don't like to think that anyone is any more special than anyone else, they are also a means of *choteo*. So don't get offended if you hear yourself or others called *Flaco* (Skinny), *Moreno* (Darky), *Gordo* (Fatty), *Güila* (Kid), or if, like me, you have green eyes, *Gato* (Cat).

Spanish names have stock nickname equivalents, such as Moncha (from Ramona), Paco (Francisco), or Nacho (Ignacio). As a foreigner, you may have your name changed with the addition of an—ito/ita as a mark of affection, especially if you have a Latin name—for example Teresita, from Teresa.

THE PULPERIA

The Tico equivalent of a favorite corner shop, *pulperías* have been such a ubiquitous feature of Tico communities that they have even figured in art and literature.

The pulpería is not a place where one buys or sells *pulpo* (octopus), but instead *pulpa* (literally, pulp), such as fruit and meat. Since the arrival of supermarkets, pulperías have been increasingly confined to the countryside and urban barrios. Unlike supermarkets, however, they represent much more than a place to stock up on groceries.

Some still accept credit or payment in kind, and most double up as a bar, games hall, local bush telegraph, and center for socializing, counseling, and advice. They may have a pool table or table football, chess and checkers, and sell everything from ice cream to machetes. The *pulpería* plays a huge role in rural areas where people live quite isolated from each other—it's a place to gather in the evening or at weekends, to sit on benches or in rocking chairs and gossip. In the poorest areas, it may provide people's only chance to listen to music, watch television, or make a telephone call.

NATIONAL PRIDE

Ticos LOVE their country. "If we ever go abroad and hear our national anthem, we cry," one butch young Tico told me.

Flag-waving schoolchildren are always at the forefront of patriotic parades, and they are indoctrinated from an early age by teachers and often parents that other countries, beset by violence, envy Costa Rica's lack of military, its stability and high living standards. With up to a quarter of the population having left or fled their own countries to live in Costa Rica, this belief is pretty understandable.

However, many Ticos have traveled surprisingly little around their own tiny country, and of a group of 20 university students I met, not one had visited La Casona, Costa Rica's foremost national monument (see History Chapter).

The Teatro Melico Salazar in San José regularly holds popular folkoric dance extravaganzas, which are not solely patronized by tourists, and Radio Nacional broadcasts programs such as *Aires de mi Tierra* (Melodies of my Land) and *Cantares Campesinos* (Peasant Songs). Even the *páginas amarillas* (telephone directory) starts with several pages of morale-boosting Costa Rican history and statistics about its high standard of living.

Some suggest the strength of national pride comes from the fact that Costa Rica is so small and dependent on the outside world. This makes people feel powerless, and leads to a desire to talk up the national heritage and defend it against foreign influence.

THE LOTTERY

Sometimes it is hard to weave your way through San José's choked streets because of the sheer number of lottery sellers taking up the

At times it's hard to put a pin between the lottery sellers lining the city streets.

pavement, either sitting at tables or wandering up and down shouting out the numbers of the cards they're selling.

The lottery is hugely popular and becoming more so with every passing week thanks to the slow decrease in the colón's power to purchase imported goods, as it depreciates at a crawling rate against the dollar.

"My wife almost bankrupts us each week, betting everything on the lottery," one taxi driver groaned. "But I can't really blame her— we're getting poorer and poorer, and there's always a chance we could get lucky."

Lottery gamblers don't choose their own numbers, but buy tickets with three pre-printed numbers. Both these, and the series number, must match up with the numbers drawn in order to win. Many people stick to the same 'lucky' numbers week after week.

The lottery itself is played on Sundays, with a top prize of 35 million colones (US$100,000), as well as *chances* on Tuesdays and Fridays, with a 10 million colones winning prize. There are also very popular instant scratch cards, or *raspas.*

Salesmen of *tablas mágicas* also do a roaring trade. These tables supposedly tell you your lucky lottery numbers.

THE ROCKING CHAIR

The pace of life in the Costa Rican countryside goes as slowly as possible, and every rural Tico home worth its salt has at least two rocking chairs (*perezosas* or *mesedoras*) on the porch outside. Sometimes these are hand-carved out of wood, with leather backs, or—more usually—made out of woven nylon cords which are much more comfortable than they sound. Here one sits for hours with family members reading the paper, snacking, or watching the world go by and chatting to it as it goes.

DRESS STYLE AND BODY IMAGE

Ticos take a great deal of pride in their appearance, although style is quite a lot more relaxed than in many other Latin American countries—partly as a result of the strong North American influence.

For example, you will see, especially among upper middle-class students, a lot of piercings and tattoos, and surf style is massive among the country's youth. However, even if some people look as laid back in style as they do at home, you will notice there is very little sense of individualism. Ticos worry about what other people will think of them, and always try to wear the 'right' label in order to *aparentar*. You are only a little more likely to see a Tico punk than a surfing tapir.

Of course, many Ticos cannot afford Quiksilver or Billabong, and in every town you will find one or more shops selling *Ropa Americana*—cheap, second hand clothing from the United States. Even if they cannot afford new clothing, however, Ticos' clothes are always spotlessly clean, being washed and ironed after nearly every wearing.

Women take a huge amount of pride in how they look, and beauty contests are popular. While men drink away their evenings in the local *cantina*, women spend hours in the *sala de belleza* (beauty parlor) having their hair dyed or fingernails painted.

The basic female 'look' involves a large amount of make-up, tight-fitting trousers, and even tighter-fitting, colorful tops. As in other Latin countries it's quite unusual to see skirts—apparently because tight trousers are better at emphasizing your shapely behind. Short hair for women is almost unheard of in Costa Rica. Ticas make the most of their long, glossy manes and have a huge amount of confidence in their feminine wiles.

With the influx of Western television culture, body image and diet are changing, and cases of anorexia are starting to rise. One rather chubby Tica anthropology student told me this was a senseless paradox in Costa Rica.

"It's really crazy, because that's not how Ticas should be," she said. "In fact, men here prefer women with *figuras rellenitas* (filled-out figures). They've been historically conditioned into it from the days when you wanted a plump and muscular wife to do heavy work and bear healthy children. When I go out at night dressed in a tight outfit I get a lot more attention than any of my skinny friends."

Men, particularly in the countryside, wear a handlebar moustache, shirt open to show off their chest hair (and if possible several chunky gold chains), cowboy boots (or ankle-length rubber boots in the rainy season), and a cowboy hat. The outfit may be finished off with a leather-sheathed machete slung over the shoulder.

Shorts are not acceptable in the city, unless, of course, they are terminally trendy three-quarter length skateboard shorts. Outside the city, shorts are fine for young people—although dress sense is still fairly proper unless you're in a surfing beach town.

At the beach conservatism is still the rule. Ticas wear bikinis which can look positively frumpy next to the 'dental floss' G-strings of Brazil and Venezuela, and some even cover up with a T-shirt while swimming.

FREE TIME

Ticos are experts at enjoying free time, although this often means doing nothing much at all. They are happy to spend hours hanging around, chatting, telling jokes (most people have an enormous repertoire), or playing practical jokes. This is often called *matando la culebra* (killing the snake)—a banana workers' excuse for idleness to their overseers.

When not enjoying a *reunión* at home, Ticos like to go out in large, giggling, screaming herds of friends or family. In the dry season, they visit parks, springs (*ojos de agua*), and beaches, where they often turn up the sound level still further with a radio played at full volume. (Unfortunately many Ticos still can't swim, and several drown each year in the country's riptide-plagued waters).

In San José, one of the busiest places on a weekend (for people who can't get to the beach) is the big Sabana Park, which is full of families flying kites, having picnics and taking horse rides.

In the rainy season, people spend more time lingering over coffee

Ticos whiling away their weekend at a local waterhole.

and cakes in cafés, window-shopping, or going to the cinema. The cinema is popular, although Hollywood films tend to arrive pretty late (so operators can pay lower licence fees). The Sala Garbo in San José also shows European art house movies, as do some university cinemas.

Nightlife

Ticos, especially those living in San José, like to go out to eat, drink, listen to live music, or dance. They'll do this pretty much any night, but the busiest evenings are from Wednesdays to Saturdays.

Away from the bright lights of the US-style city center bars, however, most drinking goes on in the ubiquitous *cantina*. The *cantina* is an almost exclusively male preserve, and can be recognized by the doorway, which will be either shrouded by a beaded curtain, swinging Wild West-style saloon doors, or a large advertising hoarding. Inside, aside from the odd peeling pornographic calendar, decoration is limited to say the least, with metal chairs often welded to the floor.

While you might be expected to drink a few shots of *guaro* and engage in discussion about football or women, you are very unlikely to get into an ugly Mexican-style tequila-drinking contest with the locals. You would, however, offend or confuse your fellow drinkers if you turned down the offer of at least a first drink.

There's not a huge amount of nightlife in the countryside, where many bars are housed under traditional indigenous *rancho* roofs, huge conical thatched structures around 10 meters high. Apart from this, there might not be a lot else to do apart from karaoke.

Sports

Many Ticos are reasonably fit, and although most people can't afford to join a gym, the Sabana park is always full of people playing basketball, soccer, tennis, volleyball, baseball, or just jogging.

It hasn't always been this way though. According to the Biesanzes in *The Ticos*, one man was even arrested in a highland village in 1976 after police caught him running, and deduced that he must be mad.

They're also interested in boxing and cycling. There's plenty of coverage of both in the papers, and you'll often see people training or meeting for cycling competitions along major roads. There is even an annual Tour de Costa Rica. (For details on soccer and surfing, see Social Indicators chapter).

Shopping

Costa Rica has several large, American-style shopping malls. The San Pedro Mall and Multiplaza in Santa Ana are the two biggest in Central America. While these malls and the numerous gringo-friendly grocery chains and supermarkets have absolutely everything you can think of under one roof, the country also has many much more interesting shopping options.

On weekend mornings, many Ticos still go to local *ferias*, or open air fresh produce markets, to buy their vegetables and other goods for the week. These are much cheaper than supermarkets, and much more fun. The vendors arrive early in the morning from the

Getting a shoe shine and putting the world to rights outside San José's Central Post Office.

countryside, and sell everything from cashew nuts, coffee beans, and pigs' trotters to cut flowers, home-made wine, and traditional cakes. Prices are progressively cut during the day, until by the end of the afternoon goods are almost given away. There are also often musicians on hand for added entertainment.

Shopping in central San José is also fun. The central zone is pedestrianized, and full of buskers, hustlers, beggars, and *limpiabotas* (shoe shiners), who for a small charge will not just clean your shoes, but also give you a run-down on what's wrong with the country and the world. If you're lucky, someone may even try to sell you a baby goat or a puppy.

Around the Mercado Central, there are so many stalls selling fruit, umbrellas, cheeses, cheap jewelry, and DIY goods that there's hardly any space on the pavement. Inside, the selection is even better, and includes some excellent cheap and cheerful Tico food outlets and fascinating medicinal herb and magic stands.

Every town has a *Ropa Americana* shop, selling a huge amount of cheap second hand clothes from the United States. If you're the kind of person that loves rummaging through charity shops and jumble sales, you will be in your element.

Increasingly limited budgets also mean that Ticos hate to throw anything away. The country is peppered with hole-in-the-wall tailors, cobblers, and odd-job men, who, for a small fee, can and will fix almost anything which would be consigned to the rubbish dump at home.

Fiestas

Ticos love an excuse for a party. All towns and villages have a fiesta at least once a year. These may be to mark the town's saint's day or the end of the year (traditionally a good time as the coffee harvest is in and everyone had been paid their Christmas bonus). Local parishes also have *turnos* (smaller fiestas) to raise money for the church.

Most fiestas last for at least a week, and start each day with rockets at dawn. They usually include fairground rides, local bands, folkloric parades, dances, beauty contests, *corridas de toros* (bull fights), sports events, and plenty of eating and drinking. Classic fiesta food includes Chinese chop suey and *vigorón* which is made of yucca, *chicharrones* (fried pig skin) and cabbage.

No fiesta would be a fiesta without the presence of *Los Gigantes* — a group of giant figures on stilts which run around taunting (and being

Fiesta gigantes *taunting children – or is it the other way around?*

127

The tope *is an essential part of any Tico fiesta.*

taunted by) the local children. The giants usually include *La Giganta* (the giant woman), *El Gamonal* (the chief), *El Diablo* (the devil), *La Negra* (the black woman), and *La Bruja* (the witch)—although their traditional violence has now been officially limited.

"When I was a kid, the *gigantes* used to go around with sticks and try to catch you," said Max, an engineer. "Sometimes they'd really whack you, but it was all part of the excitement. Now it's been made illegal because of people bleating about child abuse."

Another inevitable part of a Tico festival is the *tope*, or horse parade. Horsemen—often hundreds from all over the country—come to parade through the streets on their *caballos de paso*; highly-strung and specially-bred, high-stepping horses. Decked out in incredibly ornate and be-tasseled tack, they prance and skitter all over the streets, sometimes almost standing on the onlookers who let out high-pitched Speedy González-type screams of excitement.

CALENDAR OF EVENTS/FIESTAS
January
Copa de Café, San José. This is a big international junior tennis tour event at the Costa Rica Country Club. (First week)

Fiesta de Santa Cruz, Guanacaste. A celebration in honor of the famous Guatemalan Black Christ of Esquipulas, supposedly discovered here in colonial times after a Guatemalan miracle-peddler abandoned it. It features a two-week pilgrimage around the district, culminating in folk dancing, marimba-playing and bullfights. (Mid January)

February
Fiesta de los Diablitos. Masked dancing among the Boruca Indian community of Rey Curré. Very similar to the other Boruca festival in December. (Dates vary)

March
Día del Boyero, San Antonio de Escazú, San José. The country's ox-cart drivers gather for a colorful parade and contest, and priests bless the oxen. (Second Sunday)
Día de San José. Celebration of the capital's patron saint. (March 19)
National Orchid Show, San José. (Dates change)

April
Holy Week. Religious processions are held in towns across the country, and many Ticos make the most of the Thursday and Friday holidays by going to the beach. (Week leading up to Easter)
Juan Santamaría Day, Alajuela. Ticos celebrate the bravery of their national hero with parades, concerts, and dances. (April 11)
Día del Aborígen. National celebration of Costa Rica's indigenous population, history, and culture. (April 19)

May
Labor Day. It is particularly celebrated in Limón, with dances and cricket matches. (May 1)
Carrera de San Juan. Costa Rica's biggest marathon, starting from near Cartago and passing through the mountains to San José. (May 17)
Día de María Auxiliadora. 'Miraculous' nun Sor María Romero

129

(see religion section of Social Indicators chapter) was a big devotee of this virgin, and this is now the second biggest religious festival in the country. Novenas are said for nine nights, culminating in a 4:00 A.M. procession and mass every hour at the Casa de la Virgen in San José's Barrio Don Bosco, where Sor María's remains lie.

July
Fiesta de la Virgen del Mar, Puntarenas. Fiesta to give thanks to Our Lady of Carmen who miraculously saved storm-stricken fishermen from a shipwreck in 1913. A procession of boats decorated with yellow and white ribbons (the colors of the Catholic Church) carries the statue. (Saturday closest to July 16)

Guanacaste Day. A week of festivities in towns across the province leads up to the big day on July 25, in honor of the annexation of Guanacaste in 1824. Festivities include massive *topes*, bull fights and rodeos, folkloric processions, dancing etc. The biggest events are in the provincial capital, Liberia.

The Basílica de Nuestra Señora de Los Angeles is home to Costa Rica's patron saint and the scene of massive pilgrimages every August.

August

Fiesta de la Virgen de los Angeles, Cartago. Around a million Ticos make the pilgrimage, or *romería* to the Basílica de Nuestra Señora de Los Angeles to pay homage to the country's patron saint, La Negrita (see religion section in Social Indicators chapter). Some *romeros* walk, many on barefoot, or cycle or ride on horseback, from as far away as Guanacaste. They camp overnight outside the church before making their way to the altar on their knees to give thanks to the Virgin for miracles, or to ask for help in the coming year. (August 2)

Mother's Day. This is not a simple day for giving *mamá* a bunch of flowers and a card. Shops are crowded out for weeks before with Ticos looking for gifts—more often than not a new washing machine or car. Some people even plunge themselves into debt in an effort to out-do their siblings or friends. This is a big family day, where mothers are thoroughly pampered. People whose mothers have passed away visit their graves with flowers and gifts. (August 15)

September

Independence Day. Various festivities are held throughout the day, culminating in children's lantern-lit parades at night. (September 15)

International Beach Clean-Up Day. (Third Saturday)

October

Carnaval de Limón. Uniquely in Latin America, (where carnival is generally celebrated the week before Lent), in Limón it marks Columbus' arrival in Costa Rica. The carnival was originally the brainchild of Arthur King, who brought back tales of colorful celebrations after a stint working in Panama. This massive party mixes Tico fiesta traditions, Afro-Caribbean music, and hordes of outlandish, often skimpily-clad Rio-style street paraders. (Week leading up to October 12)

Fiesta del Maíz, Upala, Guanacaste. A celebration of all things related to corn. The highlight is a pageant, with the local beauty queens parading in outfits fashioned from the crop. (October 12)

November
Día de los Muertos. As in most of the Latin world, on the Day of the Dead, Tico families visit their deceased relatives in graveyards around the country and stage religious processions. (November 2).

December
Día de la Pólvora, San Antonio de Belén and Jesus María de San Mateo. This celebration, in which fireworks are let off, honors Our Lady of the Immaculate Conception. (December 8)
Fiesta de la Yegüita, Nicoya. According to legend, two drunken men were fighting with machetes and one of their wives prayed to the Virgin of Guadelupe to intervene. A horse appeared, biting and kicking the men until they stopped. Today's festival, along with the usual fiesta activities, involves the parade of a wooden horse (*yegua*) and the virgin, accompanied by whistle music. Some people still use the occasion to settle scores, and the horse intervenes as necessary. (December 12)
Las Posadas. Country-wide event in which children and adults, re-enacting Joseph and Mary's search for lodging in Bethlehem, go from house to house in their neighborhood singing carols. (Begins December 15)
Festejos Populares are held around the country, but particularly in San José, where there are bullfights, a *tope*, a carnival, and fairground rides in Zapote. On New Year's Eve there is a dance in the Parque Central. (Last week of December)
Fiesta de los Diablitos. Indians in the Boruca reserve perform this traditional masked dance over three days, in which the Spaniards are represented by a bull. The bull vanquishes the Indians, or *diablitos* (little devils), but—wishfully departing from historical fact—they come back in the night and symbolically kill it. (Begins December 31)

Chapter Five

SOCIAL INDICATORS

RELIGION AND WITCHCRAFT

Whichever way you look at it, Costa Ricans are overwhelmingly Catholics. Catholicism is the state religion, abortion is illegal and non-Catholics cannot be legally married in their own church without going through a civil ceremony too. The Church is state funded and has always been viewed as one of the strongest and most morally-untainted institutions in the country.

Religion is never far away from Ticos's lips. When you wake up in the morning, you will be asked how you slept: '*Cómo amaneció?*', to which the stock answer is: '*Bien, gracias a Dios*' (Well, thank God). People talking about something in the future will often also invoke God, for example: '*Iré mañana, si Dios quiere*' (I'll go tomorrow, if God wills it), and when someone leaves the house, they will be told: '*Que Dios le acompañe*' (May God go with you).

When going to someone's house, instead of knocking on the door Ticos shout: '*Upe*', which is (thankfully) a shortened version of the traditional greeting '*Ave María Purísima Nuestra Señora la Virgen de Guadalupe*' called out by arriving visitors.

Often, when setting out for even a short bus journey or passing a church, Ticos will cross themselves. Many homes are also decorated with pictures of the Last Supper, holograms of the Pope, ornaments of the baby Jesus, and palm crosses. New commercial or government offices are blessed by a priest before they open, and roadsides are littered with shrines marking the spot where unlucky motorists died.

The number of believers, however, is clearly on the wane. In a 1995 La Nación poll, 100% of respondents said they believed in God, and 84% said they were Catholics. By 2001, those numbers had fallen to 98% and 70.3%.

Evangelism is making inroads, especially in the city and in indigenous reserves. The Catholic Church has had to become more charismatic, incorporating a lot of clapping and singing, in order to hang on to its congregation. People in the countryside, however, tend to be more traditional and stick with Roman Catholicism.

Even among Catholics, most church-goers are older people, and many of them admit they *muy poco practicante* (don't really practise). The Padre Mínor furor (see *Heroes and Villains* in *People* chapter) was also a big blow to the image of the Church.

As in most Latin American countries, the forcible imposition of Catholicism failed to totally root out indigenous superstitions and practices. Although there is no syncretic religion in Costa Rica today, such as Santería in Cuba or the cult of Maximón in Guatemala, people definitely have a kind of elastic belief system which allows them to pick and choose what suits them best.

Market stalls do a roaring trade in magic herbs and potions, thanks to the faith people have in the supernatural to bring them everything from love, money, and luck in the lottery, to revenge against their enemies or a means of getting rid of annoying neighbors.

Many apparently 'normal' people will happily tell you they bathe themselves in magical herbal washes, hang aloe vera or garlic over their doors to suck up bad luck, and burn colored candles to attract love and money, drive away evil spirits, or stop gossipy tongues.

They may spread sugar on the floor to keep witches out of the house, or always sweep inwards to keep good luck inside. Just as they use social connections to cut through bureaucracy, Ticos pray to particular saints to intercede with God—Santa Clara can help with business, Santa Apolonia is good for toothache, and San Antonio Abad can help protect pigs.

People buy books of spell 'recipes,' adorn themselves with Stars of David and images of the Buddha, have their tarot cards read, and tie red ribbons around babies' wrists to protect them from the evil eye.

In this kind of catch-all insurance system, Ticos often say: '*No creo, ni dejo de creer*' (I don't believe—but I don't not believe either).

Although 'witchcraft, sorcery, or any other cult or belief contrary to civilization or good customs' is technically a jailable offence, many spells are still cast. In a 1996 survey, half of all Catholics said they believed in witchcraft.

Some of the most popular spells include rubbing the back of a black cat with salt at midnight for health and wealth. A surefire means of becoming irresistible to men is to mix together 33 drops of three love perfumes, a piece of gold and hummingbird nest, aloe vera, mint, and honey. Leave it in a bottle in the sun for seven days, and then carry it around in your handbag. If you want a man with money, add some myrtle. Most spells involve some aspect of Catholicism, such as prayers to particular saints.

Often inexplicable aches, pains or bad luck are explained by the local *bruja* (witch) as the result of spells or 'bad shadows' cast upon the victim by the envious.

One woman whose daughter was cured of the *mal de ojo* (evil eye) by a witch, told me: "We only went to the lady after conventional medicine wasn't able to do anything. It seemed crazy at first, but we

135

were desperate and would try anything. My daughter had been in a kind of trance, but she was cured. The lady wouldn't accept any money—she just wanted us to pray."

According to *De Que Vuelan... Vuelan!* by May Brenes Marín and Mayra Zapparoli Zecca, people cast bad spells on their enemies by piercing voodoo dolls with nails, burying *aportes* (bags full of nasty substances such as dead toads, chili, entrails, blood, and mercury), spraying 'evil' liquids over the entrance to their victim's house, or even simply preparing their food. *Aportes* are often buried in graveyards, where the soil is considered particularly suitable for evil-doing. In the same book, San José General Cemetery official Carlos Rodríguez says his staff find at least one set of *aportes* a month.

The most famous place in Costa Rica for witchcraft is Escazú where, historically, indigenous people secretly attempted to continue practicing their religious and magic rituals in mountain caves. Now a rich suburb of San José full of big houses and fast food restaurants, it looks more like California than Costa Rica. The *brujas,* however, are still to be found—ostensibly reading tarot cards, but often also offering a whole range of other services.

Luis 'Billy' Acuña Araya, who runs a magic stall in the San José Mercado Central, told me: "People come a lot to buy the ingredients for *aportes*—particularly to get rid of neighbors they don't like. They put black salt, mercury, and other unpleasant things in a red bag along with a message saying "You will never find happiness until you leave this house" and throw it up on the roof."

Even though Billy says that most people use magic for nothing more than attracting love and money, it is not surprising that many people carry some kind of *contra* (amulet) to protect themselves.

Of course many Ticos these days don't resort to magic, herbs, or witchcraft, but they are still very superstitious people. For example, if a '88' butterfly (with a mark looking like this number on its wings) flies into their house, they will rush out and buy a lottery ticket with the same number, hoping for a big win.

These are some of the most important members of the Costa Rican pantheon of popular saints.

La Virgen de los Angeles

According to tradition, La Negrita—the tiny black virgin which is Costa Rica's patron saint—first appeared in 1635 to a girl named Juana Pereira on a rock in a forest. Every time the virgin was removed, she miraculously reappeared in the same spot. A shrine was built at the site, and the first pilgrimage took place in 1653 after La Negrita apparently cured a serious illness.

Although black virgins and Christs were popular in Europe in the 17th century, many people believe the appearance of a black virgin was particularly significant, as it allowed the indigenous Costa Ricans to identify with their new religion. La Negrita was made the nation's patron saint in 1824, displacing the original patron saint, and represented the triumph of the *mestizo* religion over Spanish domination.

Today, visitors to the shrine, often patients from the nearby Max Peralta hospital, still 'walk' up the whole aisle of the basilica on their knees. In an ante-room, glass cases house literally thousands of silver *exvotos*, or tiny charms, which can be anything from legs, ears, and livers to guns, babies, and airplanes. These graphic requests for miracles are surrounded by thousands more offerings representing thanks for help granted, such as football trophies and university degree certificates. Downstairs at the shrine of the rock, people pray in groups, sometimes with the help of a professional prayer leader.

On August 2, around a million people from all over the country, including the president, finish the pilgrimage to Cartago on foot, by horse, or on bicycle in order to fulfill their promises to the Virgin.

Dr Moreno Cañas

Dr Moreno Cañas became well known in the 1920s and 1930s as a helper of the poor. He was murdered in 1938, and after his death, he

137

became a mythical figure. People claimed he was communicating with them from beyond the grave, doling out medical advice, and occasionally performing supernatural surgery.

Now a popular saint, he has even been officially honored by being named a *Benemérito de la Patria* and having an obelisk placed in front of the house where he was killed. Special Dr Moreno Cañas photographs and prayers are available for people who want the ghostly doctor to intervene on their behalf. Some people claim a glass of water containing a lemon cut into a cross and placed overnight on a prayer card will be turned by morning into the required medicine.

Sor María Romero

Costa Ricans passionately hold this nun, in the process of being beatified by the Vatican, to be their own, despite the fact she was actually Nicaraguan. In 1989, she was made an honorary citizen of Costa Rica, and her portrait hangs in the Legislative Assembly. Sor María, widely held to have been psychic, came to Costa Rica at the age of 29 and died at 75 in 1977. When her body was exhumed to be relocated 14 years later, it was found to be almost intact. The Pope has accepted as miraculous her cure of a Costa Rican baby with a hare lip.

Thousands of people visit her sepulcher in the Casa de la Virgen in San José's Barrio Don Bosco to ask for help (especially on the feast day of María Auxiliadora on May 24), and many leave with bottles of supposedly miraculous water from the building.

CRIME

Costa Rica was once a peaceful country, experiencing its first bank robbery only in 1970. Now, like the rest of the world, it is experiencing a rapid rise in crime, and by 1993 private guards outnumbered police.

Petty crime is notorious, especially around San José's Central Market, where gangs of young thieves known as *chapulines* (grasshoppers) pounce on their prey and melt away into the thick crowds. When a friend had her handbag stolen in a city center bar,

the bar owner told us this was a regular event. He had had the hat stolen from his head that same day as he sat in his car at traffic lights. The week before, investigating a flood, he found thieves had even wrenched out and pilfered the steel pipes from the bar toilet.

Many thieves use a particularly common scam, which I once fell victim to myself: a man started walking ridiculously slowly in front of me while going through a narrow area near a fruit stall. Unable to pass him or turn around, I could feel his 'team mate' opening my rucksack and rummaging through it. Luckily for me, I had my money and documents in my front trouser pocket.

"It's not just the quantity of crime that's changed, it's the type," said Steve Brown of the Residents' Association, an organisation which lobbies for foreign residents' rights. "Fifteen years ago, the worst you could expect was to have your purse snatched, or your washing stolen from the line. Now, things seem to be a lot more violent."

Costa Rica is used as a corridor by narcotic traffickers shipping consignments north from Colombia and Panama. Drugs are often moved through the jungles of Talamanca, and also by boat. Joint patrols by the US Drugs Enforcement Agency and Costa Rican coastguards have been set up to crack down on this trade, though without a great deal of success to date.

The country also has something of a reputation as a haven for foreign crooks. It is weak on extradition, has secretive banking laws, and a big expat community in which it is easy to disappear.

In addition, the burgeoning tourist trade offers an ideal front for the investment of unlaunderable money, with Colombian drugs barons and the Italian mafia reputedly behind the construction of many of the country's biggest hotels and shopping malls. Michel, a shaven-headed French friend traveling the country, told me he had been approached by members of a Corsican organized crime gang asking if he wanted to join their operations in San José.

Mr Brown voiced a disturbing trend. "Today, whenever the police catch criminals, it nearly always seems to be a group of Ticos plus a Guatemalan or a Colombian who has taught them new tricks. While most of the immigrants are entirely legitimate, a lot of criminals have also flooded in, and unfortunately they've had a big impact."

In street crime at least, the figures do not seem to back up this view. In 1993, 96% of those convicted for such crimes were Costa Ricans. Many feel that the country's much-lauded universal education has in fact bred in Ticos an unwillingness to do low-paying menial jobs, meaning that some people would sooner turn to crime than take on demeaning work. Reduced government spending on education, job cuts and an increasing underclass have only increased the problem.

Whatever the cause, Costa Rica is still safer than the United States or most of Europe, and murder or physical attacks on strangers are extremely rare. In the city, the situation really only requires common sense, while in the countryside honesty and calm still reign—at least for now. Several times I have forgotten something in a café or on a park bench, only to go back half an hour later and find it still there, or even have someone run after me to give it back.

Many Ticos who grew up in a cocoon of 1960s stability, however, are paranoid about crime. In a 2001 Universidad de Costa Rica survey, more than 60% of respondents said they were frightened to leave their house, and 91% felt that San José was either unsafe or very unsafe.

In the capital, most people live behind barred windows, their garden fences festooned with razor wire and broken glass, and their properties guarded by big dogs or even geese. Many people will not leave their home untended, and in one house where I stayed all expensive items, such as the television, had a string with bells tied to it to alert the owners if anyone tried to move them.

Guns have become much more commonplace in Costa Rica since the civil wars in Nicaragua and El Salvador, when weapons were smuggled through the country. There are an estimated 30,000 guns in the country today, only one-third of which are legally-owned. To buy a gun legally you only need to show your *cédula* (identity card). You are also supposed to take a course and get a certificate of psychological fitness—but not until after you have already bought the weapon.

In a non-militarized country with a traditional lack of crime, little was invested in training, equipping, or paying the 13,000 Costa Rican police officers. This is now changing, however, with numerous armed police now seen on foot or on bicycles in city centers. Professional, non-military training focuses on issues such as human rights and domestic violence.

CULTURE

Even being generous, it is hard to describe the country's historical cultural production as anything more than pitiful. Poor, rural, and with a population below 200,000 in 1860, Costa Rica has little architecture remaining from the colonial period, as most buildings from that era were made from straw and adobe.

Costa Rica did not get its first printing press until 1830 (compared to 1539 in Mexico and 1660 in Guatemala), so it's not surprising that writing was slow to develop. The country certainly didn't produce any literary giants, and in fact, apart from Manuel González Zeledón and Aquileo Echeverría, hardly anyone appears to have made a stab at anything very creative until the 20th century.

What did happen, however, was that from around 1860 onwards the country started to have more contact with all things European as a result of the coffee trade and development of the railway. The children of newly-rich families were sent away to be educated in Europe, creating an intellectual class obsessed with imitating European—especially French—styles. At this point any home-grown innovation would have been sneered at.

San José's beautiful Teatro Nacional, built in 1897, and described soon after by foreign visitors as 'a jewel in a mud hole', was designed and built by French and Italian artists. Every stone, pane of glass, and lick of gold paint was brought from Europe too.

An exact small-scale copy of Paris' Opéra Comique, the Teatro Nacional was built with funds raised by the coffee barons through a self-imposed export tax. The tax was implemented after Italian opera singer Adelina Patti, who was touring Central America, refused to sing in Costa Rica as she felt that there was no venue worthy of her.

European-style marble tombs still dominate San José's main cemetery.

Likewise, the General Cemetery in San José is full of European-style marble angels, replica pyramids, and Greek temples carved by Costa Rican sculptors who had trained in Italy.

In fact, the only truly Tico invention was the intricately hand-painted ox-cart used to transport coffee. Covered in geometric designs reminiscent of Moorish art in southern Spain, replicas of the carts are now the most ubiquitous example of creole *artesanía*, and are available as souvenirs in the tourist town of Sarchí.

In this environment, innovative artists, such as the great sculptor Franciso Zúñiga, found themselves with little choice but to leave the country because of the prevailing belief that everything foreign was better. Zúñiga settled in Mexico, where his modern styles made him one of the most famous artists of his era (see Heroes and Villains in People chapter).

University of Costa Rica anthropologist Sergio Chávez said: "The problem is that we're passive and self-congratulating. We've never had to fight for anything. We didn't have an independence struggle from Spain or the ravages of a guerrilla war in the 1970s. We're relentlessly middle class, and that's just not the kind of background that favors the development of new art forms."

Minds did start to broaden in the 20th century, and a great debate arose over whether art and literature should continue to be influenced by foreign styles, or rather reflect the realities of the country. With greater consciousness of the exploitation of peasants by wealthy landowners and foreign companies, daily life started to figure more heavily in local art, and literature became peppered with *costumbrismo* (rural color and dialect). The arts, however, remained the preserve of the elite until 1960, when the state-funded publishing house Editorial Costa Rica opened doors for many new authors.

A decade later, during his third presidential term, José Figueres sparked what Ticos like to call their cultural revolution, by setting up the Ministry of Culture and the National Theatre Company.

Figueres said: "Why should we have tractors if we don't have

143

violins," and took it upon himself to revitalize the limping National Symphony Orchestra which was on the point of collapse. The orchestra is now world class, with soloists playing all over the globe, while the state-funded Youth Orchestra has wowed audiences at the White House and the United Nations.

The arts blossomed. In the new climate, Costa Rica developed a huge national library with 300,000 volumes in nine languages and dozens of museums and galleries. In San José, some of these developments are housed in former jails or military barracks.

The capital also has at least 14 theatres, around as many per capita as in London or New York. Costa Rican theatre has been important even in continental terms—especially during the 1970s and 1980s, when playwrights fleeing as refugees from dictatorships in Argentina, Chile, and Uruguay took up residence. Opening nights are packed, and while it's hard to imagine that there could be sufficient audience in San José to keep a play running for more than a few days, the Teatro de Barrios program took many plays all around the country, swelling the average audience size from 2,000 to 30,000 or more.

Although state funding of the arts has fallen dramatically since the economic crisis of the 1980s, pushing many actors, directors, and writers into more populist work such as television sitcoms, the show still goes on. While many theatres concentrate on risqué sex comedies, there are always classics showing by Moliere, for example, or Aristophanes. On Sundays, bands play for free in parks all over the country, while flyers posted on lamp posts advertise discussions on philosophy or politics.

Samuel Rovinski, a top Costa Rican author, and an advisor to UNESCO said: "What took 300 years to develop in Europe developed in 30 years here. We went through all the phases in extreme acceleration, and the whole national mindset has been permanently changed."

Today, in something of a reversal of history, many foreign artists actually settle in Costa Rica to make the most of the relaxed pace of life, stunning scenery and clear air. Many Ticos earn a living making artwork for sale to tourists.

However, the all-pervasive influence of Hollywood and MTV is seen as a huge threat to Costa Rican cultural development today.

Mr Rovinski said: "It might seem impossible that we can survive any real and concrete competition from the US, the biggest empire in the history of the world. However, the Romans absorbed Greek culture without it destroying them, so let's hope our encounter can also be enriching rather than destructive."

Some of the best Tico painters to look out for are Max Jiménez, Francisco Amighetti, Margarita Bertheau, Luisa González de Sáenz, César Valverde, Isidro Con Wong, Rafa Fernández, and Ricardo 'Negrín' Rodríguez Córdoba, a black artist from Limón. Top sculptors are Francisco Zúñiga and Jorge Jiménez Deredia.

The most important authors are Fabián Dobles (look out for his archetypal 'proletarian' novel *Ese Que Llaman Pueblo* and *Historias de Tata Mundo*), Joaquín Gutiérrez (*La Hoja de Aire*), Carlos Luis Fallas (especially *Mamita Yunai*, his classic tale of oppression and misery among 1930s banana plantation workers), José León Sánchez (wrongly imprisoned on the notorious prison island of San Lucas—most famous is *La Isla de los Hombres Solos*), Carmen Naranjo (Costa Rica's foremost female writer—look out for *Los Perros no Ladraron, Sobrepunto*, and *There Never Was Once Upon a Time*), Carmen Lyra (*Mi Tía Panchita*, based on traditional tales told in the Caribbean by African slaves), and Samuel Rovinski (especially plays such as *Las Fisgonas de Paso Ancho*). Quince Duncan is the country's major black writer, and Eulalia Bernard (*Ritmohéroe, Negritud, My Black King* and *Griot*) the top black poet. For more literary suggestions, see 'further reading' after the Strategic Directory chapter.

Some of the more popular bands in Costa Rica are Editus, Marfil, the Brillanticos, and Calle Ocho. On the Caribbean coast, look out for Shanty (Calypso), Charro Limonense, and Chakra.

EDUCATION AND LITERACY

Even in the days when they had a military, Ticos used to boast that they had more schoolteachers than soldiers.

In what used to be a poverty-stricken rural backwater, it is understandable that the country's high standards of schooling are a source of enormous national pride. With foregone military budgets funding the massive education system, the only armies these days are hordes of neatly-uniformed schoolchildren on their way to and from school—one of the most ubiquitous images of Costa Rica.

Ticos have a 95% literacy rate, almost the highest among Latin American countries. Many people sport *anillos de graduación*, or high school graduation rings, bearing chunky jewels and flowery inscriptions, given by proud parents.

The country's first president was a teacher, and believing that education can ensure democracy, Costa Rica was one of the world's first nations to introduce free, obligatory education in 1869.

Education is seen as the means to income (salaries are determined by academic level) and status—everyone wants to be *culto* ('cultured'). As nearly every job, however menial, requires a high-school education, many adults study at evening classes or through distance learning, choosing from the huge array of courses available.

The school system is in decline though. The average adult now has only 5.7 years of schooling, compared with 6.6 years in Panama, 7.5 years in Colombia, and 8 years in Cuba. Although Ticos are legally supposed to remain in school until age 14, half of all children do not finish their education. The number of school dropouts reached 14,080 in 2000 and the Ministry of Education seems helpless to staunch the flow. Traditionally, many children missed weeks of school each year to help with the coffee harvest. Today, many drop out altogether through their family's need for them to work. Figures from the Ministry of Economy show that by 1998 more than 15% of children aged between five and 17 were already working, 39% of them for 57 hours a week (21 hours more than the legal maximum). Those aged

Education is a prized asset and children use all means to get to school.

five to 11 received on average only 11.6% of the minimum wage.

Despite efforts to provide a standard level of nationwide education, many rural schools are poorly equipped. Most teachers would rather work in the cities than far-flung rural backwaters, increasing still further the gulf between education standards in urban and rural areas. The curriculum (like much else in Costa Rica) is centrally controlled, meaning little provision is made for the different history, culture, and circumstances of indigenous and Afro-Caribbean children.

According to the Biesanzes in *The Ticos*, per capita funding for education fell by 35% in the 1980s alone, and a 1994 United Nations survey revealed the country now actually invests less money per capita in education than most other Latin American countries. The average class size in public schools is 40 children.

As a result of these factors, around 20% of children now attend private schools. Public school teachers are badly paid, so the best ones end up in the private schools. As most politicians send their own children to private schools, education has become less and less important in the national budget.

147

While the level of education in Costa Rica is clearly high for the region, and one of the reasons why the country is so popular with foreign business investors, it seems that a good education is increasingly becoming an issue of wealth.

Reluctant LITERACY

So, despite the much-trumpeted statistics, it is not a shock to learn that Ticos are not big readers. Real LITERACY levels may actually not be as high as the figures suggest, as the tests measure little more than the ability to write your own name. In fact, many people from the lower classes clearly have trouble writing. Although Spanish is a phonetic language—meaning spelling mistakes should theoretically be all but impossible—misspellings are commmon everywhere. It is common, for example, to see welcome signs saying *bienbenido* (instead of *bienvenido*), vendors selling *copoz* (instead of *copos*), and no-smoking notices saying *grasias por no fumar* (instead of *gracias por no fumar*).

Shop assistants use calculators to do the simplest of sums and, according to the Biesanzes, directory inquiries staff waste large amounts of time dealing with people too flummoxed by alphabetical order to use telephone directories.

Nearly every time I have seen a Tico reading a book, it has been the Bible. While reading novels in public, I have even been told by well-meaning strangers that I could ruin my eyesight or make myself sick.

The government is clearly concerned. Newspapers and advertising hoardings carry messages from role models such as football trainers urging young people to read, but apparently to little avail.

Book shop owner Darren Mora said: "People don't get into the habit of reading because books are too expensive for many people. In any case most book shops only stock text books and literary classics."

Libraries are not exactly user-friendly either. You can't just browse among the books, but have to fiddle through old-fashioned card files, fill in a form for each book and ask the librarian—who will probably demand your *cédula* (identity card) or passport—to bring the books to you. You may not remove the books from the library and can only use them for a few hours.

"How are you going to read a novel in an environment like that?" asked Mora. "My nephew, who's in university, has never read a non-academic book in his life, and I know there are many others like him."

Although most Ticos say they're too busy to read, many people—especially women—spend hours watching the variety of addictive Mexican or Venezuelan *telenovelas* (soap operas) which they freely admit are a bad habit. Most houses have several televisions, and flickering screens can be seen even in the tiniest shack in a San José *tugurio* (shanty town).

Higher education

Following the closure of the University of Santo Tomás in 1888, the country didn't have another university until the University of Costa Rica was established in 1940. The number of universities, however, has mushroomed out of control since then. With the higher status and better job prospects associated with having a degree, demand for university education is massive. Now, there are four state universities and almost 40 private ones that together churn out tens of thousands of graduates each year. Many of these private institutions offer only specialized courses and standards are often low.

This rapid growth in the number of graduates, combined with the decline in public sector jobs (traditionally a huge source of graduate employment) since the crisis-hit 1980s, means the number of graduates now outstrips professional jobs available.

UCR student Tomás Fernández said: "This is a small country, so opportunities are limited. Soon we're going to be in a situation like Cuba, with lawyers and doctors driving taxis. Already most of us are looking for work abroad as it's really the only way forward."

PRESS AND JOURNALISTS

Ticos are big newspaper readers (even though a lot of people read little more than the football pages). The conservative La Nación, set up in 1936, has the largest circulation of 500,000, about an eighth of Costa Rica's population.

Other papers include the pro-PLN (but also pretty conservative) La República, and the more left-wing afternoon paper La Prensa Libre. Tabloids, such as Al Día and Diario Extra, concentrate heavily on sensationalist crime stories and sports. The controversial Chavespectáculos is the local equivalent of a girlie newspaper like England's Sun, except that it reflects Latin males' tastes by focusing much more on bottoms than breasts.

The Tico Times, the longest-established and largest circulated English language paper in Central America, is targeted mainly at the older expat audience, with pictures of fluffy animals, recipes, and lightweight opinion columns. The Tico Times covers the main bases, but isn't exactly a hotbed of incisive reporting and investigation. All attempts at competition have so far folded.

Of the terrestrial television channels, Teletica has the most in-depth local news coverage, while Sinart fashions itself as a national cultural channel. The other stations telecast hefty servings of imported soap operas, football matches, and evangelical sermons.

Given the country's credentials in other areas, press freedom is not as progressive as you might expect in Costa Rica. Journalists are expected to verify all information, no matter how impeccable the source, and have no right to keep their sources secret—a huge blow to investigative journalism. Since 1994, they have also been forbidden to identify anyone being investigated for a crime.

Most famously, La Nación journalist Mauricio Herrera was sentenced to 160 days' imprisonment for defamation (later commuted to a large fine) for a 1995 article in which he quoted a reputable Belgian newspaper, which had accused a Tico diplomat of links with the mafia. The action against Herrera was harshly criticized by the

Interamerican Press Society.

However, things may start to loosen up somewhat. The hit-style murder of outspoken radio journalist Parmenio Medina in 2001 (see Heroes and Villains section in the People chapter) shocked the country, prompting widespread calls for a change in the somewhat heavy-handed attitudes towards the press.

SOCCER

'Perdemos, pero somos los mejores.'
We lose, but we're still the best.
          – Anonymous soccer fan.

If a Costa Rican male approaches you, holding one hand limp-wristed and palm down, slapping the back of it with the other hand, don't panic! He is not accusing you of being gay, but is actually inviting you to join in a *mejenga*, or informal football (soccer) game.

Likewise, there's no cause for alarm at the sound of an enormous, almost inhuman roar coming from the bowels of your neighborhood *cantina* (well, not on a Sunday or a Wednesday night anyway). This, or a sudden chorus of frenzied horn honking from surrounding traffic, is a guarantee that a favored team has just scored. People who can't be at the match or in the bar, will be listening in on car radios.

Costa Ricans are, quite simply, obsessed with *fútbol*, which has even altered the structure of many Tico towns. A settlement without a soccer pitch can't legally qualify as a political district. In a large number of towns, the shady trees that once graced the Spanish-style central *plazas* have been uprooted and replaced with a grass pitch and goalposts, sometimes made from bamboo.

The social life in some small towns has been quite drastically changed by soccer. The young people, both boys and girls, are happy enough practising their dribbling, but many older folk complain that there's now nowhere to have a *paseo* on Sunday after Mass, or to sit out in the evening with an ice cream and watch the world go by.

151

Soccer coverage in the local press is massive, often to the total exclusion of any other sport, and sometimes to the exclusion of the news itself. Sandwiched between baseball-mad Panama and Nicaragua, Costa Rica is the only Central American country, aside from Honduras, with a big tradition of soccer. The sport was introduced to the country in the early 1900s by the sons of rich coffee barons who attended school in England.

Soccer is now such a big part of the culture that sociological texts have been written on its impact. Sociologist Sergio Villena Fiengo, the author of one such tract, says soccer is not just a game for Ticos, it also gives them a sense of 'anonymous belonging' and a means of venting emotions which are normally repressed in this relatively reserved society. Combined with a strong sense of national pride and patriotism, matches are, he says, "moments highly charged with tension, but at the same time free of social controls, which create a kind of social catharsis."

Soccer is a popular pastime and Costa Ricans, both young and old, enjoy watching and playing the game.

Getting to the 1990 World cup quarter-finals was one of the proudest moments in Costa Rica's soccer history, leading the president to declare a national holiday. People still talk about the event with misty eyes more than a decade later. The Ticos reached the World Cup again in 2002, although they failed to get through to the last 16. They now have their hearts set on Germany 2006.

Before international matches, newspapers are flooded with letters from fans to their favorite players, as if they were warriors going away to war. These letters often praise the players for their *humildad*, that top Tico trait of humility.

The country has produced some international-level players, such as Paulo 'Chope' Wanchope, who has played for Manchester City and other clubs in England, Hernán Medford, Ronald Gómez, Wilson Muñoz, and Jafet Soto. The press follows the fortunes of the players' foreign teams in minute detail, and the players, said Villena, are expected to fulfill a symbolic function even more important than that entrusted to ambassadors.

Back at home, however, players frequently actually threaten to go on strike, claiming they have to work too hard, that the season is too long and that they want their own union. This griping may not be quite as petulant as it sounds. With so many teams in the country, there are 56 matches in the national league alone.

Ticos boast that they're the best players in the region, and often attribute their fairly frequent defeats not to any failing on their own part, but like so many of the country's other problems, to external factors. Villena says: "The referee picked on us, it was too cold, it was too hot, the pitch was in a bad state... people nearly always say: 'We lost, but we're still the best', 'We have talent, it's just organization we lack'."

Universidad de Costa Rica anthropologist Sergio Chávez added: "We're too anarchic and individualistic to be good team players as everyone wants to be the star."

The best way to make up your mind about such criticism is by attending a game, a frenzied and near-deafening experience. The season runs from August to May, and seats are cheaper and the atmosphere crazier in *sol* (sun) than in *sombra* (shade). For the few weeks when the local teams are not playing on home turf, Ticos make do with watching them playing abroad in international contests and qualifiers.

Like Europe, Costa Rica has its share of *barras* or hooligan gangs, such as the Ultras and the Doces. In the finals of the national championships in 1993, fighting between the supporters of Cartago and Heredia got so out of hand that the National Guard had to be called in, and the match was abandoned in chaos. It later had to be replayed in an empty stadium. Generally though, in typical Tico fashion, actual violence is very rare. Pregnant women and children attend soccer matches without any worries, although one important point to bear in mind is to duck if someone shouts: '*Suelo! Suelo!*' (floor)—Tico fans don't like to have their view of the game blocked.

Usually, the worst kind of post-match violence reported by police is between two groups of *barras* pelting each other with fruit. Several injuries were reported after Costa Rica's defeat of Honduras in the 2001 World cup qualifiers, although these were mostly broken ankles suffered by people who had indulged in too much joyful jumping. Traffic in San José also came to a standstill for almost an hour as fans sat in the street doing Mexican waves.

One ex-*barra* member told me: "We were never really interested in real violence. Sometimes we'd take a bag full of wasps into a match to throw at the other side's fans. Other times we'd throw rotten eggs or pods from the *pica-pica* plant, which has irritating hairs which get into the skin and itch like crazy."

For many supporters, alcohol is a big part of the soccer experience. Unfortunately, but tellingly, indices of both alcohol-fueled car accidents and domestic violence shoot up after matches, and announcements are even flashed on television screens during football matches saying '*mantengamos la paz familiar*' to remind fans not to take their frustrations out on their spouses.

The biggest rivalries are between supporters of the two top clubs. Saprissa (the San José team) is also known as *Los Morados* (purples) for the color of their strip, while Alajuela is called *Los Manudos* (big hands) or *Los Erizos* (hedgehogs), the nickname for people from Alajuela. The other major top team is Heredia or *Los Florenses*—so called as women from Heredia are supposed to be the most beautiful 'flowers' in the country. As of 2001, Saprissa had won the National League 22 times, with Heredia and Alajuela tied on 21. Heredia, which won the first ever championship in 1921, has not won since the 1992/93 season.

The teams are divided into two divisions, with 12 teams in each. At the end of the season the bottom team from the first division is relegated to the second, while the top team from the second division is boosted up. The 11th team in the First Division and the runner-up in the Second Division also have a play-off to determine which division they will play in the next season.

The colors of the top Costa Rican teams are:
- Club Sport Herediano   – red and yellow.
- Deportivo Saprissa   – purple.
- Liga Deportiva Alajuelense   – red and black.

SURFING

Although Costa Rica has the perfect conditions for surfing, the sport only really started to take off among locals in the early 1990s. Now it has become, for many, a passion.

José, a sun-bleached, dreadlocked surfer who lives in a hut right on the beach in Jacó so he can be in the sea in seconds, said: "We're more organized now, with competitions and stuff. Before, everyone in Costa Rica thought surfers were just layabouts and drug addicts."

The attitude in surf towns is the most laid-back you will find anywhere in Costa Rica, and is in particularly sharp contrast with the conservatism of the Meseta Central.

155

Surf towns are also some of the places where you're most likely to come across the open sale of illegal drugs—mainly *mota* (marijuana), *perico* (cocaine), and *piedra* (crack), all served up by the *doctor* (dealer).

Those that pride themselves on being 'real' surfers will not take drugs, or even smoke or drink, because they have to be up and alert for the best waves early in the morning. They also have a tendency to sport tattoos, eat macrobiotic food, and sit on the beach, waxing their boards and staring out to sea with a faraway look in their eyes.

"It just gives you a really different outlook on life," said Oscar Arguedas, one of the country's pioneer surfers and arguably the most mellow human being on the planet. "My wife left me, my dog was run over, and I was duped out of US$750,000 by a friend. But when you go out there and confront death in the middle of those huge waves you get the kind of adrenalin rush that makes all the bad things just melt away."

While all the surfers tend to spout the same kind of New Age philosophy, their simple way of life can be very seductive. It's also usually easy to find someone to give you some tips or lend you a board. Be very careful, however. Many Costa Rican beaches are riddled with *corrientes* (rip tides), and several people drown each year.

While Tico surfers, like all Ticos, are polite and hate confrontations, you should remember that surf etiquette applies just as much here as elsewhere. Gringo surfers have a bad reputation, and the locals will not take kindly to you stealing their wave (although they probably won't say anything to your face).

Traditionally, some of the best surfing was in the Caribbean (particularly the famous and enormous *salsa brava* wave in Puerto Viejo). The 1991 earthquake, however, pushed the reef up in some areas, making surfing now difficult or dangerous. Most of the big surf areas are now on the Pacific coast.

Chapter Six

FOOD AND DRINK

Costa Rican food is based on two main ingredients: black beans and rice. In most homes, especially in the country, these will crop up in every meal of the day masquerading under various names, and in some places rice and beans are even thrown on newlyweds like confetti. Incredibly, Ticos really do not get bored of this combination. "If my wife doesn't have *gallo pinto* on the table in the morning, I'm really annoyed and she has to give me a pretty good excuse," said a middle aged Tico friend. Unlike Mexican food, Tico fare is not spicy.

BASIC TICO FARE
Gallo Pinto. Literally 'spotted rooster,' this is beans and rice mixed together and fried (traditionally in pork lard) with onion, bell pepper,

garlic, and herbs. Usually eaten for breakfast, it's often served with eggs, small corn tortillas, and *natilla* (sour cream). Gallo pinto is pretty much the national dish, even McDonald's serves McPinto. Many Ticos will proudly say they are 'as Tico as gallo pinto,' although this is also the national dish of Nicaragua.

Casado. Literally 'married man,' this strictly lunchtime dish is beans and rice (separately this time) served with beef, chicken, fish, or liver, along with fried *plantain* (green banana), salad, tortillas, and maybe some *picadillo* (See *Popular Food* Section) and pasta. Yes, if you were at all worried about not getting enough carbohydrates in Costa Rica, your worries will evaporate after a hefty serving of rice, *plantain*, tortillas, AND pasta all on one plate.

Arroz con frijoles. If you're wondering what Ticos eat for their evening meal, it's very often a lighter dish of *arroz con frijoles*, which is—you guessed it—rice and beans.

Sopa Negra. This soup is made out of black beans, usually with some onion, green pepper, cilantro, a poached egg, and a squeeze of lemon juice. It rates along with Alka Seltzer as Costa Rica's number one cure for a *gotera* or *goma* (hangover).

If the above selection makes Tico cuisine sound less than exciting, remember that until recently the country was poor and rural, with a diet designed to keep people going for a day in the fields. Well, the diet simply hasn't kept pace with changing times. These (and the dishes below) are still what you'll find served in *sodas* (cafés) in the country.

Without all that coffee-picking to burn off the calories today, obesity is definitely on the rise, although you still don't see too many rolls of fat forced sausage-like into skin-tight luminous boob tubes – an alarming sight in some other Latino countries. Diet may also play a large role in the fact that Costa Rica suffers from the western world's highest rate of stomach cancer (see end of chapter).

In urban areas at least, diets ARE slowly starting to change. "Just 10 years ago in San José, if you wanted to eat out you could basically only choose from Chinese and Italian cuisine," said a Tico friend. "Today we have Peruvian, French, Thai restaurants—whatever you can think of." Despite the fact that San José does have some really excellent restaurants, the bulk of eateries are still fast food joints that suit Tico pockets.

Although they still love their rice and beans, many younger Ticos are starting to take more care with their diet. A lot are semi-vegetarian, and one of San José's most popular restaurants, Vishnu, serves only vegetarian food.

Another point to remember is that many Tico dishes are family specials to be had only in homes—just as you'd be lucky to find toad-in-the-hole or Lancashire hotpot in any restaurant in the UK. Some delicious dishes Ticos cook up include soups, picadillos, meat stews, and a huge range of stuffed squashes, pumpkins, and gourds, such as *chayote* and *ayote*.

In Costa Rican restaurants, the *entrada* is the appetizer, while the *plato fuerte* or *segundo plato* is the main dish. A good bargain on weekday lunchtimes is to order the *menú ejecutivo*, which usually offers a specific main dish, soft drink or coffee, and sometimes dessert, for a reasonable price.

Ticos take their lunch any time between about noon and midnight, although long Spanish-style lunch hours are no longer the norm. Most people eat their evening meal fairly late, around 8:00 P.M. or 9:00 P.M.

Meat

Beef is plentiful, thanks to the Guanacaste cattle industry, but can be on the tough/stringy side. Chicken (*pollo*) is good and cheap, often served as *arroz con pollo*—chicken fried rice.

A word of advice to **vegetarians**—it is no good asking whether a dish contains *carne* (meat), as in Costa Rica this only refers to beef. If you ask for a dish *sin carne* you run a high risk of being given something containing ham. It's better to say you are *vegetariano/a*— a bizarre concept for many Ticos, especially in the countryside.

Fish and Seafood

In the Meseta Central, the fish you're most likely to come across is *corvina* (sea bass). The selection is bigger on the coast, but still not huge, featuring a lot of *atún* (tuna) and *pargo* (snapper). Lobster (*langosta*) and shrimp (*camarón*) are available but very expensive as nearly all seafood is exported.

Cheese

Costa Rican cheese is either *blanco* (white) or *amarillo* (yellow), and is generally pretty bland. The Monteverde cheeses (originally made by the Quakers) have become some of the most popular in the country, and include Cheddar, cheese spreads, and smoked cheeses.

POPULAR DISHES

Arreglados: meat or cheese-stuffed puffed pastry or sandwiches.

Ceviche: this traditionally Peruvian dish is a firm favorite in Costa Rica. Ceviche is either white fish or seafood marinated in lime juice and spiced up with some onion, garlic, red peppers, and coriander.

Chorreada: a Guanacaste speciality, this is a big, fat corn pancake, usually served with cheese.

Elote: Corn-on-the-cob either boiled (*cocinado*) or roasted (*asado*).

Empanadas: these can be savory; made from deep-fried corn flour and stuffed with meat, cheese, potato (*papa*), or beans, or sweet; made from baked wheat flour and stuffed with fruit preserves: usually pineapple, guava, or *chiverre* (a kind of stringy melon).

Enchiladas: savory pastries stuffed with potato, sometimes with meat, and a little chili.

Gallos: a small serving of meat or chicken with tortillas.

Olla de Carne: literally 'meat pot,' this hearty dish is made of beef, yucca, plantain, corn, ayote, and chayote.

Picadillo: usually made from chayote, plantain, or potato, this is a kind of chopped vegetable stew, often with a little meat or egg, and flavored with spices.

Pupusa: this Salvadorean speciality has become ubiquitous throughout Costa Rica since the large immigration of refugees from war-torn El Salvador during the 1980s. It is a thick grilled tortilla stuffed, usually, with beans, cheese, salad, and *chicharrones*— artery-clogging chunks of fatty fried pig skin.

Sopa de Mondongo: tripe soup.

Tamales: steamed maize dough wrapped up in a corn or banana leaf with meat in the middle.

Salad and Condiments

Ticos are not big eaters of greens, and salad is usually a disappointing affair, consisting of some grated cabbage and carrot in vinegar topped with a tomato. Wherever you eat, your table with usually have a big jar of *curtido* (pickled vegetables and chilies) to mix with your food.

Rice is often cooked with garlic and/ or red pepper, and sometimes *achiote*, a traditional red food coloring prepared from a native plant.

Sandwiches, burgers, and *gallos* usually come slathered in *salsa rosa* (Thousand Island dressing), ketchup, and mayonnaise.

Bocas

Bocas (literally 'mouths') are snacks traditionally served with alcohol. Somewhat like tapas in Spain, *bocas* are sometimes free—although these days you usually pay a small amount extra. *Bocas* could be anything from meatballs to *ceviche*, stuffed tortillas or fried fish, and grazing on a few of these as the night progresses is a cheap and delicious way of soaking up excess alcohol. Sometimes turtle eggs— widely held to be an aphrodisiac—are served as *bocas*. Costa Rica is one of the Caribbean's major egg-laying sites for these ancient animals, which are in danger of extinction. A certain quantity of the eggs can be officially harvested, but unfortunately many turtle egg *bocas* are illegal, so it's best to avoid them.

Cakes and Desserts

Ticos, like most Latinos, have an incredibly sweet tooth, and you will come across cake and pastry shops (*pastelerías* or *reposterías*) every few meters selling all manner of sweetmeats, often slathered in bright pink or blue icing.

Merienda, the Tico equivalent of afternoon tea, is an important part of the day, especially in the rainy season, when many people spend hours sitting out the afternoon downpours in *sodas* (cafés) and kitchens. Some favorites are:

Alfajores: shortbread-type round biscuits sandwiched together with *dulce de leche* or fruit jam and dusted in icing sugar.

Cachos: literally horns. Tubes of croissant pastry stuffed with cream. Regular shaped croissants are called *cangrejos* or 'crabs.'

Churros: six-inch long sticks of deep-fried doughnut mix, usually stuffed with some kind of sweet cream.

Dulce de Leche: mind-blowingly sweet concoction of milk and sugar boiled together to the consistency of condensed milk. Sometimes eaten alone as a treat, used to sandwich together cakes such as torta chilena, or used as a cake filling—often sweetened still further by mixing with, say, guava jelly.

Ensalada de frutas: fruit salad; a healthier option, though it's often out of a tin and accompanied by *gelatina* (jelly) and *helado* (ice cream).

Orejas: literally ears. Dinner plate-sized pastry covered in sugar.

Púdin: heavy, moist, bread pudding.

Queque Seco: literally dry cake. Basically a sponge cake cooked in a ring shape.

Suspiros: meringues.

Tamales Asados: sweet corn tamal made with sour cream and sugar.

Tres Leches: incredibly sweet and soggy cake steeped in boiled milk and sugar.

SWEET STANDS

Roadside stalls and street vendors also sell a colorful variety of homemade sweetmeats, which are great for a snack if you're off on a long road journey. These include:

Bananos a la leña: wood-smoked bananas.
Bolis: frozen flavored ices in a tubular plastic bag, made either with water or milk.
Cajeta: basically fudge, which can contain nuts, raisins, dried fruit, or coconuts, and is often colored pink.
Copos: a cup of ice shaved off a huge block and mixed with milk powder, condensed milk, and a choice of brightly-colored fruit syrups.
Higos and **Toronja**: preserved, sugared figs and grapefruit.
Tarteletas: little coconut tarts.

FRUITS AND VEGETABLES

Ticos might not be huge vegetable eaters, but they love to snack on fruits. The most fun kind of fruits are those you pick yourself. Often, traveling with Ticos, you will find they screech to a halt by the side of a road, whooping with delight, to collect jocotes or throw rocks and sticks into mango or guava trees in an effort to bring down the fruit. Be warned that in the countryside howler monkeys often hang out in mango trees, and will mercilessly pelt you with unripe fruit if you try to steal their mangoes. If you bother them too much they will urinate on you... or worse! If your efforts are fruitless, there are always plenty of roadside stalls selling just what you were looking for.

Carámbola: starfruit.
Cas: a small, many-seeded fruit, which is almost unbearably sour when eaten raw. Ticos add salt to make it more palatable, but as a soft drink, with plenty of sugar, it is refreshingly delicious.
Guaba: this is not guava (which is *guayaba*), but instead the giant brown pod from a leguminous tree. The idea is to break them open

and suck the sweet fluff off the shiny seeds, which are sometimes used to make jewelry.

Jocotes: reddish plum-sized fruit with a dry, tart flavor. The tree is often used as a living fence—its cut branches being stuck in the ground as posts, where they take root and grow. Ticos love them as they're ideal for roadside-picking.

Mamones Chinos: Rambutans, whose hairy red covering is removed to reveal a white, lychee-like fruit.

Manzanas de Agua: Asian water apples, a dark pink fruit which looks like a small bell pepper, with a delicious, refreshing texture.

Manzanas Rosas: again from Asia, these are rose apples. Small pinkish-white fruits with a highly perfumed flavor.

Marañón: the fruit of the cashew nut. It's a large, capsicum-sized fruit with the nut dangling from the end. The delicately-perfumed fruit is used for jams and wines. The nut is poisonous until roasted.

Nances: tiny yellow berries whose indescribable taste is both bitter and sour. Often pickled or made into wines.

Pejibaye: an indigenous staple, this fruit comes from the same palm whose growing shoot provides *palmitos* (palm hearts)—a salad ingredient grown in plantations in some parts of the country. You will find pejibaye cooking in big metal pots on roadsides or in supermarkets (they must be boiled for about four hours). Tasting like a cross between chestnut and potato, they're usually eaten with mayonnaise.

Pitahaya: known as the strawberry pear, this baroque-looking dark pink fruit comes from a cactus. Found most commonly in the north.

Plátanos: giant green bananas, or plantains. When roasted or fried, these have a delicious starchy, sweet flavor.

Zapote: orange-fleshed fruit with a huge, black, avocado-like stone and dusty brown skin. The taste and texture is rather like an orange sweet potato.

You'll also see a lot of stalls selling nothing but apples and grapes. These are hard to grow in Costa Rica and are mostly imported from the United States—an expensive treat.

AFRO-CARIBBEAN FOOD

On the Caribbean coast, food reflects the West African, Jamaican, and British traditions. At the market in Limón you can buy turtle meat and salt cod, a huge range of roots such as yam, cassava, and sweet potato, as well as breadfruit and ackee. Food is generally a lot spicier than anything you'll find in the highlands, often flavored with cumin, chilies, cloves, and groundspice. Coconut milk is also used a lot.

Ackee: the national fruit of Jamaica, it is known in Spanish as *seso vegetal* (vegetable brain) as it looks a lot like a small brain. The fruit comes in three-inch pods and is poisonous until the pods have opened. When boiled, the yellowish fruit has the taste and consistency of scrambled eggs. It's often served with fish—a favorite dish is ackee and codfish.

Calalu: stewed leaf vegetables.

Jonny cakes: originally from 'journey cakes,' these are heavy, dry bread buns, ideal for taking along for a day's walking.

Pan bon: the name comes from either the French 'good bread,' or is a corruption of the English 'bun.' It's a heavy, glazed gingery-spiced fruit cake.

Patacones: deep-fried green banana chips.

Rice and beans/peas: this is the Afro-Caribbean version of *gallo pinto*—you can't get away from it anywhere in the country. In the Caribbean, however, it's cooked with coconut milk, which gives a very different, aromatic flavor.

Ron don: really delicious, hearty meal, which is cooked slowly for several hours. Either meat or seafood stewed with root vegetables and breadfruit in coconut milk.

COFFEE

Given the historical importance of coffee to Costa Rica, a surprising number of city dwellers these days prefer herbal teas. Ticos, however, still have one of the highest per capita caffeine consumption rates

in the world. Most people have a coffee shot up to three times a day—often even just before bedtime, and coffee dispensers can be found in banks, bookshops, and supermarkets. Ticos will tell you that "coffee is good for you," for example using black coffee as a migraine cure; the caffeine opens up constricted blood vessels in the brain.

Coffee normally comes very heavily sugared and either black (*negro*) or milky (*con leche*) in a tall glass. *Agua chacha* is coffee with a lot of milk. You will hardly ever find an espresso, cappuccino, or frothy milk, and in many homes coffee is still prepared using a *chorreador*, a kind of muslin sock supported on a wooden frame. The coffee filters through this and into the cup.

Despite their world class coffee, Ticos regularly commit crimes against coffee which would never be tolerated in places such as Venezuela, where each cup is prepared individually in a gleaming coffee machine. In Costa Rica, cold coffee is often re-heated and (horrors!) some people even use instant.

While there is a difference in the price and quality between export coffees (such as Café Britt and Volio) and those for local consumption (such as Rey), you won't find any foreign brands on sale here. Costa

Rica's coffee always tastes great as it is generally grown over a mile above sea level, where low air pressure results in hard beans. (Soft beans burn when roasted, creating a bitter taste.)

Coffee tasters, or *catadores*, who decide which coffees to buy, are as important in Costa Rica as wine tasters in France. They train for five years to learn exactly how to slurp the coffee off a big spoon onto their taste buds, and they taste it cold—a good coffee should taste just as good cold as hot.

Coffee still gives many Ticos a feeling of pride and cultural tradition. The landscape of hillsides is covered in the shiny-leaved plants. At blooming time they are covered in white flowers called *nieve* (snow). The only kind of snow you'll see in this Switzerland of Latin America is a classic image of the Meseta Central. Until recently, children would work during school holidays in the coffee fields, which were a place of healthy fun and fresh air flirting. These days, however, Costa Rica relies almost entirely on Nicaraguan workers to pick the coffee crop, as highly educated young Ticos are no longer interested in the hard work and low pay involved.

Historically, by law, Ticos could grow only Arabica beans, in order to maintain a special market niche. Today, however, many higher-yielding hybrids are grown. Most coffee plants can produce beans for 30 years, and Costa Rica produces more coffee per square meter than any other place in the world. The processing of a red coffee berry picked from the bush takes a week, involving pressing, peeling, fermenting, sun drying, raking and roasting at about 250 degrees Centigrade. The least roasted beans give a light roast coffee and the longest a French roast.

OTHER DRINKS

Ticos really excel on the soft drink front. Every house, no matter how humble, has a liquidizer, which is usually used to whip up fantastic and delicious fruit concoctions. Some of the best are made out of fruits such as *guanábana* (soursop), papaya, *piña* (pineapple), mango, *tamarindo* (tamarind), *banano* (banana), *sandía* (watermelon), *mora* (blackberry), or *fresa* (strawberry), and can be made with either *agua* (water) or *leche* (milk). Fruit juices may have salt added.

You will find drinks such as *chan* and *mozote* particularly in the countryside. Chan is made from small black seeds which have both the look and consistency of frogspawn—definitely an acquired taste. Mozote is a rather acrid drink made from the bark of a tree. Coconuts, (*pipas*) are sold with a hole tapped through the shell so you can drink the milk. *Caldo de caña* is sugar cane juice crushed from the cane in a kind of giant mangle, and *agua dulce* (sweet water) is made from raw cane sugar dissolved in water. The big, brown slabs of cane sugar called *dulce*, are sold in supermarkets.

In Guanacaste, corn is a much bigger part of the diet, and many drinks are based on this and other cereals. Some drinks are milky, such as *horchata* (ground rice and cinnamon), *resbaladera* (barley, rice, and cinammon), and *pinolillo* (maize and cocoa). Others include *avena* (oats), *cebada* (barley,) and *linaza* (linseed).

Ticos also drink a lot of carbonated bottled drinks. One of the most popular is ginger ale, which is confusingly known as *gin*. If you want to take a soft drink away from a *pulpería* or *soda*, it will be poured into a plastic bag so that the salesman can claim the refund on the bottle.

On the Caribbean coast, tea and herb teas are more popular than coffee. Traditional wild 'bush' teas include sorrel, lemon grass, ginger, wild peppermint, and soursop.

ALCOHOL

The Costa Rican government has a near monopoly on the country's alcohol production, producing both beer and *guaro*, a rough firewater made from sugar cane. The most popular brands of beer are Imperial (also called *Aguila* for the unfortunately Nazi-looking eagle on the label), Bavaria, and Pilsen.

Guaro can be pretty deadly stuff, and is often known by its brand name of Cacique. It is staple fare in *cantinas*, usually knocked back neat, or with salt and lemon, like tequila. In more classy establishments, you can order a *guaro* with any mixer. On the coast, a shot of *guaro* may be mixed with *pipa* (coconut juice) to make a *coco loco*. A stiff *guaro* with lemon juice is also taken by many as a cold treatment. It might not cure you, but it will definitely numb the misery!

A small glass of neat *guaro* is ordered as *techo bajo* (low roof); a full glass is *techo alto* (high roof).

On the Caribbean coast, rum is more popular than *guaro*, and is often drunk with fresh milk or coconut milk.

A typical Guanacaste alcoholic drink is *vino de coyol*, which comes from the sap of the coyol palm. Traditionally, it must be cut only during certain phases of the moon, and ranges from *vino dulce* 'sweet wine' after 24 hours of fermentation to *vino fuerte* 'strong wine' at eight to 22 days. After that, it's vinegar.

ALCOHOLISM

Costa Rica has the dubious distinction of having the highest rate of alcoholism in Central America. Experts estimate that up to 20 per cent of the population has a drinking problem ranging from abuse to addiction, and even the tiniest country hamlet has an Alcoholics Anonymous office.

This may seem incredible to visitors, especially those from hard-drinking northern European countries, because in Tico restaurants it is common to see many people—especially women—drinking nothing but fruit juices, and there are also many hard-core teetotalers.

"The thing is that we have a very problematic relationship with alcohol," said Dr Luis Sandí Esquivel, director of the government's Instituto Sobre Alcoholismo y Farmacodependencia (IAFA).

"Our actual alcohol consumption is quite low compared with Europe but we don't drink with our meals or regularly throughout the day, as many Europeans do. Instead, people go on a huge binge at the weekend, during football matches, or once a month on pay day with the express aim of getting drunk as quickly as possible. Their bodies have no resistance."

Ticos, traditionally reserved mountain farmers who only saw their neighbors sporadically, needed an alcoholic boost in order to loosen their tongues enough to maintain a conversation, suggests Constantino Lascaris in *El Costarricense*.

While it is quite common, especially in poor barrios, to see dozens of drinkers strewn on the pavements sleeping off the effects of a Sunday spree, and thousands of students swigging pitchers of beer in San Pedro's Calle de la Amargura, it is unusual to see drunkenness descend into public violence. In fact, in the worst drunken behavior I ever saw, a man who was *muy bien tomado* repeatedly delayed a bullfight by jumping into the ring and dancing in the spotlights, wiggling his bottom like a madman.

A lot of drinking also goes on in the home, and Dr Sandí says one of the most worrying statistics is that 16% of children over the age of 10 already have a drinking problem.

"With both parents working, children are now spending more time alone, and also have more access to money," said Dr Sandí. While in their parents's age group, male drinkers outnumber females by three to one, among the children just as many girls drink as boys.

One-third of all traffic accidents in Costa Rica are alcohol-related

—the rate of accidents shoots up on the weekends—as well as 70% of domestic violence, murder, and suicide.

Dr Sandí sees no conflict with the fact that the government itself monopolizes alcohol production in the country and makes seven billion colones (US$23.3 million) from sales each year. "It's better this way," he said. "If the business was privately-run, production and advertising would probably be even more efficient."

The institution, however, is currently locked in a battle for funds with the government, which legally must give IAFA 15% of its income from alcohol. In 1999, IAFA received 4%, and in 2000 nothing. The government says that in times of limited budgets it has to prioritize.

STOMACH CANCER

Costa Rica also has the odd reputation of having the highest rate of stomach cancer in the western world and ranks fourth in the world after Japan and North and South Korea.

Dr Horacio Solano, head of the government's stomach cancer detection and prevention program, said: "We really can't say for sure why the rate is so high. Stomach cancer is multi-factorial, but it's definitely got something to do with our diet—we eat a lot of carbohydrate, fat, salt and alcohol and not much in the way of fruit and vegetables."

Other factors could include high nitrogen levels in the volcanic soil (the highest cancer rates are on the volcanic Meseta Central, and other countries with a high rate, such as Japan and Chile, also have a lot of volcanoes), as well as bacteria in food and genetics.

Worldwide, stomach cancer incidence and death rates from it are falling—but not in Costa Rica, where 85% of those currently diagnosed will die. It's the top cause of cancer among men and the third among women.

"The problem is we haven't been able to afford early enough detection," said Dr Solano. "Widespread screening is expensive, and the government economists have said our over-burdened social security system can't stretch to it. Now we're trying to persuade them that early detection means less days in hospital, less intervention, and so in the long run will work out cheaper."

Due to its high health indices and First World disease profile (most people die of heart disease, cancer, and strokes), Costa Rica is often caught in the Catch 22 situation of being ineligible for foreign aid, but at the same time unable to afford expensive medical techniques. Japan, however, has provided funding and training for Tico doctors to help them set up a broad screening program—in the early stages of the cancer, the cure rate is over 90%. However, no-one knows if the government will be able to afford to keep the program going.

— *Chapter Seven* —
BUSINESS PRACTICE AND CUSTOMS

Foreign investors flock to Costa Rica for several reasons—its stable politics, relatively low costs (though more expensive than most of the rest of the region), peaceful labor relations, and well-educated workforce, much of it bilingual. There is now an education initiative to expand on this by turning Costa Rica into a country with a population fluent in high grade technical English.

The infrastructure is good too. The country has a self-sufficient power supply with the highest level of connection and cheapest rates in the region. It also has two international airports and ports on both the Pacific and Caribbean coasts.

All this adds up to make Costa Rica the easiest working environment in Central America. It has the highest level of foreign investment, proportionately, in Latin America, and a 2001 World Economic

Forum survey showed that it was also the most competitive country in Latin America after Chile. In addition, it has a young, mainly urban population, which means the productive work force and consumer group are set to grow rapidly.

The country is fast moving towards an economy dependent on tourism and high technology industries. This, however, doesn't spell new opportunity for everyone. In fact, the changes brought by the apparently terminal decline of coffee prices and huge workforce reduction of the government bureaucracy since the 1980s means a large part of the population is getting steadily poorer. Currently, about 20% of Costa Ricans do not earn enough to support themselves.

More than a fifth of the labor force is now employed in the informal sector, working as anything from shoe shiners, street vendors, and prostitutes to scavengers, door-to-door salesmen, or illegal taxi drivers (*piratas*). Many people *camaronear* (literally go shrimping), looking for various small jobs on the side, which usually pay below the minimum wage, in order to help them make ends meet.

Costa Rica is working hard (through the urgent need to tackle its massive internal debt) to open up its traditionally protectionist economy to foreign investment and competition. It is a signatory to many regional and international trade agreements, such as GATT, the World Trade Organization, and the Association of Caribbean States. It has been granted preferential conditions in the USA and Europe, and has signed bilateral trade agreements with several countries in the region. It also has bilateral investment treaties with many countries (mostly European). The oft-mooted idea of full Central American trade integration still seems a long way off, with nearly every country of the isthmus having a territorial dispute with at least one other.

Business customs in Costa Rica are not wildly different from anything you'd expect at home, largely because of the influence of the country's large North American population over many years. There are, however, hints on dealing with local partners and workforce, which will help any business venture run more smoothly and fruitfully.

WHAT KIND OF BUSINESS?

The Costa Rican economy is changing rapidly, with agriculture being downgraded and clothing factories declining in the face of cheaper competition from Asia. The country is now trying to remodel itself as a suitable location for high technology industries, foreign companies's operation centers for human resources, call centers, conferences, and conventions.

Intel opened a huge microprocessor plant in the country in 1998 (the country's GDP figures are now given both 'with' and 'without' Intel), while Procter and Gamble has set up its services and payroll division here to cover all its operations from Alaska to Tierra del Fuego. Lucent Technologies, Panasonic, Siemens and many others have their bases here too.

As an investor, it's important to think extremely carefully about the sort of business you want to set up, especially if your scope is small. In particular, remember that you can't set up anything that will compete with a government monopoly (of which there are several in Costa Rica), such as a brewery or domestic Internet service provider.

In fact, for nearly all small foreign investors, the safest bet is tourism—the fastest growing area of the economy.

That's not to say that other businesses are doomed to failure, but long-term San José resident and bar owner Julian Smith, offered some warning: "This is a small market, and local consumers don't have a lot of money. You need to decide what clientele you're aiming for—the small, rich class, or the much larger, but poorer, middle class. Having seen many people try and fail, I would say the classic mistake is to come here on holiday, see something that's missing compared to what you have at home, and automatically think that it would go down well here. It's hard to make money here, and it's crucial to find out if there is a real demand for your product."

Ricardo Rouillon, a jet-setting Peruvian entrepreneur who tried to import high quality foods such as gourmet asparagus and octopus, learned the hard way about the need for good market analysis.

175

"Basic food here, if you look at it charitably, is simple. Uncharitably, it's a disaster—rice and beans in the home, and fast food if you eat out," he said. "I would have thought my products would go down a storm among wealthy people with more refined tastes. But in fact, it turns out that rich people here are not at all ostentatious and they live very simply. Costa Rica is rarely what it seems on the surface, and I have never had to do so much research in any other country."

There are other factors to be taken into account when investing in the country. Absentee ownership is particularly inadvisable. "You really must be here, unless you have a manager you would trust with your life—especially if your business involves a property," said Lynda Solar, executive director of the Costa Rican-American Chamber of Commerce (Amcham). "There are problems here with squatters, because they gain all rights to your land after a year and you will then be unable to return to it or sell it."

She also warned against the investment programs which have proliferated in recent years in Costa Rica, such as teak plantations offering huge returns within a few years. Many people buy into these to fund their (often early) planned retirement in the country, but frequently find the dividends a lot less than they were led to believe, or even non-existent.

OPPORTUNITIES FROM THE DISMANTLING OF GOVERNMENT MONOPOLIES

While it still maintains monopolies in many areas, the government is keen to offload many of these responsibilities as part of its long-term scheme to bring down internal debt, which will provide many new options for foreign investors.

It is likely that the National Insurance Institute (INS) will be dismantled in the near future, which would create definite business opportunities in an almost untapped market, and another institution which may open up to private investment is the Instituto Costarricense de Electricidad (ICE).

Although widespread riots in 2000 scuppered the 'ICE Combo' plan to break up this monopoly, the government no longer has the funds to invest in major new infrastructure projects, such as hydroelectric plants (nearly 80% of the country's power comes from hydroelectricity).

A proposed dam to be built in Boruca would enable the government to meet the country's power needs over the coming decades, as well as exporting more power to its neighbors in the region. Costing about US$2 billion—around 20% of the country's GDP—the project would be impossible without private sector participation.

In the meantime, small private power companies are currently allowed to generate and sell electricity to ICE on a long-term build-operate-transfer (BOT) basis. ICE has recently asked for bids for BOT projects totaling 150MW (ICE has a total installed capacity of about 1,400MW). If there is enough participation in this scheme, it may eventually displace the need for larger projects such as Boruca, which have met stiff opposition from environmentalists.

WORKING AS A FOREIGNER IN COSTA RICA

State protectionism means that as a foreigner you may own a business, but you cannot legally work in it or anywhere else—unless you are a legal resident. Becoming a resident is not a simple task. You must either be married to a Tico, have children born in the country, or have held one of the other types of Visas (see *Survival Skills* chapter) for at least two years.

This leaves you able to do only a limited number of jobs—basically those which could not be done by a Tico, for example teaching English or writing for an English language newspaper. Of course many, many people work illegally; often in bars, hotels, or with travel companies, and usually with no problem—especially in areas furthest away from the capital. If you do this and get caught, do be aware that you run the risk of deportation.

Even if you are a permanent resident it can be hard to find work unless you're working in your own business. Few Ticos are used to the idea of foreigners seeking local employment, and local wages are not likely to be attractive either. So many people choose to work without pay—Costa Rica has a huge variety of volunteer opportunities, usually on environmental projects (see *Strategic Directory* chapter).

TYPES OF COMPANIES

Four forms of business organization are recognized in Costa Rica: a corporation (*sociedad anónima*), limited liability company (*sociedad de responsabilidad limitada*), limited partnership (*sociedad en comandita simple*), and general partnership (*sociedad en nombre colectivo*). Corporations are by far the most common and most flexible. They must be formed by at least two parties, although one party may obtain 100% of the stock immediately afterwards.

LEGAL AND OTHER REQUIREMENTS FOR SETTING UP A BUSINESS

The first step for setting up a business in Costa Rica is to get in touch with a notary public—the only person allowed to register a company with the Costa Rican Mercantile Registry. Without this registration a company cannot operate legally. All information about the new company and the people who will administer it must be submitted. This includes names, nationalities, the legal form of the business being organized, the company's purpose, amount of capital, and how this will be paid.

An extract of this registration is then published in *La Gaceta*, the official legal journal, and payment on initial equity (usually ranging from US$100 to $1,000) must be deposited in *colones* with a local bank until registration is complete.

There is usually no minimum investment required to set up a Costa Rican business corporation, except of course in the financial or banking sectors.

Companies may also have to secure a municipal patent or permit. Any foreign business with branches in Costa Rica, or which intends to open branches, must appoint and retain a legal representative with full power of attorney regarding the business or branch.

Recording fees for the registry are low but lawyers's fees can vary greatly. Lynda Solar of Amcham, which represents 400 North American, Costa Rican, and multinational companies, advised: "You really cannot cut corners in this country, and it's worth paying extra for a real professional, if possible bilingual, not only to set up the business, but also to find distributors or buyers. A good lawyer will help you to avoid potentially costly confusion over technical legal terms, and to get a business set up in a week rather than a month. If you get a cheap lawyer, you'll get a cheap job done."

Another requirement to be aware of is that new companies must secure an environmental impact certificate before they start operations. These are generally strictly enforced—building work was stopped for some time during the construction of the massive Intel plant outside San José after archaeological remains were found at the site. Foreign firms might find they get especially tough treatment in this respect.

For recommendations of good local lawyers, approach the commercial office of your embassy or Amcham. For more in-depth legal advice, as well as other information on how to estimate operating costs, tax and other investment questions, contact CINDE (Costa Rican Coalition for Development Initiatives) or PROCOMER (Costa Rican Foreign Trade Corporation). (See *Survival Skills* chapter).

WORK FORCE

"One of Costa Rica's greatest untapped resources is its workforce," said Julian Smith. "I have had no problems at all with staff. If you treat people well, they really appreciate it—especially women, who may be subject to sexual harassment in a locally-owned workplace."

A foreign bistro owner agrees. "One of the nicest things about working here is the great respect Ticos have for themselves and

179

others. Ticos are very humane and equality-conscious and my dish-washer will feel quite comfortable talking to me on an equal footing."

But, as he points out, this also underpins one of the most important issues for maintaining good relations with your staff: Ticos are proud and reluctant to accept criticism.

He said: "If you're going to criticize someone, you must never embarrass them by doing so in front of others. However much you may be itching to shout at someone who has done something seriously wrong, doing so will just result in them and their co-workers losing all respect for you. You must find a more consensual solution."

Ricardo Rouillon agreed: "You really cannot exploit people here the way you can in poorer Latin American countries. They simply will not accept it.

"This is a good thing, of course, but you must be very careful about how you tell your workers what to do. My head waiter resigned in a huff because I told him to set the tables my way, rather than the way he had always done it. People here get very upset by directness and confrontation. They go all around the houses to make everyone happy and save face."

Julian explained how to get around the problem: "Our company van was damaged after the driver allowed his underage son to drive it. Even though it might seem ridiculous, the correct solution was to start off by admitting that I was partly at fault for not having made it clear that we only wanted him to drive it."

At the other end of the scale, he points out, being too nice may lead people to take advantage of you so you must find a happy medium.

Similarly, if you want an employee to work harder, Julian says, the best approach is to appeal to their sense of *pobrecito*, or 'poor old you'. "I would make them feel that they're doing me a real favor," he explained. "I would say, for example, that we've been having a really awful month, and so could they please help me to get the work finished quickly."

RULES FOR EMPLOYERS

After years of state paternalism, Ticos jealously hang on to their long holidays and other benefits—even though these can at times reduce a firm's competivity. Ridley Scott, director of the Columbus movie *1492: Conquest of Paradise*, which was filmed in Costa Rica, was baffled when local extras refused to work 12-hour days, even after having signed contracts agreeing to the long shifts.

Lynda Solar said: "Workers here are very savvy when it comes to their rights. Labor codes here are stricter than in the United States, although thankfully the rules are much clearer and easier to understand than they once were. You must follow the rules or you could easily find a complaint lodged against you with the Ministry of Labor."

It's also important to be aware that the rules governing child labor are very strict too, unlike in many other Central American countries where minors commonly work in factories. Although you do see young children who have been sent out by their parents to work selling chicks or pencils on the street, it is absolutely illegal to hire them to work in the formal sector.

The most important workers' benefits are as follows: all salaried employees must be registered with the CCSS, into which the employer must pay 22% of the total salary amount. An additional 9% is deducted from the employee, all of which goes to cover medical costs and their personal pension fund.

The minimum monthly wage (as of July 2001) ranged from approximately US$230 for unskilled workers rising to US$530 for employees with a university degree. Starting salaries are dependent on an employee's academic level.

Workers also get a big Christmas bonus or *aguinaldo* (8.33% of salary) and hefty severance pay if they are laid off after three months or more service. Pregnant women are entitled to four months' maternity leave, while new mothers get an hour a day for breast-feeding. All Ticos must have a one-hour lunch break, plus 15 minutes in the morning and afternoon for coffee.

In many offices, people come dressed casually on a Friday in order to 'get ready for the weekend.' Workers are also entitled to one day of vacation for every month of employment, as well as the national holidays listed below.

Jan 1	New Year's Day
April	Thursday and Friday of Holy Week
April 11	Juan Santamaría Day (Costa Rica's national hero)
May 1	International Workers's Day
July 25	Guanacaste Day
Aug 2	Day of Nuestra Señora de los Angeles (Costa Rica's patron saint).
Sep 15	Independence Day
Oct 12	Día de la Raza (to mark Columbus's 'discovery' of the New World)
Dec 8	Immaculate Conception Day
Dec 24	Christmas

DOING BUSINESS A LA TICA

With Costa Rica being so small, virtually all the big firms involved in import or export belong to the handful of inter-related, old money families which still run the country. This can make it hard to break in with any kind of serious competition, so you must be very resilient.

It seems that most people are more concerned with price than anything else. There is only a very small market for quality products, and for many buyers quality means a label saying 'Made in the USA.'

How can you sell anything in such an environment? It is possible, said Ricardo Rouillon, but you will make life a lot easier for yourself if you play by the Ticos' rules.

"In this country, an aggressive sales pitch will turn people off straight away," he said. "You have to be humble, but get the balance just right. If you look too eager to sell, or offer it at a low price, people will not buy it either; they think there is something wrong with it.

"After some time, I finally learned that one of the most useful tricks is to make yourself out to be more important than you are. If I tell a prospective client I have been knocking on doors here for two years, it could take me weeks or months to get an appointment.

"They'll be much more impressed and see me straight away if I say I have just flown in for a few days and am leaving soon for a meeting in Europe. In my experience, people here do not value your time. They will turn up late for meetings, and sit around drinking coffee without getting to the point.

"I take a leaf out of the Ticos' book, and never give away too much about myself; I keep them guessing. It's not really being untruthful, because nearly everyone here presents him or herself as having more authority than they actually do. This means you should know the chain of command in a target company, or you could waste a lot of time talking to the wrong person."

THE BUSINESS ENVIRONMENT

Before heading for a business meeting, be fully prepared for the fact that you could become a victim of 'Tico Time' and be left hanging around kicking your heels waiting for the other parties to arrive.

If this does happen, don't complain over wasted time as it will get you nowhere. There's no point getting off on the wrong foot with people who simply have less of a cultural sense of urgency. Costa Rica's business community is small and your reputation, good or bad, is likely to travel before you. Instead, try to keep your schedule fairly open by not planning too many back-to-back meetings.

Lynda Solar said that such delays are thankfully becoming less and less acceptable among the business community. "There are so many American companies working here that we really work under US culture in Costa Rica now. While an 8:00 A.M. meeting in the US may begin at 7:45 A.M., we're still not at that stage here. It would generally start at 8:00 A.M. or at the latest 8:10 A.M. here rather than at 9:00 A.M. as would be the case in many other Latin countries."

Personal relationships and conversation are still valued more highly than punctuality, and there is usually quite a bit of friendly chitchat before meetings get seriously started. Getting straight down to business as you would at home might seem rather rude or brusque. There are few topics off-limits when talking with Ticos, but don't waste the opportunity to strengthen your new business relationships by moaning about their country, bureaucracy, or government. Ticos may well do this themselves, but if a foreigner starts carping too much they may take offence.

Costa Rica is a very business card-oriented culture, and everyone from your taxi driver to a company president will whip out a card (*tarjeta de negocio*) at the slightest opportunity. Costa Ricans, however, set a great deal less store on formality than many other Latin countries. While many of these cards will show the person's educational status, for example *licenciado* (graduate) or *doctor* (Ph.D.), this is not the norm, and you are not expected to greet anyone in a business setting in this fashion as you would do elsewhere in Latin America.

You should, however, use *Señor, Señora* or *Señorita* (the equivalent of Mr., Mrs. or Miss), plus the person's surname, when you first meet them. Once your relationship becomes closer, it is okay to swap to their first name, although you should prefix the terms of respect *don* or *doña* for people appreciably older than yourself (*señorita* plus first name for an unmarried woman).

In terms of business dress style, it is best to go for formal, i.e. suit and tie, especially in San José. Altitude and clouds can make weather in the capital surprisingly chilly for a country so close to the equator, so it's wise not to scrimp on a jacket. Trouser suits or skirts are fine for women, although Tica style is dressier than in America or Europe.

Outside San José most foreign businesspeople are involved in tourism, in which case dress codes are obviously much more relaxed. In the hotter coastal areas, men very occasionally wear *guayaberas* (traditional, embroidered shirts with four patch pockets) which are not tucked into the trousers.

As with everything else in tiny Costa Rica, networking is the key, so you should have good people skills. Although many Ticos, especially in the business community, have been educated abroad and speak excellent English, any effort to speak some Spanish on your part will definitely be appreciated. You should try to learn at least enough to be polite.

Lynda Solar said: "In a small business community there are a lot of opportunities for people who know how to work the system, but this will often depend upon who you know."

But how do you actually get to meet the people in the know? Tico society is generally more reserved than in most other Central American countries and the United States, and you're unlikely to be invited to a business colleague's house. There are, however, several business chambers such as Amcham (see *Strategic Directory*) many of which organize events such as golf contests—a lot of business in Costa Rica gets done on the fairway.

They also host plenty of social events where, as anywhere else, alcohol can be an important part of the bonding process. But Ms. Solar said: "Unlike some other Latin countries, you won't be expected to get roaring drunk, or even to drink at all. Alcohol consumption is definitely not a vital part of doing business here, and not nearly as prevalent as it once was."

She added that although Costa Rica is a Latin, often *machista* country, there is little sexism in business, especially at the higher levels. "In Latin America, Costa Rica is the vanguard in terms of participation of women in the business community," she said. "It has a lot to do with the level of education. More than half this country's university population is female, and we have a lot of female CEOs."

BRIBERY AND DODGY DEALINGS

By Latin American standards, Costa Rica is very 'clean' when it comes to corruption, although it did slip in the stakes from being the least corrupt country in South America in 2000 to the third least corrupt

185

country in 2001—behind Uruguay and Chile—in a Transparency International survey. However, bribery still exists, people still pay *mordidas* (literally bites), and underpaid, overworked public employees look for illegal income in the form of *chorizos* (literally sausages).

Julian Smith said: "The country is so small that anyone with access to the president or other avenues of power is constantly besieged by people wanting favors. This can easily result in bribery and corruption."

Another American businessman added: "No official person has ever even insinuated to me that unless I paid a bribe the work wouldn't get done, but I have bribed people in order to speed things up, particularly tax issues and getting things cleared through customs. I have always been the one to suggest the payment, but no-one has ever been offended or refused to accept."

Everyone agrees that excessive red tape is one of the major causes of corruption, with desperate businessmen willing to pay bribes in order to cut through the morass of bureaucratic delays to simply get work done. For example, all contracts must be scrutinized and approved by a government office called the *controlaría*. The intention is to ensure that no money is changing hands. In reality, however, it just makes things proceed at a frustrating snail's pace and breeds more corruption than it prevents.

The government is now making serious efforts to slim down bureaucracy, having set up an office called the Programa de Simplificación de Trámites.

Irene Vizcaíno, an official in this department, said: "*Mordidas* have become common because of the hundreds of hoops people had to jump through. You'd go to one office only to be told to go to another and then another. Any procedure could take months, and you never knew how long it actually should be taking.

"The idea behind this was that the greater the bureaucracy, the greater the safeguards against corruption. But in fact it just created a kind of Kafka-esque nightmare for businessmen, with lawyers and middlemen being the only winners."

The office is now working to weed out duplications and unnecessary procedures, and has also produced an excellent CD and information pack laying out exactly what the steps are in setting up a business, the maximum time limits for completion of each procedure, investors' rights and options for legal action (see *Strategic Directory* chapter).

Ms. Vizcaíno said that, with the Costa Rican economy attempting to diversify, the streamlining plan is deliberately aimed at attracting more foreign investment. However, with a huge backlog of papers waiting to be cleared, it could take years to get the system running smoothly, she warned. She added that bribery has always been, and still is, very definitely illegal and punishable by jail and/ or deportation.

Do take note that US law does have a "Foreign Corrupt Practices Act" which means that an American businessman could be charged in the US for bribing a Costa Rican official.

In the meantime, in order to minimize the amount of bureaucratic pain you may suffer, most businessmen recommend the use of a *despachante* or *gavilán* (hawk), so called because they make a profession out of spending hours waiting around in government offices or banks and then swooping down to collect important papers. These people know all the ins and outs of the system, are fairly reasonably-priced and indispensable, unless you want to wait yourself in interminable lines only to find out you're in the wrong office, or to be told to 'come back tomorrow'.

SHADY CHARACTERS

Tens of thousands of foreigners do business happily in Costa Rica—but it's also good to be aware that the country has its fair share of fraudsters and con artists (most famously Robert Vesco—see *Heroes and Villains* in the *People* chapter). These characters often come to hide from the law back home, and are attracted by the country's secretive banking laws, vagueness concerning extradition, and large expat community, which provides an ideal environment to hide in.

A foreign book shop owner said: "Most of my worst business experiences have actually been with other foreigners. In less than nine years, we've had six attempts to con us out of money by professional con artists in 'bust out' scams.

"Another problem is that the legal system here is labyrinthine. It's very hard to pierce the corporate veil, and with the legal system based on the Napoleonic code, there is no case law as in the US or UK. This means there has to be a specific law for absolutely every eventuality—if a law has not been written to address your particular issue, then it's simply not covered.

"An example of one of the legal deficiencies is that someone can run out of cash, shut down their business and start another one in another name across the street. The current system means their debts will all be erased. If that person owes you money, it will be impossible to get it back. I can't tell you how important it is in this country to have a good, trustworthy lawyer."

UNIONS

The first union was set up in 1916. However, since the banana strike of 1934, employers have tended to see union activity as tantamount to communism — anathema in Costa Rica.

In 1995, unions represented only one worker in 16 in the private sector but three out of five in the public sector. In the private sector, potential union activists are frightened of being sacked, while workers often view union leaders as corrupt and self-serving. Unsurprisingly, nearly all strikes are among public sector workers, which can effectively hold the state to ransom.

As a result, private sector workers often organize around *solidarista* associations, which are little more than management-controlled savings and low-interest loan bodies financed by payroll deductions.

There are also 22 *colegios* (guilds) of professions such as lawyers, doctors, and architects. These regulate the people allowed to work in each profession, and are often also required to oversee contracts and procedures in their speciality area.

PERSONAL AND BUSINESS SECURITY

Amcham advises businesspeople to take the same kind of sensible precautions they would take at home.

Lynda Solar said: "Despite the rise in petty crime and car theft, Costa Rica, unlike the rest of Central America, does not suffer from kidnapping or other violent crime against businesspeople. The Organismo de Investigación Judicial (Costa Rica's equivalent of the FBI) is over-worked, but generally does a good job."

Remember that in businesses where you're taking cash, for example restaurants and stores, it's extremely important to have an ultra-violet bill checker. There are many professionally counterfeited bank notes in circulation.

INTELLECTUAL PROPERTY RIGHTS

Intellectual property rights laws in Costa Rica are far from perfect, especially in terms of the policing infrastructure. As in so many areas, Costa Rica has forward-looking legislation that meets WTO requirements, but no means of implementing it. Even the Supreme Court admitted in 2001 that it was still using some unlicensed software.

"With the boom of high-tech business in the country, biotechnology and software could become fantastic industries here," said Lynda Solar. "But if patents and other rights are not respected, the country is going to find it is shooting itself in the foot."

The chambers of commerce provide an ideal venue for getting the most up-to-date news on changes in the situation as well as legislation regarding intellectual property rights and other issues.

TRANSLATION

Although you can get by to a large extent with English in Costa Rica, a good translator is fundamental and well worth the cost (around US$100-150 per day, ask your embassy or chamber of commerce for recommendations). Business jargon can be quite different from conversational language, and you don't want to lose out on a deal by missing the point. Legal documents that must be recorded in the National Registry or logged in a Notary Protocol book MUST be written in Spanish. However, foreign businesses have done leases in English with an official Spanish translation, and have ligitated these leases in court in Costa Rica.

Translation is also crucial if your company plans to produce local brochures or advertise in the widely read Costa Rican media— a good way of drumming up business. You don't want to blow your chances with badly worded Spanish, which is a possibility unless you speak with perfect fluency.

In addition, you will probably attract more customers by using local Tico slang words, which you may not know. For example, many Ticos hate the creeping infiltration of '*tú*' (the informal word for you) instead of '*vos*' (the local equivalent). As a result, many international companies have changed the grammar on their adverts in Costa Rica, and you would be advised to do the same.

TAX INCENTIVES

Costa Rica offers major tax incentives in key industry areas where it is trying to attract investment. These are significant in a country where import taxes can be very high.

- Import taxes are waived on materials to be used in tourism developments.
- For forest conservation, land and asset taxes are exempted and special police anti-squatter protection is guaranteed if land owners can certify that no lumbering has taken place during the two previous years and will not take place over at least the next 20 years. The same benefits are offered to those who replant deforested land.
- Import duty and other taxes are also waived for businesses involved in mining or agriculture.

For income tax rates etc., see *Survival Skills* chapter. Be aware of recent legal changes, which will impose strict punishments for tax evasion, including a prison term of up to 10 years. These sanctions were previously unknown.

FREE TRADE ZONES

Zonas francas are special business parks in which major tax incentives are offered to companies making new investments in the country and making an initial new investment of at least US$150,000. The free trade zone benefits apply only to companies manufacturing goods for export or companies involved in science or technology.

STOCK EXCHANGE

The *Bolsa Nacional de Valores* (stock exchange) is the biggest in Central America, having operated since 1976, and trading is focused almost entirely on government securities. It publishes daily, weekly, and monthly bulletins with complete disclosure of all transactions (for contact details see *Strategic Directory* chapter).

— Chapter Eight —
LANGUAGE

One of the most commonly bandied-around misconceptions about Spanish is that it is an 'easy' language. Of course, it is much easier, if you are a native English speaker than, say, Japanese. But while it is reasonably easy to learn to speak basic survival Spanish, it can take longer than you might expect to learn to speak it well unless you can already speak another Latin language. Sadly, many people become disillusioned or give up after being initially told how 'easy' it was.

The major problem, for English speakers, is that Spanish has a LOT of grammar, including two noun genders, two different verbs for 'to be' and a verb mood that can be very hard to grasp (the subjunctive). With verb conjugations, there are generally only four possible permutations in English: for example, 'say, says, said, and saying.' With Spanish verbs, there are nearly 50.

In addition, Spanish in Costa Rica varies widely from both the Spanish spoken in Spain and most other Spanish-speaking countries, in terms of both pronunciation and vocabulary.

But don't get downhearted! On the plus side, Spanish, unlike English, is at least based on rules, which can be learned. It's also 100% phonetic—so you'll never agonize over the pronunciation of the Spanish equivalents of 'enough', 'cough', and 'thorough'. Costa Rican Spanish is spoken relatively slowly and clearly, and, along with that of Colombia, is usually recognized as the best in the whole of Latin America (usually put down to the high levels of education in both countries).

There are dozens of very good Spanish schools in the country, and most educated younger Costa Ricans—especially in the urban areas —can speak at least a smattering of English. This can be a huge help at the beginning when you get stumped. Ticos are also endlessly patient. Most of them have had to deal with so many English-speaking tourists or residents who can't or won't even say '*gracias*,' that they are delighted at anyone making the effort, however ham-fistedly, to speak their language.

Unless you're pretty fluent in Spanish, Ticos may try to help you out by reverting to English. I've known some foreigners who are really determined to speak only in Spanish and so tell a white lie, saying they don't speak English. Of course, if you are asked where you're from this means you'll have to plump for somewhere unusual like Norway—and hope no-one asks you to teach them any Norwegian!

Once your Spanish skills improve, you will find that soap operas can be a good way of picking up (admittedly rather melodramatic) conversational slang. Another big help is that Hollywood movies in Costa Rica are always subtitled into Spanish— reading the subtitles while you hear the dialogue can be a massive learning boost.

It is beyond the scope of this section to provide more than the most basic of pointers for readers who can't yet speak Spanish—a good phrase book, dictionary and, if possible, a few weeks in a

Spanish school are strongly recommended. Much of the information in this section is aimed at people who already speak some Spanish and want to learn some of the peculiarities of the language as spoken in Costa Rica.

PRONUNCIATION

A – like the 'a' in 'cat'.
E – like the 'e' in 'bed'.
I – like the 'ee' in 'meet'
O – like the 'o' in 'top'.
U – a short 'oo', as in 'Oops!'

Most consonants are pronounced like their English counterparts. Exceptions are:

C – like the hard 'c' in 'cat' before 'a', 'o', and 'u'. Like the soft 'c' in 'centre' before 'e' and 'i'.
D – like the 'd' in 'dog' at the start of a word. Like the 'th' in 'this' elsewhere.
G – like the hard 'g' in 'give' before 'a', 'o', and 'u'. Like the 'h' in 'his' before 'e' and 'i'.
GU – like the hard 'g' before 'e' and 'i'. Like the 'gw' in 'Gwen' before 'a', 'o', and 'u'—but pronounced more softly, almost like a 'w'.
Gü – the same soft 'gw' as above, but used before 'e' and 'i'.
H – silent.
J – like the 'h' in 'his'.
LL – like the 'y' in 'yellow'.
QU – like the 'k' in 'kite'.
R – in the middle of a word, sounds like the lazy 'tt' in American pronunciation of 'butter'. At the start of a word, is should be rolled. However, if you have problems with

rolling the Spanish 'r', worry not! Uniquely, many Ticos, especially older Ticos, do not roll it either. Instead it is a rounded 'r' pronounced pretty much as it would be by an American or an Englishman with a Westcountry burr.

RR – rolled, as above.

S – like the 's' in 'soap'.

Y – at the start of a word, pronounced like 'j' in 'jam'. Elsewhere pronounced like 'y' in 'yellow'.

Z – like the 's' in 'soap'.

As already mentioned, Costa Rican pronunciation is good. Outside the Meseta Central, however, you will find that people often speak much faster. In Guanacaste, the accent is the same as in Nicaragua—very fast, and with only an aspirated pronunciation of the letter 's'.

Much 'realistic' Costa Rican literature, especially from the early 20th century, faithfully reproduces countryside pronunciation that you will still hear today. For example, many words starting with a consonant followed by 'ue', such as *'huevo'*, *'fue'*, or *'vuelvo'*, may sound more like *'güevo'*, *'güe'* or *'güelvo'*. Less educated Ticos may also leave out various consonants, running words together—so that *'entonces'* (then, well, so) sounds more like *'to'es'*, while 'de nada' (you're welcome) becomes *'e na'a'*. In coastal areas people often replace a final 'r' with an 'l', for example the verb *'decir'*, to say, becomes *'decil'*.

STRESS

The stress comes on the last syllable if the word ends in a consonant other than 'n' or 's' e.g. *la mujer* (woman), or *universal*. If the word ends in a vowel, an 'n' or an 's', the stress comes on the penultimate syllable, e.g. *la cama* (bed), *la imagen* (image) or *interesante* (interesting). An accent above a vowel, e.g. *difícil* (difficult), or *la química* (chemistry), shows irregular stress, that is placed on the accented syllable. For words ending in 'io' or 'ia', these letters are

195

pronounced as a diphthong, i.e. one syllable, (e.g. in *el misterio*, where the stress is on the 'e'), unless a stress accent shows differently (e.g. *la panadería* meaning bakery).

COGNATES

Though English is a Germanic language, more than 50% of all its vocabulary actually has Latin roots. This gives rise (helpfully) to thousands of related words in Spanish and English, which means a beginner can expand his or her vocabulary very quickly.

For example, hundreds of words in Spanish ending in '*dad*' end in 'ty' in English, e.g. *libertad (*liberty), *posibilidad (*possibility), while words ending in 'tion' in English end in '*ción*' in Spanish, such as *información* (information) and *violación (*violation).

English words ending in 'ly' are often equivalent to those in Spanish ending in '*mente*', such as really (*realmente*), naturally (*naturalmente)*, while those ending in 'ry' in English end in '*rio*' in Spanish, such as territory (*territorio)* and commentary (*comentario)*. 'Ism' in English becomes '*ismo*' in Spanish, e.g. communism (*comunismo)* and individualism (*individualismo)*.

There are many other cognate forms. Be warned, however, of many 'false friends'—for example, *actualmente*, which means 'currently' rather than 'actually', and *sensible*, which means 'sensitive', not 'sensible'. When I was first learning Spanish I regularly caused hilarity by saying: '*Estoy embarazada*', whenever I was embarrassed —not for a moment intending to announce that I was pregnant!

GENDER

In Spanish, nouns are either masculine (mostly ending in 'o') or feminine (mostly ending in 'a'), e.g. *la muchacha* (the girl), *el muchacho* (the boy). There are exceptions to the above, e.g. *el programa*, *el planeta*, *el problema*, and *la mano* (hand), *la foto* and *la dinamo*.

Nouns ending in '*ión*' or '*dad*' are also feminine (e.g. *la organización*, and *la unidad*). Those ending in any other letter simply have to be learned e.g. *la piel* (skin), but *el nivel* (level), and *la mujer* (woman), but *el amor* (love).

IMPORTANT POINTS OF GRAMMAR

Unlike English, adjectives nearly always follow the noun, e.g. *un programa interesante* is 'an interesting programme'. They also agree in gender and number with the noun, e.g. *el gato negro* ('the black cat'), but *las vacas blancas* ('the white cows').

Spanish has two verbs 'to be': *ser* and *estar*. *Ser* refers to a permanent state, and *estar* to a temporary state or location. For example, *el perro es gris* (ser) = 'the dog is grey' – permanent state, but *el perro está afuera* (estar) = 'the dog is outside' – location. *Es aburrido* (ser) means 'he is boring', *está aburrido* (estar) means 'he is bored'.

USEFUL BASIC SPANISH PHRASES

Good morning/good day – Buenos días
Good afternoon – Buenas tardes
Good evening – Buenas noches

Yes – Sí
No – No
Please – Por favor
Thank you – Gracias
What's your name? – Cómo se llama (usted)?
My name is Pedro – Me llamo Pedro (literally 'I call myself Pedro')
Excuse me! (when trying to pass someone) – Permiso!
Excuse me! (when trying to attract attention/ apologising for standing on someone's foot etc.) Disculpe! (Generally, to summon any person under the age of about 35, particularly a waiter or shop assistant, call them *muchacho/a* (boy/girl) or *joven* (youngster). While in many other Latin countries this would sound incredibly rude, and one would use *señor* or *señorita*, Ticos find this form of address endearing.)
How are you? – Cómo está (usted)?
I'm fine thank you (and you?) – Estoy bien gracias (y usted?)
I would like... – Quisiera, quería or me gustaría... (more polite than 'quiero' – 'I want')
Do you have... ? – Tiene... ?
Not at all/ My pleasure – Con mucho gusto.
What do you do? – A qué se dedica?
How do you say? – Cómo se dice...?
Goodbye/see you later – Hasta luego.
I (don't) understand – (No) entiendo.
Good/bad – bueno(a)/malo(a)
Big/small – grande/ pequeño(a)
Old/young – viejo(a)/joven
Fat/thin – gordo(a)/delgado(a)
A lot/a little – mucho(a)/poco(a)
Happy/sad – feliz/triste
More/less – más/menos
Right/wrong – correcto(a)/equivocado(a)
Open/closed – abierto(a)/cerrado(a)

Entrance/exit – la entrada/la salida
When? – Cuándo?
When does the next bus leave for... ? – Cuándo sale el próximo bus
    para... ?
Tired – cansado(a)
How? or Come again? – Cómo?
Why? – Por qué?
Do you like... ? – Le gusta... ?
I like it/I love it – Me gusta/me encanta
I don't like it – No me gusta
I feel bad/I am sick – Me siento mal/estoy enfermo(a)
Where is... ? – Dónde está... ?
The toilet – el baño
Hospital – el hospital
Bank – el banco
Market – el mercado
Policeman – el policía
Doctor – el médico
Post office – el correo
Embassy – la embajada
Church – la iglesia
Airport – el aeropuerto
North – norte
South – sur
East – este
West – oeste
To the right/left – a la derecha/izquierda
Up/down – arriba/abajo
(Round trip) ticket – un tíquet (de ida y vuelta)
How much? – Cuánto cuesta/vale?
It's too expensive – Es muy caro
Do you have anything cheaper? – No tiene algo más barato?
Do you take credit cards? – Aceptan tarjetas de crédito?

Do you have a free room? – Tiene un cuarto libre?
With a single/double bed – Con cama individual/matrimonial
Air conditioning – el aire acondicionado
Fan – el abanico/ ventilador
With a private/shared bathroom – Con baño privado/colectivo
Hot/cold water – Agua caliente/fría

Food
Bon appetit! – Buen provecho!
Breakfast – el desayuno
Lunch – el almuerzo
Dinner – la cena
Dessert – el postre
Could I see the menu, please? – Podría ver la carta, por favor?
I'm a vegetarian – Soy vegetariano(a)
The bill please – La cuenta, por favor

Time phrases
Today – Hoy
Tomorrow – Mañana
Yesterday – Ayer
This morning – Esta mañana
This afternoon – Esta tarde
Tonight – Esta noche
Week/month/year – la semana/el mes/el año
Next week – la semana que viene
Last month – el mes pasado
Early/late – Temprano/tarde
Summer (dry season) – Verano
Winter (rainy season) – Invierno/temporada verde

Telling the time

What time is it? – Qué hora es?
It's one o'clock – Es la una
It's two o'clock – Son las dos
It's half past three – Son las tres y media (literally three and half)
It's 4.15 – Son las cuatro y quince
It's 4.40 – Son las cinco menos veinte (literally four minus twenty)

Days of the Week

Monday   – lunes
Tuesday   – martes
Wednesday – miércoles
Thursday   – jueves
Friday   – viernes
Saturday   – sábado
Sunday   – domingo

Months of the Year

January   – enero
February   – febrero
March   – marzo
April   – abril
May   – mayo
June   – junio
July   – julio
August   – agosto
September – septiembre/setiembre
October   – octubre
November – noviembre
December – diciembre

Numbers

1 – uno
2 – dos
3 – tres
4 – cuatro
5 – cinco
6 – seis
7 – siete
8 – ocho
9 – nueve
10 – diez
11 – once
12 – doce
13 – trece
14 – catorce
15 – quince
16 – dieciséis
17 – diecisiete
18 – dieciocho
19 – diecinueve
20 – veinte
21 – veintiuno
30 – treinta
40 – cuarenta
50 – cincuenta
60 – sesenta
70 – setenta
80 – ochenta
90 – noventa
100 – cien
200 – doscientos
300 – trescientos
500 – quinientos

1,000	–	mil
1,000,000	–	un millón
1,000,000	–	mil millones/ un millardo
1,000,000,000	–	un billón

Be aware that Costa Ricans reverse the commas and points in numbers that English speakers are used to. For example 4,982 (four thousand nine hundred and eighty two) in Costa Rica is written 4.982 or 4.982,00. You will even see this with dates, for example the year 2.003.

VOSEO

Vos is an archaic form of 'you', which is now only widely used in Argentina, Uruguay, Nicaragua, and Costa Rica, where it is an intimate, informal means of address (the formal form is *usted*), used instead of *tú*.

Originally, however, the *voseo*—which descends from the Golden Age and was used in Spain until the 19th century—was actually the polite second person singular form, equivalent to 'thou' in English. It was the way in which the *hidalgos*, or noblemen, who settled Costa Rica, addressed each other.

For those who have studied Peninsular Spanish, *vos* conjugates exactly like *vosotros* (the informal plural 'you' of Spain). The only difference is that where verbs in *vosotros* end in *áis, éis* or *ís*, in *vos* they end in *ás, és* or *ís*, always maintaining the same stress as the *vosotros* form.

Alternatively, you can usually take the *tú* form and just stress the last syllable (e.g. *tú miras = vos mirás*). *Vos* uses the infinitive as a root, so doesn't share the irregularities of *tú*. Therefore:

Tú entiendes (vosotros entendéis) = *vos entendés* (you understand)
Tú piensas (vosotros pensáis) = *vos pensás* (you think)
Tú dices (vosotros decís) = *vos decís* (you say)
• Importantly, note *vos sos* (tú eres/ vosotros sois) – you are.

In the simple past, *vos* adds an 's' to the *tú* form, so *tú supiste* (you knew) = *vos supistes* (*vosotros supisteis*).

In the imperative, *vos* simply removes the 'r' of the infinitive (or the 'd' of the *vosotros* imperative).

Pon (tú) = poned (vosotros) = *poné (vos)* put!

Mira (tú) = mirad (vosotros) = *mirá (vos)* look!

Ven (tú) = venid (vosotros) = *vení (vos)* come!

Unlike *vosotros*, *vos* takes *'te'* rather than *'os'* in the reflexive, for example: *Tenés que vestirte enseguida* (You have to get dressed straightaway).

VOS OR USTED

The use of *vos* is becoming something of a hot potato in Costa Rica. While you'll still hear it a lot in the countryside, you will rarely hear *vos* these days in the city. Many, many people in Costa Rica now exclusively use *usted*, even with family members, children and pets.

Some towns are also more likely to use *vos* than others. Two Tico friends, university students Rebeca, from Cartago, and Ariana, from San José, have known each other for years, but while Ariana always calls Rebeca *vos*, for Rebeca, Ariana will always be *usted*.

Some people may switch from *vos* to *usted* and back again during the course of a conversation to emphasize a slight change in mood. Unlike most other Spanish speaking countries, there may well not be a symbolic moment in your relationship with a Tico when you cross the intimacy threshold from *usted* to *vos*—particularly among middle-class Ticos, who like to be thought of as cultured and educated. If you hear someone saying *vos*, there's a good chance they may be from Nicaragua, where it's still used more widely.

"*Vos* sounds nice and old-fashioned, but it's the way I think of farmers speaking," a San José taxi driver said. "It's just way too informal for me. I don't really have any kind of relationships where I'd be comfortable calling someone *vos*."

Ticos will not expect you to know how to use *vos*. *Tú* is fine for a foreigner, unless you're planning on staying for a long time. If you do use *vos*, it goes without saying that you should never do so with people much older than yourself. It's really easiest to avoid the whole minefield by sticking with *usted* until the Tico you're talking to suggests you change.

In addition, *tú* is slowly starting to appear in the country through the influence of foreign movies and soap operas, with occasional Ticos using it as a 'classier' alternative to *vos*. There is a big backlash against this, however.

"If another Costa Rican called me *tú*, I wouldn't even respond to them," said Ariana. "It's not part of our language or culture—it just smacks of people trying to be something they're not."

Many multinational companies, such as Burger King, take such strength of feeling on board, changing their advertising for Costa Rica from *tú* to *vos*.

TIQUISMOS

Despite being such a small country, Costa Rica has as much or more country-specific vocabulary and slang than many other much bigger nations. Many of these 'Tiquismos' arose because of the country's historic isolation, and have their roots in farming or religion, or more recently in the Ticos' unusually heavy exposure to English.

Of course you will also find many diminutives ending in '*ito*' or '*ico*' (the very reason for the Costa Ricans being called Ticos), either for emphasis, or to make words sound more cute or friendly; such as *ahorita* from *ahora* (now/right now), *despuesito* (afterwards), *hasta lueguito* (bye), *chiquitico* (teeny) from *chiquito* (tiny), and ultimately *chico* (small), and *a la vueltica* (just around the corner).

This is a list of some of the most common Tiquismos (a few are used more widely throughout the region). There are hundreds more, lots used by speakers of *pachucho*, a kind of street slang. For a more exhaustive selection, an excellent website to visit is: http://www.geocities.com/SouthBeach/Jetty/1875/ticoac.html

Adiós! – Hi! (when passing someone in the street, especially in rural areas) – usually means 'goodbye'

Andar – to have (literally 'to walk'), e.g. *Sólo ando cien colones*

Apear – to get down (used instead of *bajar*)

Birra – beer (usually *cerveza*). Also *rubia* – (literally blonde)

Blanco – cigarette (usually *cigarro*)

Bomba – petrol station

Brete – job (*bretear* means to work)

Buenas – short for *buenos días*, *buenas tardes* or *buenas noches*

Cabra/o – girlfriend, boyfriend (literally goat)

Cachos – shoes (literally horns)

Campo – space, e.g. on a bus (literally field). *Hay campo?* – Is there space?

Cerrado – stupid, pig-headed (literally closed)

Chamaco/chavalo – child/kid

Chepe – San José

Chile – a (usually sexual or scatalogical) joke

Chinamo – a street stall

Chiva/chivísima – brilliant, cool (literally goat). Used mainly by younger people

Cien metros – one city block

Chorizo – illegal business (literally sausage)

Chunche – thing

Diay! – crucial Tico interjection, which can mean anything from 'hey!' to 'what a shame' to 'hmm... '

Que dicha/por dicha – thankfully, luckily

Este – often a drawn-out *eeeeeste...* Used much as 'like' in lazy English, to fill a space while you're thinking of what to say

Gato – person with light-colored eyes (cat)

Güeison – bad quality. This originally comes from the phrase *buey sólo*, or 'single ox'. A pair of oxen are needed to pull a cart, so a *buey sólo* is something that's pretty useless.

Güevon – literally big egg (or big testicle). Term of address used between men, often insultingly.

Güila – child/kid. Be careful as this means prostitute in Mexico!

Hijo'eputa – literally son of a bitch. Widely used as an expression of surprise or annoyance, and sometimes toned down to *juepucha*.

Jale! – Let's go!

Jupa – head

Limpio/quedarse limpio – to have no money

Macho/a – light-skinned or haired person

Maicero – hick

Maje (usually ma'e) – literally crazy or stupid. This word is the equivalent of 'mate' in English, *tío* in Spain or *che* in Argentina.

Maso – short for *más o menos*. 'More or less', 'pretty much'.

Nerdo – nerd.

Nota – as in *que buena nota*, or *que mala nota* – fantastic or what a pain

Ocupar – used instead of *necesitar* (to need), e.g. *ocupo ir al banco* (I need to go to the bank).

Platero – a gold digger.

Porta amí? – What do I care? So what?

Que pereza! – What a pain! How boring!

Pesos – colones

Playo – homosexual (another word is *guineo* – a type of small banana)

Porfa – please (short for *por favor*)

Pura vida – the absolutely ubiquitous Tiquismo. Literally pure life, it can mean cool, great or thanks, and even be used as a greeting. It can be applied to people, places, events, etc.

Regalar – literally to give as a gift. This is widely used instead of *dar* (to give). Asking for a beer in a bar, for example, you would say *regáleme una cerveza, por favor*.

Roco – old man

Rojo – 1,000 colón note. Literally 'red' (the color of the bill). This also means a taxi—all Tico taxis are red.

Salado – an unlucky person. Literally salty.

Suave/suave un toque! – hang on/wait a minute

Teja, tejita – 100 colón bill

Tomado – drunk

Torta – a big cock-up

Tuanis – from 'too nice' in English. Basically 'cool!' Can also be used as a greeting

Tucán – 5,000 colón bill (it has a toucan on it)

Tugurio – shanty town

La U – university (especially UCR)

Upe! – greeting/warning shouted when approaching someone's house instead of knocking on the door

Vacilar – to have a good time/pull someone's leg; *vacilón* - funny (person, experience)

Vieras que... – you should see... , or you wouldn't believe...

Vina – nosey, *vinear* – to gossip, try to find out about something

GESTURES
Greetings

Ticos aren't as big on cheek-kissing as many other Latin Americans. When meeting someone for the first time, it's best to follow their lead rather than lunging in for the embarrassment of a potentially unrequited kiss. You may not reach kissing status until you know someone better. Among non-intimate acquaintances, kissing is more common between women than between men and women—usually reserved more for family members and close friends. When you do find yourself in a kissing situation, remember that double cheek European-style kissing is not the Tico way—instead you kiss just one cheek, making quite a loud lip-smacking noise rather than a 'mwaa' air kiss.

Men greeting other men shake hands firmly. With good friends they swoop in for a giant handshake, with the hand swinging down theatrically from head height. This is often followed up with some hearty shoulder-slapping for good measure.

In the Caribbean, men often greet each other with a tapping of clenched fists, or with an African handshake in which the fingers are slipped out from the 'normal' handshake and the fingertips hooked together, before slipping back into the handshake.

Other gestures

While someone you've only just met may quite happily prod you in the shoulder to emphasise a point during conversation, Ticos generally aren't really very big on gesticulating or body contact. Below are some of the gestures you are most likely to come across:

- To beckon someone to come towards you place your arm straight out in front of you, hand palm down, and flap the hand up and down. Beckoning with the index finger is considered rude. Also rude—but often used for this purpose—is a hiss.
- To ask for the bill across a crowded restaurant, mime signing a check to the waiter.
- To signify a place or room being full of people, place palm towards you and fingers up, bring all fingertips together.
- To signify something incredible, fast, unbelievable or outrageous, hold forearm horizontally in front of the chest, palm facing inwards and shake hand vigorously up and down (often hard enough to make fingers snap loudly against each other).
- To signify that something is finished and you no longer care about it, usually a relationship, place palms facing towards each other at chest height, and rapidly wipe one palm over the other about three or four times.
- While driving, if on-coming cars flash their headlights, this means there are police, a landslide, a flood, or some other unpleasantness up ahead.
- To say 'cheers' while drinking, Ticos often use the popular Spanish ritual of holding the glass up high and shouting *Arriba!* (up), down low shouting *Abajo!* (down), in the middle, shouting *Al centro!* and then swallowing the drink, with a *Y adentro!* (inside).

CONVERSATION TOPICS

It's never difficult to strike up conversation with a Tico—in fact you might have to feign sleep on public transport in order to avoid chatting with your neighbor. There are no explicitly off-limits areas, although be aware that many Ticos are quite conservative. If you get a sense of this, it's obviously best to avoid risqué topics such as your impending sex change or fascination with Satanism.

Ticos are big newspaper readers and, being such a small country, generally have a good grasp of affairs in the region and the world. They generally respect the perceived discipline and organization of the US and Europe, and will be fascinated to find out more about your country, and also your opinion of Costa Rica. Score points by reading the local press so you're up to date with what's going on.

Be warned, however. While they're cynical about their own political situation, don't criticize it too much yourself—or anything else in the country for that matter, with the possible exception of the roads. Ticos are enormously patriotic, and while they can be as critical as they like, they may take offense if you do so.

Family is more important to Ticos than just about anything else (with the possible exception of football—the conversation starter *par excellence*). They will want to tell you all about their relatives, and will expect you to reciprocate. If your family is not with you, carry pictures.

Football is an ideal gambit—especially for men, who will often be invited to join in an informal kickabout. But other hobbies can spark conversation too. Coin collection is very big among Ticos, and they will often want to swap foreign currency with you or show you their collection. If you're lucky, someone will give you one of the beautiful (now phased out) five colón bills—with orchids on one side and a copy of the coffee-harvesting painting from the Teatro Nacional on the other.

Ticos are only a step removed from their agricultural heritage. Many people will talk for hours about farming, countryside lore and customs, and the weather. Despite the country having only two rather predictable seasons, the onset of climate change (which has already had drastic effects in Central America) now means that each downpour and passing cloud has become almost as worthy of comment as in Britain.

INSULTS

Like many Latinos, Ticos love their mothers to the point of worship. Consequently, one of the worst things you can call someone is *hijo'eputa* (son of a bitch), although it really depends upon the tone of voice used. (This term is widely used as an exclamation with no hint of insult). Some Ticos prefer: *Tu madre puede ser una santa, pero vos sos un hijo'eputa*—your mother might be a saint, but you're a son of a bitch. Ticos are quite *delicados* and easily offended. Personal criticism can be taken as a huge insult.

AFRO-CARIBBEAN ENGLISH

Most black people in the Caribbean, at least among older generations, speak English much better than Spanish. Younger people tend to speak more and more Spanish, however—often to the chagrin of their parents.

However, there are two kinds of English: One is perfectly intelligible, though with a Caribbean lilt. The other is *mekatelyu* (make I tell you), more a kind of code language originally designed to bamboozle British slave masters. This is a mixture of Victorian English with some Spanish, French and completely invented words— all spoken at break-neck speed with a strong Jamaican accent. It has evolved individually to some point at least in Costa Rica, as people cannot always communicate perfectly with the black speakers of *guari-guari* just over the border in Bocas del Toro in Panama.

The most ubiquitous phrase you'll hear in the Caribbean is: *Wh'apin?* (what happen?), which can mean anything from 'how are you?', to 'what's up' and 'what's wrong?'. It can also be used in explanation, like *lo que pasa es que...* in Spanish, e.g. 'Wh'apin, rain wet me up and I catch a draft.'

You'll also hear a hooting 'cho man!', used to express disbelief, disgust or surprise; 'go good!' for 'goodbye'; and some bizarre grammar—e.g. 'his friends' would be 'him friends dem'.

An equivalent of the Spanish *don* and *doña* is used for politeness with older people, who are called 'Mr. Edwin', 'Miss Edith,' etc. (not 'Mrs.'). Black Costa Ricans speaking Spanish may well affectionately call you *mami* or *papi*.

NAMES AND SURNAMES

Although, like all Hispanic people, Ticos have both a paternal and maternal surname, in daily life the paternal one is often the only one used, which makes life a lot less confusing for non-Latins. For legal purposes or on business cards, they will probably use both (and often their middle name too—usually the name of the saint on whose day they were born).

Confused? Don't be. Ernesto Tomás, son of Daniel Luis Alvarez Gómez and María Fernanda Rodríguez Mora, will be called Ernesto Tomás Alvarez Rodríguez (or just Ernesto Alvarez). Both men and women keep their surnames at birth throughout life, regardless of marriage or divorce, although Ernesto's mother María Rodríguez may at times be referred to as María Rodríguez de Alvarez.

In a telephone book or in official documentation, surnames usually come first, so Ernesto would be Alvarez Rodríguez Ernesto Tomás.

For the dual surname purpose, an illegitimate child may take its mother's paternal surname twice, e.g. Ernesto Rodríguez Rodríguez.

While religious first names are still popular, the fascination with all things American has ensured a growing number of Anglo-Saxon first names (often bizarrely phonetically spelt), such as Maikol, Randall, Warner, and Leidy. Others are nonsensical, such as Email and Pulmitan (a bus company). There is even reportedly one child in Limón who goes round with the name of Usnavi after his parents, with no idea of what it meant, decided they liked the sound of a sign painted on a ship in the bay: 'US Navy.'

COMMON ABBREVIATIONS

Avd   – Avenida (avenue)

Bo   – Barrio (neighborhood)

C   – Calle (street)

Cía   – Companía (company)

CCSS – Caja Costarricense de Seguro Social. The sprawling, obligatory government social security system which covers more than 90% of Ticos for medical expenses and personal pensions.

EEUU – Estados Unidos. The United States of America.

INS   – Instituto Nacional de Seguros. A government-run insurance monopoly.

OEA – Organización de Estados Americanos. Organization of American States which has its headquarters in Costa Rica.

OIJ   – Organismo de Investigación Judicial. Costa Rica's equivalent of the FBI.

ONU – Organización de las Naciones Unidas. United Nations.

PB (in elevators) – Planta Baja (ground floor).

PLN – Partido de Liberación Nacional – the more left-wing of Costa Rica's two main political parties.

PUSC – Partido Unidad Social Cristiana. The PLN's conservative rival.

S.A.   – Sociedad Anónima. Ltd., plc, corporation.

UE   – Unión Europea. European Union.

Chapter Nine

SURVIVAL SKILLS

GETTING THERE

People of most nationalities don't need a visa to enter Costa Rica, but you should check first. With a passport valid for six months, you will generally be granted 30 days' or three months' stay upon arrival. US, Canadian, most western European, Israeli, Japanese, and some other citizens get three months. In any case, if you want to extend your stay, you can easily hop over to Nicaragua or Panama for a couple of days at the end of your time limit and come back in again. It is not worth overstaying your visa and trying to sort it out later. While the immigration police rarely check tourists, I have met people being deported with no chance of returning within 10 years after being caught overstaying their visa by just a couple of weeks.

VISAS AND RESIDENCY

If you want to stay more permanently in the country, the most common types of residency are: retired residents (*pensionados*), earning residents (*rentistas*), investor residents (*inversionistas*), those on company Visas (*representantes*), and permanent residents (*residentes*). All can own companies and receive income in Costa Rica, but pensionados and rentistas may not actually work in the country.

WHERE THE STREETS HAVE NO NAME...

"I crossed the Atlantic, got all the way to Costa Rica, and then found myself up against the utter necessity to buy... a compass," said Greek academic Constantino Lascaris in his definitive work on the Ticos, *El Costarricense.*

Lascaris was not exaggerating. Finding your way around is one of the most bizarre and infuriating experiences you will have in the country, especially if, like me, you have little sense of direction.

The country was, until recently, largely rural. Villages didn't need street signs as everyone knew where everyone else lived. Unfortunately, this means that today, except in city centers, the streets remain largely nameless and numberless.

Instead, all directions are based on landmarks. You will be told, for example to look for 'the pink building 200 meters (219 yards) east and 50 meters (55 yards) north from the south-east corner of the Supreme Court'. Note that 100 meters (110 yards) means a city block, 50 meters half a block, etc. It often bears no relation to the actual distance, and sometimes meters may not be called *metros* at all, but *varas.*

Even worse, directions are often based on something well-known to locals, but which no longer exists—such as the old Coca Cola plant in San José, or a mango tree in Escazú which has been chopped down. One foreigner I met said that in a small village he had been instructed to: "Go 200 meters west from where Juan's cow gave birth last year".

In addition, some people, when going to their house, will say they are going *arriba* (up), or if going to the town center that they are going *abajo* (down). This is because most Tico towns were built in mountain valleys, with the church and official buildings on the valley floor and houses built up the slopes above. In reality, however, *arriba* may be down and *abajo* up.

215

Tico directions may be just about manageable if you can tell your cardinal points from the sun (as Ticos, uncannily, do). But what if you arrive in a town you don't know on a cloudy day, or at night?

Of course Ticos are very helpful, so you can always ask. However, they may well give you the wrong direction if they're not really sure, because it might seem rude or embarrassing to admit they don't know. They're also quite likely to tell you it's *a la vueltica* (just around the corner).

If in doubt, there are some handy tips to follow. If you are in the Valle Central, the closest mountain range is always to your south. If you're looking for something near the plaza, it's good to know that the main doors of all Tico churches point to the west.

In towns, where the central streets are numbered and laid out on a grid plan, the situation is initially quite confusing, being made up of *calles* (streets), which run north-south and *avenidas* (avenues) running east-west. The *calle* and *avenida* which cross closest to the town's central plaza are *calle central* (or 0) and *avenida central* (or 0). From there on, the calles go in odd numbers (1, 3, 5 etc.) to the east of the plaza, and in even numbers (2, 4, 6 etc.) to the west, while the *avenidas* go in odd numbers to the north and even numbers to the south.

Street addresses are given by the avenida or calle and the two closest intersecting avenidas or calles. If you're looking for a building on Calle 13 between Avenidas Central and 2, the address would be written Calle 13, Avenidas Central y 2. In a telephone directory it would be C13, ACtl/2 or C13, A0/2.

Unsurprisingly, although some streets and buildings do have numbers, very few letters in Costa Rica ever get delivered to anyone's door. Nearly everyone has an *apartado postal*, or post office box.

GETTING AROUND
By Car

The Ticos' famed niceness evaporates the second they get behind the wheel of a car. The streets of San José, particularly, are too small for the volume of traffic. The center is a maze of one-way, traffic-clogged

Rains in Costa Rica are torrential, and don't mix well with city center congestion.

streets noisy with (often unprovoked) horn-blowing. As a driver you need your wits about you. As a pedestrian, be warned that traffic lights turn immediately from red to green with no lip service paid to amber. If you're half way across the city center's six-lane Paseo Colón as the lights change, you'll be lucky if the traffic stops to let you get across.

Although you will find large, two or three-laned autopistas on the outskirts of San José, once you're outside the city, conditions change drastically. The Interamericana, the biggest road through the country, is single-lane for nearly all its length. Huge tailbacks of traffic stuck behind crawling *camiones* have been very common ever since the railways to Puntarenas and Limón were closed, as all freight is now transported by truck. Other common causes of hold-ups are landslides, herds of cattle, rainstorms, and thick mist (especially passing over the Cerro de la Muerte at 3,491 meters/11,454 feet).

Costa Rican roads are also notoriously holey. A popular joke runs: "How can you spot a drunk driver?" Answer: "He's the one driving in a straight line." Although to be fair, the pothole (*hueco*) situation has improved a lot in the past few years.

217

The excruciating slowness combined with *machismo* generally leads Ticos to overtake at the slightest opportunity—usually around one of the (very many) blind curves—which in turn leads to one of the world's most horrific accident rates; four times higher than in the United States. Around 700 people died in road accidents in 2000 and 1,500 were injured. In fact, the country's laudable life expectancy has actually fallen by 1/10 of a year for men in the past few years—as a result of the rise in traffic deaths.

Things are not helped by the fact that driving licenses can be bought for US$200. Costa Rica must also be one of the only countries in the world to repeal a previously compulsory seat belt law, after the Sala Cuarta constitutional court ruled that it should be a matter of personal choice.

Speed limits are fairly low, a maximum of 100km/hr (62 miles/hr), but generally around 60km/hr (47 miles/hr). Wherever the limit changes, it is painted on the road surface. People exceed the limits whenever possible and often resort to bribing the traffic police if caught. Fines are around 5,000 colones for going up to 20 km/hr (12 miles/hr) over the limit and 20,000 colones for anything faster.

Off the main routes, many roads, often along the edge of precipices, have yet to be asphalted, and are littered with boulders and potholes. Some are barely passable in the rainy season. For this reason 4x4 jeeps are by far the best option for off the beaten track driving. In many places people use *cuadriciclos* (all-terrain quad bikes) to get around.

You can drive in Costa Rica with a drivers' license from your own country. Gasoline is relatively inexpensive, and is available in either *regular* or *super*. The price difference between the two grades of petrol is very small.

By Rail

Both lines to the Pacific and the 'Jungle Train' to the Caribbean have been closed down since the earthquake of 1991. However, plans are allegedly afoot for foreign consortia to re-open them.

By Plane

Flying is a good alternative to spending hair-raising hours on the road. The two domestic airlines are Sansa (part of Grupo Taca), which flies out of the Juan Santamaría airport in Alajuela, and Travelair, which flies out of the Tobías Bolaños Airport in Pavas, San José. Return flights cost on average from US$100-150. Book well in advance during the high season as planes are small. Baggage weight is also limited to 12 kg per person.

It's also possible to charter small planes from the Tobías Bolaños Airport, which can be surprisingly economical if you are a group of four or five (see *Strategic Directory* for details).

By Bus

Local buses run regularly and have the route (and often the fare) posted on the windscreen. To hail a bus like a Tico, you should stand in the road, arm pointing skywards Saturday Night Fever-style. You nearly always have to pay the full set fare, whether you're going only for one stop or for the full route.

In the cities, buses have electronic *barras contadoras,* which count passengers on and off the bus. One of the only times in Costa Rica you are likely to encounter rudeness, or be shouted at, is if you hang around for too long between the bars as you wait for your change—the counting will be screwed up and the driver will have some explaining to do to his supervisors. Angry Tico bus drivers can be surprisingly scary.

When you want the driver to stop, shout *parada* (stop) or, if you have a loud and distinctive whistle, whistle like a Tico. Many bus drivers will drop you off or pick you up wherever you like. In the countryside, local buses are often old yellow US school buses with tiny seats—although you won't have to share your seat with farmyard animals as in most of the rest of Central America.

Long distance buses between Costa Rican towns run regularly. However, they all set out from different terminals in San José, in a move intended to cut down on congestion. Taxi drivers know where all the terminals are, and many travel agents have maps of the city showing their location.

Most buses do not have toilets or air conditioning, though on long journeys they will stop every few hours for a coffee break.

International buses to Nicaragua and Panama are modern, roomy, and equipped with savage air conditioning, so remember to take plenty of warm clothes. Most nationalities do not need Visas for these Central American countries, although rules do change, so it's worth checking with the embassy before you set off.

By Taxi

Taxis in Costa Rica are all red, and are therefore called *rojos*. The rates are very good (around US$1.50 for a ride within San José). The taxis have a meter which you should make sure the driver switches on at the start of the journey. Taxi rides are also a good opportunity to get to grips with the way Ticos find their way around, as you'll have to give the kind of contorted directions the driver will understand, such as '*de la esquina sureste de la catedral, cincuenta metros al norte.*'

Traveling by pony cart – the taxi cab of Costa Rica's countryside.

By Colectivos

In rural areas colectivos are common. These are small trucks or pick-ups, which operate like either a taxi or bus, and will pick up and drop off people as they go.

By Horse

Many parts of rural Costa Rica are still horse country, where you'll see people riding from the age of about four, often without saddles or shoes. Most horses do not wear bridles with bits, but just a *jáquima* (rope halter). However, the horses are so well-trained and sensitive that the touch of the rope rein on their neck is enough to steer them. If you are used to English-style riding, be aware that you steer one-handed and that the horse moves AWAY from the rope on its neck, so pressure from the right rein on its neck will make the horse turn left. *Monturas* (saddles) when used, are of a semi-Western style. The stirrups are worn long, and often have full leather foot covers designed for barefoot riders.

BUYING A CAR OR BRINGING YOUR CAR TO COSTA RICA

The tax you must pay to bring a car into the country is extraordinarily high—more than 50% of the value of the car, and up to 86% if it is more than five years old. Until a few years ago, the government, in a move to encourage foreign retirees to settle in the country, allowed them to bring a car in tax-free. This allowed people to sell their cars later at a huge profit and live quite comfortably on the earnings. The scheme has now been stopped due to abuse as people were bringing in several cars at a time.

On top of the tax payable, you also have to contend with shipping costs, customs delays etc. It is therefore not advisable to import a car which is not in excellent condition. It's really less of a hassle to buy a car in Costa Rica, although prices are obviously still pretty high (around US$19,000 for a five-year-old 4x4 Mitsubishi Montero, or

US$9,500 for a five-year-old Nissan Sentra). You will therefore see a lot of old, patched-up cars on the road, and many of the newer cars have actually been 'bought' under hire/purchase schemes.

Due to the high value of cars, vehicle theft is rampant, and you should have a car alarm plus another safety device, such as a gear stick lock. Most Ticos keep their car inside a kind of caged garage, or *cochera*. There are protected car parks in the cities, which charge less than a dollar an hour, but there are not enough to meet demand. If you have to park your car on the street, leave it under the watchful eye of a *cuidacarros* or *guachimán* (from the English word watchman), whom you should pay around 200 colones.

Your car will also need to be fitted with a catalytic converter, and get the *marchamo* (obligatory liability insurance—cheaper than in the UK or US) and *ecomarchamo*—a sticker showing that exhaust emissions are within certain limits. In case of breakdown, labor is reasonable but parts may be expensive and hard to find if you drive a car that is not commonly found in the country.

ACCOMMODATION

Costa Rica has a huge proliferation of hotels, but when you first arrive one of the best options is a homestay. Much less impersonal than a hotel, and a good means of immersing yourself in the local culture, this will place you with a well-vetted Costa Rican family. (See *Strategic Directory*).

If you want to make your stay permanent, do note that foreigners are allowed to rent and own houses and property in Costa Rica. Costs vary widely depending on location.

In San José, at one end of the scale, you could rent a room in a student house near the universities in the lively area of San Pedro for around US$80 per month. At the other end, you could rent a luxurious pad with swimming pool and jacuzzi in flashy Escazú (otherwise known as *Gringolandia* for its huge number of expat residents) for around US$5,000 per month. Areas on the east side, such as Barrio Escalante and San Pedro, are cheaper, cooler and a little more rainy (yes, the climate can really change within just a 15 minute drive here) than the west (Sta Ana and Escazú).

The best areas outside San José in the Meseta Central area are Heredia (Sto Domingo and San Isidro) or Moravia. Somewhat further away (around 45 minutes drive) are Atenas, Grecia, and San Ramón. Areas such as Heredia are cheaper than San José and may have a more 'genuine' feel.

Generally, prices to both rent and buy are around half the price you would expect to pay for accommodation of a similar standard in the United States. In the countryside, you can rent a house for around US$200 per month and up, and entire farms are for sale for between US$150,000 and US$250,000. Beachfront locations carry a premium. Condos and other residences on the beach can be bought from around US$125,000 up to several million dollars.

Look for the best bargains via the Residents' Association (see *Strategic Directory*), in local newspapers, or even on supermarket and shop notice boards. Sometimes you will even find free deals in return for house-sitting a foreigner's house for six months while they winter back home. If you're buying, remember to use the services of a recommended lawyer as there are con artists out there.

Another option is to build your own dream house, although this may involve more red tape than you would anticipate. Importantly, if your heart's set on building on the seafront, remember that the first 50 meters of beach from the mean high tide mark is public and cannot be built on. The next 150 meters is concession property, on government leasehold, and cannot be leased by a foreigner unless more than half the leasing company is owned by a Costa Rican.

Also beware of squatters. Landless *invasores* frequently move onto property, and may gain 'rights of possession' if they live there for a year and either construct a dwelling or work the land. You will then be unable to sell it. If you have bought a large piece of property and are absent, it's essential to employ a guard.

HEALTH

Costa Rica has one of the best health systems in Latin America, and an average life expectancy of almost 77 years in 1999.

Many people take advantage of the country's relatively cheap, but highly professional, medical care to combine a holiday with medical procedures (often cosmetic) they could not afford at home. For more information, contact Health Holidays of Costa Rica on 506-240 6645 or visit their website: http://www.health.co.cr

You are extremely unlikely to get ill while in the country, apart from—at worst—a spot of stomach trouble, but you should, of course, have health insurance.

Most communicable diseases are totally under control, and drinking tap water in the towns is safe (although bottled water tastes better). Food is generally very clean too—to the extent that cutlery in *sodas* and restaurants arrives in miniature plastic bags. However, if you have a weak stomach, it may be sensible to avoid ice in drinks, salads, and fruits (apart from bananas and others which can be peeled).

You don't legally need any jabs to enter Costa Rica, though the following are sensible if you're going to spend much time in the region: hepatitis A, typhoid, tetanus, yellow fever, and rabies (if you are planning to work with animals or are likely to be exposed to a lot of bats). Don't forget that vaccinations need several weeks to take effect, so see your doctor at least six weeks before you leave.

There have been some very occasional and limited outbreaks of malaria and dengue fever, usually on the Caribbean coast. Prophylactics are a good idea if you are staying in the depths of an affected area for a long time. However, anti-malarial drugs do no favors to your body, and offer no protection against dengue fever. It is important to take precautions to avoid being bitten by mosquitoes (high deet content insect repellent, long pants and sleeves, and mosquito nets—all particularly at dusk), and seek medical help in the extremely unlikely event that you do become ill—even if it's months after you left the country.

Chagas disease is another potential problem, especially if you're staying in old adobe huts with thatched roofs, where the culprit, the 'kissing bug' likes to live. The beetle bites you and tramples its parasite-ridden excrement into the wound. Over the course of many years the parasites reproduce quietly, leaving you with heart, esophagus and colon failure. The early, acute stage involves low-grade fever and headaches for a couple of months—seek medical help if you have these symptoms.

There are all sorts of other poisonous creepy crawlies to look out for, particularly snakes—but you would have to be extremely unlucky to receive a fatal bite. The golden rule is to wear boots in forests and to be careful where you put your feet and hands. If someone is bitten, try to identify the snake (important for administering the correct anti-venin), immobilize the limb and get help as soon as possible. Do not use tourniquets or slash open the wound—many snake venoms contain anti-coagulants, so the person could bleed to death. Don't try to suck out the venom either—you may end up with two people poisoned instead of one.

Finally, remember that Costa Rica is on the equator, so use high protection sun cream and drink plenty of water.

AIDS

Around 2,000 cases of AIDS (SIDA in Spanish) have been diagnosed in Costa Rica. There could be up to 10 times this many people infected with HIV (VIH in Spanish), although many may not yet know it. Around 60% of cases are among the gay community, and many women sufferers have been infected by gay/bisexual husbands who married to avoid having to come out of the closet.

Problems have also arisen because of Church opposition to the use of condoms (*preservativos*), and the prevalent *machista* attitude that 'real' men don't use them.

Although prostitutes have to have regular health checks and carry a health card, HIV and other conditions may not be picked up by the tests for some time after infection. Many male prostitutes do not have these checks at all.

The country has the best AIDS treatment in Central America, with all the latest medication available to sufferers.

Hospitals and Health Insurance

If you're moving to Costa Rica, you can get health insurance from the Caja Costarricense de Seguro Social (CCSS)—the national socialized medical system. Monthly premiums (very reasonable and almost half price for those over 55) cover all illnesses (including pre-existing conditions) for the member and their immediate family.

An alternative choice is the Instituto Nacional de Seguros (INS), the semi-autonomous government insurance company. There is less cover than with the CCSS, but members can choose their own doctor and make appointments with less red tape. Costa Rican hospitals are generally good, and the doctors excellent. Most doctors (although probably not their receptionists) speak English. However, don't forget this is a developing country so lines can be long.

You can also see doctors in private practice, and there are a number of excellent private hospitals (see Strategic Directory).

Pharmacies

Unlike many Latin countries, Costa Rica does not have *farmacias de turno*, or pharmacies which stay open overnight on a rotating basis. Many pharmacies are open until 9:00 P.M. or even midnight, and the pharmacies at the Clínica Bíblica in downtown San José and Hospital La Cima in Escazú are open 24 hours. Pharmacies are well stocked, and you can buy many things over the counter that you would need a prescription for at home, such as strong antibiotics.

BANKING AND MONEY

If you're using your cash card from home, you won't find as many compatible ATMs as in some other countries. Cirrus and Visa cards can be used in Red Total and Scotia Bank machines.

For changing money, the rate is the same at all banks but black market changers on the street offer a slightly higher rate. It's very hard to change any dollar bill in Costa Rica that has even the smallest imperfection or tear. You can also actually pay with dollars instead of *colones* for almost anything.

If you want to set up a bank account, be aware that there are state and private banks. The state-owned banks are the Banco Nacional, Banco de Costa Rica and Banco Crédito Agrícola de Cartago. Money in these banks is guaranteed, and can also be accessed at branches all over the country. Service, however, can be very slow and limited. Lines can extend outside the building, especially on the second and last Fridays of the month—payday for many Ticos. Loans are also expensive and difficult to arrange, so this is not a practical source of capital for a foreign investor.

Service is faster in the private banks, around 20 of which have been set up since 1996. Privatization came after a 1994 scandal when the country's oldest bank, the Banco Anglo-Costarricense, collapsed with the loss of US$136 million following huge unsecured loans made by its inexperienced directors on the basis of political favoritism. Banco Elca, for example, takes only five to eight days to cash a foreign check, while in Banco Nacional this could take up to a month. However, branches of private banks, and especially ATMs, can be limited outside the Meseta Central.

Most banks offer saving and current accounts in dollars or colones. Interest rates can vary widely between banks, so shop around. It is much higher on colón accounts, but because of the monthly devaluation against the dollar, you won't be earning as much as you think. Most banks require a deposit of around US$500 to set up a current account, and many also require two letters of recommendation. Costa Rica has strong banking secrecy laws.

Inflation and Currency

The colón is devaluing at a creeping rate of about one or two colones per month against the US dollar. In January 1992, there were 138.65 colones to the dollar. By December 2000, there were 318.30.

This is bad news for Ticos as their salaries buy gradually less and less over time and most consumer goods are imported. However, the currency is stable and major shocks and devaluations are unlikely. Inflation is around 11%.

Tax

As a foreign resident, you don't pay any tax on income generated outside Costa Rica, but have to do so on money made within the country— although rates are low. There is no tax for salaries below US$700 per month. Thereafter, it rises from zero up to a maximum of 15% on salaries over US$1,100 per month. If you are self-employed, the rates after all deductions are: 10% from around US$3,000 to US$5,000 up to 25% above US$16,000.

There is no capital gains tax, but corporate income tax rates on income earned within the country start from 10% of net profit on revenue of US$50,000. This rises up to 30% for net profits above US$100,000.

The tax year ends on September 30, and forms must be filed and taxes paid by December 31. Tax evasion, traditionally considered a national sport, is now punishable by a jail term.

TIME

Costa Rican time is six hours behind GMT—the same as Central Time in the US.

BUSINESS HOURS

- Government offices are open from 8:00 A.M. to 4:00 P.M.
- Stores are open from 8:00 A.M. to 6:00 or 7:00 P.M. from Mondays to Saturdays. Do take note that there is often

a lunch break (sometimes of two hours) especially in rural areas.
• Banks are generally open between 8:30 A.M. to 3:30 P.M.

POWER AND BILLS

Costs are generally reasonable. Costa Rica has the cheapest electricity rate in Central America (mostly generated by local hydro- and geothermal plants) and by far the biggest connection to the power grid in the whole of Central America. The voltage used is 110V AC at 60Hz, the same as the USA.

Bills can be paid in banks and supermarkets, but if you don't pay on time, your service will be cut off, usually within two to three weeks. Although you may be able to negotiate a little, once the service is cut off you will have to go to the main San José or regional office to pay a fee to get reconnected.

MAIL

The recently-privatized Costa Rican mail service isn't bad for Latin America, but that doesn't mean it's great. The general lack of street addresses means that most Ticos have a post office box (*apartado*)—but a much faster and more reliable service is Mail Boxes Etc. Using this, mail is sent to you at an address in Florida, and then couriered down to the Mail Boxes Etc San José office. (See Strategic Directory). To send mail, you must go to the post office (*correo*) itself as there are no post boxes.

TELEPHONES

Costa Rica is too small to have a code system. Costs vary with distance, and are measured in pulses. For a call within San José, for example, one pulse lasts 90 seconds. To call Limón, Puntarenas or Guanacaste from the capital, the pulse lasts 15 seconds.

The telephone system is generally good, cheap, and calls are half price overnight and on Sundays, as well as on holidays such as Christmas, Valentine's Day, and Mother's Day.

229

Cell phone service is around US$10 per month plus 10 cents per minute prime time. However, there are insufficient lines, so you can wait a long time to be connected. The British Embassy in San José waited over a year just to get a cell phone.

There are various types of public phones: Chip phones, which take a regular telephone card, and coin phones (put the coin in the slot at the top; it will drop when the phone is answered—do NOT try to push it in!). There are also Viajero 199 cards (the only ones you can use for international calls). To use these, you dial 199 on any phone and punch in the code on the card. With a US$10 card you can call Europe for about 13 minutes (compared to two minutes for the same price in Panama, for example). Colibrí 197 cards are used in the same way for local calls. On the downside, the service is so cheap that you can often wait for hours for a public phone as the person in front of you chats away.

In rural areas too small for payphones, private homes, garages, *pulperías* and bars will often 'rent' their phone.

TELEVISION & RADIO

Companies which offer cable television services include: Cable Color (Tel: 231 3838), Cable Tica (Tel: 254 8858), and Cable America (Tel: 238 1756). These companies offer Latin American Spanish language channels and dozens of US channels including CBS, NBC, ABC, Fox, HBO, CNN, ESPN, TNT, the Discovery Channel, etc. There is an initial sign-up fee of around US$25 and a monthly charge of about the same amount.

The satellite-based DirecTV (Tel: 296 7681, fax: 296 7684, email: galaxia@racsa.co.cr) gives you up to 100 channels including NFL and NBA sports. The basic cost is US$499 and US$23 monthly for the basic package, although some special packages are being introduced to reduce costs. DirecTV systems purchased in the US will not work with the satellite systems in Costa Rica or the rest of Latin America.

Most radio stations play Latin music. Radio Dos 99.5 FM and Radio 107.5 FM offer 100% rock and also have regular programs in English.

INTERNET

Government-run Racsa is effectively the only provider in the country, meaning service is often infuriatingly slow. There are, however, reasonably-priced Internet cafés nearly everywhere. It is useful to know, when wanting to write @ on a Spanish keyboard, that you must usually simultaneously type Alt and Q (or Alt, Ctrl and Q or Alt, Gr and Q) or else Alt and 64 (from the number pad on the right hand side of the keyboard).

GIFTS

If coming from home or abroad, bring something typical or special from your country. Costa Rica is a small country, and Ticos are very interested in the outside world.

If you're living in Costa Rica, bring something that can be treasured and won't get thrown away. Charity worker Milena Badilla

231

said: "An ideal present would be, say, some flowers in a beautiful vase. That way, you can enjoy the flowers, but get to keep the vase. Ticos love to be able to show off and say to friends 'oh, my friend so-and-so from Canada brought me this.' It's something to remember people by."

Unless you know your host fairly well, it is advisable not to give alcohol. The family may be teetotal, or a family member may be an (recovering) alcoholic.

SHOPPING

In many stores, particularly bakeries and pharmacies, you select what you want and tell the assistant, who will give you a ticket. You then take this to the *caja* (cash register) where you pay and your purchase is handed over. When clothes shopping, be aware that Ticos generally work in American sizes.

TIPPING

There is not a big culture of tipping in Costa Rica, and Ticos rarely do it. A service charge of 10% is usually already included in restaurant bills, as well as the 13% sales tax levied on all goods and services. Most menus have two columns—one for the actual price of the dish, and another for the price including tax. If service was really great, tip 5%.

PLUMBING

Don't flush toilet paper down the bowl! Water pressure in Costa Rica is poor, and blockages frequent. A bin is provided in every bathroom for used paper.

Chapter Ten

RESOURCE GUIDE

THE RESIDENTS' ASSOCIATION
This is the one-stop shop for most people moving to Costa Rica. A non-profit organization, it can help you with anything from bringing your car or pet into the country to building your own house, sorting out residency applications, or making friends.

Association of Residents of Costa Rica
Tel: (506) 233 8068 or 221 2053; fax: (506) 233 1152
Email: arcr@casacanada.net
Website: http://www.casacanada.net/arcr

Casa Canadá Avd 4 C 40
PO Box 1191-1007
Centro Colón, San José

KEY TELEPHONE NUMBERS

Emergencies: 911. Includes fire, *Organismo de Investigación Judicial* (OIJ—the Costa Rican equivalent of the FBI), traffic police etc.

International calls through operator	:	116
Directory enquiries	:	113
International directory enquiries	:	124
Speaking clock	:	112
Cruz Roja (Red Cross Ambulance)	:	128
Fire brigade	:	118

EMBASSIES

American	(506) 220 3939
Belgian	(506) 225 6633
Canadian	(506) 296 4149
Dutch	(506) 296 1490
French	(506) 234 4167
German	(506) 232 5533
Israeli	(506) 221 6011
Italian	(506) 234 2326
Nicaraguan	(506) 222 2373
Panamanian	(506) 257 3241
Spanish	(506) 222 2128
Swiss	(506) 221 4829

HOSPITALS

Clínica Bíblica (private)	(506) 257 5252
Clínica Católica (private)	(506) 225 5055
Hospital Calderón Guardia	(506) 257 7922
Hospital Cima (private)	(506) 231 2781
Hospital de la Mujer (women's hospital)	(506) 257 9111
Hospital de Niños (children's hospital)	(506) 222 0122
Hospital México	(506) 232 6122
Hospital San Juan de Dios	(506) 257 6282

MOVING

Recommended by the Residents' Association, ABC Mudanzas offers a complete delivery, storage, insurance, and customs brokerage package. Tel: (506) 286 0075 or 227 2645; fax: (506) 226 8134. Email: movers@sol.racsa.co.cr

NEWSPAPERS ONLINE

Tico Times   http://www.ticotimes.net
La Nación   http://www.nacion.com
La República   http://www.larepublica.com

TELEPHONE AND THE INTERNET

To have a telephone installed or set up a local Internet account, contact the Instituto Costarricense de Electricidad (ICE) on (506) 220 7720 or 225 0123.

ACCOMMODATION

There is a bewildering array of hotels in San José and around the country to meet the requirements of every pocket. Contact the ICT (see below), scan the Internet or look in a web directory such as http://www.costaricapages.com for details. (Be warned that the very cheap hotels around San José's Mercado Central can be really scummy, and this is a pretty dodgy area after dark).

A highly recommended alternative is Bells' Home Hospitality, with many years of experience placing newcomers with hospitable Tico families. Run by Vernon and Marcela Bell. Tel: (506) 225 4752; fax: (506) 224 5884. Email: home-stay@racsa.co.cr

MAIL

Mailboxes Etc. (office in Rohrmoser)
Tel: (506) 232 2950 or 232 2925. Email: mbeetc@racsa.co.cr

CHAMBERS OF COMMERCE/BUSINESS CONTACTS
American Chamber of Commerce (AMCHAM)
Tel: (506) 220 2200; fax: (506) 220 2300
Email: chamber@amcham.co.cr

CINDE (private, non-profit organization for assistance in establishing a business in Costa Rica. Highly recommended).
Tel: (506) 299 2823; fax: (506) 299 2868
Email: aheilbron@cinde.or.cr (Armando Heilbron)

PROCOMER (Government-funded organization to assist companies looking to locate in Costa Rica).
Tel: (506) 256 7111; fax: (506) 233 5755
Email: info@procomer.com
Website: http://www.procomer.com

Cámara de Comercio de Costa Rica
Tel: (506) 221 0005; fax: (506) 233 7091
Email: camaraco@racsa.co.cr
Website: http://www.camara-comercio.com

Costa Rica Stock Exchange (Bolsa Nacional de Valores)
Tel: (506) 222 8011; fax: (506) 255 0531

Office for Simplification of Procedures (Oficina de Simplificación de Trámites)
Tel: (506) 222 0944; fax: (506) 221 8358
Website: http://www.tramites.go.cr

MAPS
Most travel agents and tourist offices give away fairly decent free maps, such as the 1:12,500 Central San José map, the 1:1,000,000 Costa Rica Road Map, and 1:700,000 Costa Rica Tourist Map. If you

need maps before you go, a variety of detailed maps are available from publishers in North America and the UK. Write for details to:

International Travel Map Productions (ITM), 530 West Broadway, Vancouver, British Colombia, V5Z 1E9, Canada.

Treaty Oak, PO Box 50295, Austin, TX 78763-0295, USA.

Website: http://www.treatyoak.com

Stanfords, 12-14 Long Acre, London, WC2E 9LP, UK.

CHILDREN'S EDUCATION

In Costa Rica's private schools (including those with education in English or bilingual education — see following listing), some follow the American school year schedule with vacations in June, July, and August, while others follow the Latin American calendar, with the school year beginning in February and ending in November or December.

Schools which also offer day-care facilities include:

- Lincoln School: pre-kindergarten through grade 12 with classes in English. Tuition about US$350 monthly. Address: Apdo. 1919, San Jose. Tel: 506 235 7733; fax 506 236 1706. Email: rfishel@ns.lincoln.ed.cr.
  Follows the Costa Rican academic year.

- American International School: pre-kindergarten through grade 12. Classes in English, US-style education. Pre-kindergarten: US$1,070 per year, kindergarten to grade 12: US$3,130. Address: Apdo. 4941-1000, San Jose. Tel: 506 293 2567; fax: 506 239 0625; email: aiscr@cra.ed.cr
  Follows the US school year.

- International Christian School has classes from pre-kindergarten through grade 12. Annual tuition: pre-kindergarten US$990; preparatory and kindergarten $1,300. Apdo. 3512-1000, San Jose. Tel: 506 236 7879; fax: 506 235 1518

The following private schools offer bilingual education (cheaper than the above):

Anglo American School. Tel: (506) 225 1723
Canadian International School. Tel: (506) 224 2844
Colegio Internacional. Tel: (506) 253 1231
Escuela Británica. Tel: (506) 220 0131
The European School (Heredia). Tel: (506) 237 6815

LANGUAGE SCHOOLS

There are literally scores of language schools in Costa Rica. These are among the best, many offering homestay, field trips, and cultural activities.

Academia Tica. Tel: (506) 229 0013.
Email: toyopan@intercentro.net
Berlitz. Tel: (506) 204 7555; fax: (506) 207 5089.
Website: www.berlitz.com
Centro Lingüístico Conversa. Tel: (506) 221 7649;
fax: (506) 233 2418. Email: conversa@racsa.co.cr
Centro Cultural Costarricense Norteamericana.
Tel: (506) 225 9433; fax: (506) 224 1480.
Intensa. Tel: (506) 225 5009; fax: (506) 253 4337.
Email: intensa@racsa.co.cr

ENGLISH LANGUAGE BOOKSHOPS

Getting hold of English reading material isn't a problem. Even big Tico bookstores such as Lehmann's in San José (Avd 0, Cs 1 and 3) have a large English section. The posher hotels and some book stores also have foreign language magazines and newspapers. Some of the best English book stores are:

Seventh Street Books (new, used, English, Spanish, novels, travel, nature, etc.) Calle 7 between Avd 1 and 0.
Mora Books (huge selection of second hand books and magazines) Omni Centre, Avd 1, Cs 3 and 5.
Librería Internacional, Multiplaza Mall (near Sta Ana)

VOLUNTEER OPPORTUNITIES

Many people choose to work as volunteers, usually on some kind of conservation project, while in Costa Rica.

To work in one of the national parks, (usually cleaning and heavy work—but with plenty of opportunities for wildlife-spotting) contact the Volunteer Association for Service in Protected Areas (ASVO) on tel/ fax: (506) 233 4989 or Email: asvo89@sol.racsa.co.cr (You must normally be prepared to work at least 30 days).

For other opportunities try:
Instituto Monteverde (various projects in Monteverde cloud forest)
Tel: (506) 645 5053. Email: mviimv@sol.racsa.co.cr
Website: http://www.mvinstitute.org

Pacuare Nature Reserve (turtle protection).
Tel: (506) 233 0451; fax: (506) 221 2820
Email: fdezlaw@sol.racsa.co.cr

Caribbean Conservation Corporation (turtle tagging—July/August)
Tel: (506) 710 0547. Email: ccc@cccturtle.org
Website: http//www.cccturtle.org

Talamanca Dolphin Foundation (dolphin data collection)
Tel: (506) 750 0093; Email: info@dolphinlink.org
Website: www.dolphinlink.org

Genesis II (private high mountain reserve).
Tel: (506) 381 0739. Email: genesis@yellowweb.co.cr

Asociación ANAI (organic farming and sustainable forest management in Talamanca)
Tel: (506) 224 6090/ 3570; fax: (506) 253 7524

TOURISM

The Instituto Costarricense de Turismo (ICT) is excellent and staffed by friendly, English-speaking employees who can give you advice on anything from fiestas and the best surfing spots to hotels and where to track down the resplendent quetzal or Baird's tapir. They also give away free maps, and provide publicity material and great assistance to anyone setting up a tourist facility. The walk-in office in San José is located underground in the Plaza de la Cultura next to the entrance to the Precolombian Gold Museum. Tel: (506) 223 1733/ 257 6057, website: http//www.tourism-costarica.com

CAR RENTALS

Rates range from around US$40 to US$120 per day, with most companies offering weekly discounts.

Avis	(506) 232 9922
Budget	(506) 223 3284
Dollar	(506) 257 1585/ 222 8920/ 223 9642
	Website: http://www.dollarcostarica.com
Economy	Website: http://www.economy.com
Hertz	(506) 221 1818
Prego	(506) 257 1158
Toyota	Website: http://www.toyotarent.com

DOMESTIC AIRLINES

Sansa	(506) 221 9414
Travelair	(506) 220 3054

CHARTER AIRLINES

Tobías Bolaños Airport (for charters)	(506) 232 2820
Aerolíneas Turísticas de América	(506) 232 1125
Viajes Especial Aereos	(506) 232 1010
Helicópteros del Norte	(506) 232 7534

Chapter Eleven

CULTURAL QUIZ

SITUATION ONE (FOR GIRLS ONLY)

During a break at a roadside café during a long bus ride, a friendly
older male passenger holds the door open for you, calling you
mi reina (my queen), and offers to buy you a drink. Do you:

    A   Snort in disgust at his sexism and walk off.

    B   Insist on your buying him a drink instead (after all,
you probably earn four times more than him).

    C   Accept and thank him, but say that next time you meet
(which you both know will probably be never), you will
buy him a drink.

Comments

If you answered A, you're going to end up very irritated, very quickly,
and possibly rather lonely, in Costa Rica. Try to accept the omnipresent

chivalry with a sense of humor—you will get on a lot better, and probably meet a lot of interesting people along the way. B would injure your friend's pride and embarrass him in front of anyone watching—a Costa Rican *caballero* NEVER lets a lady buy him a drink, and definitely not a first drink. C is ideal. Everyone is happy and now you can sit back for a chat.

SITUATION TWO

You're in a small town and need to catch a bus back to San José. Your taxi to the bus stop has to stop to allow a large herd of cows to pass on the road, and you arrive 20 minutes after the bus has left. Do you:

A   Sit down with a coffee and wait, fuming with frustration, for the five hours until the next bus leaves.

B   Hire a taxi to drive you the 150 miles back to San José.

C   Think laterally. Hail a passing taxi or pick-up and ask the driver to chase down the bus.

Comments

A is a possibility if you have time on your hands and a good novel to read, or something else to do in a one-horse town. B is another option if your budget stretches to it, but if you answered C, you're thinking like a Tico. The driver will go like a bat out of hell to run down that bus in record time. When you overtake it, horn honking, both you and the driver should lean out of the windows waving furiously until the bus stops to let you aboard.

SITUATION THREE

You meet a Tico at a party, hit it off right away and swap phone numbers. You call your new friend shortly afterwards to ask him to dinner a few days in advance. He gladly accepts—but on the night in question never turns up. Next time you bump into him, he offers no apology or explanation. Do you:

A   Feel insulted and resolve to reduce your circle of friends to those who take social engagements seriously.

B   Decide, next time, to only ask him out on the spur of the moment when there's no chance for forgetfulness or mind-changing.

C   Invite him to dinner again in a week's time.

Comments

If you answered A, there's no point taking it to heart or feeling paranoid—Ticos are just notoriously *incumplidos*. To you, simply forgetting about an arrangement, or turning up two hours late may seem tantamount to rudeness, but if you confine yourself to friends who share your attitudes about time, you will probably find yourself with a rather small social circle. Answer C will probably see you being stood up again. B is probably the best answer. Call up one evening and ask what your friend is doing. If he's going out, he'll probably invite you along. If he has no plans, suggest meeting up.

SITUATION FOUR

It's a rainy afternoon and you go into a clothes store to have a leisurely look around. You're hardly over the threshold when a sales assistant pounces on you asking if you're looking for anything in particular. You say no, but she proceeds to follow you around the store at a distance of approximately six inches. Do you:

A   Feel horribly intimidated, tense and leave the store in a hurry.

B   Round on her and ask if she suspects you of shoplifting.

C   Tell her your size and ask what she has that might look good with your coloring. Oh, and are there any discounted clothes?

Comments

A will mean you're going to miss out on some great deals in Tico stores. While it is easy to feel 'oppressed' by the constant shadowing of shop assistants, in Costa Rica this is considered customer attention.

B will shame and baffle the poor girl, who is simply attending to you as she has been taught. Never react in anger in Costa Rica—and especially not in public. C is the best solution—simply take a leaf out of Tico shoppers' books and bask in the attention. Sit out the rainstorm trying on a whole selection of clothes you might never have thought of, and you may well come away with a whole new outfit.

SITUATION FIVE

You're taking a crowded bus home after a long day at work when a browbeaten man stands up and starts telling a heart-breaking story about losing his job and having six children to feed. Can any of the passengers please help, he asks. Do you:

- **A** Shake your head as he approaches you. You've already given to three of these beggars today.
- **B** Tell him he's just a lazy opportunist. A survey on the TV last night showed that beggars in San José can make US$30 a day—much more than a blue collar worker.
- **C** Meekly give him a few *colones*. You don't really believe his story, but then again, you can't be sure. Plus you don't want to look stingy in front of your fellow passengers.

Comments

There's nothing wrong with A, but if you were a Tico you would probably find it hard not to fork out a few coins for the *pobrecito* (poor little thing). B will not earn you the round of approving nods it might get in New York or London. Fellow passengers will be deeply unimpressed by your uncultured behavior towards someone who has fallen on hard times. If you want to blend seamlessly into your environment, C is the right answer. Many Ticos grumble privately about the number of beggars on their streets, but in reality most people give. Ticos are generous, good-hearted people —who are also driven by Catholic guilt and a fear of looking bad in public.

SITUATION SIX

You are setting up a new business in Costa Rica. After a few weeks, nothing seems to have got done. Calls to potential clients are going unanswered, people turn up for meetings on 'Tico time', and visits to government offices involve interminable queues and confusing bureaucracy. Do you:

    A   Try to hurry up potential clients by telling a white lie—you are only in the country for two days before flying off for an important meeting in the United States, you say.

    B   Ask around and employ a trustworthy *gavilán* to take care of the confusing document-processing in government offices.

    C   Discreetly offer a bribe, or *mordida*, to the relevant officials in the hope of speeding up the slowly grinding wheels of bureaucracy.

Comments

A is a good answer. People are much more likely to call back promptly if you make it seem that you are an important type who has to jet around to international meetings. B is also good—*gavilanes* know all the ins and outs of the local system. Combined with A, this will help to free up a lot of time. C is definitely illegal. While many people do still pay *mordidas*, and many underpaid civil servants accept them, if you're caught out you could end up being deported.

SITUATION SEVEN

You've only had a Tico acquaintance for a short while when he starts to call you *gordito* (fatty). You've always been rather self-conscious about your size. Do you:

    A   Feel terribly offended. He seemed to be really nice, so why would he say such a hurtful thing?

    B   Laugh it off and start calling him *flaquito* (skinny).

    C   Tell him in no uncertain terms that he is an ignorant, size-ist pig and never see him again.

Comments

There is no point in being offended. Ticos use all kinds of nicknames based on a person's physical weak or strong points, but with no hint of malice. In fact, they are usually a strong form of affection. It's best to develop a thick skin and go for answer B. If you really and truly can't do this, there's no point suffering in silence (A) or offending his Tico sensitivities by getting angry with him, thus risking wrecking the friendship (C). Maybe it's better to ask him to call you by a special pet name which, you say, you only allow close friends to use.

SITUATION EIGHT

An employee is very sweet, but regularly late for work and doesn't seem to get much done while she is there. You often catch her putting on make-up or chatting to friends on the telephone. Do you:

A   Grin and bear it. She's really popular with the rest of the staff and could turn them all against you if you say anything.

B   Wait until she has made you so angry that you storm up to her in the middle of the office, shouting that she is taking advantage of your good nature and that you will have to sack her if she doesn't pull her socks up.

C   Take her aside and explain how much you value her strong points. The organization is going through a bit of a difficult patch at the moment, and you need her to help you get the whole team pulling together. She would be doing you a real favor if she could get in on time and put 100% effort into the job.

Comments

A will drive you crazy, and you do not want to be metaphorically held hostage by your staff. Offending a Tico in public, B, especially if you are commenting on his or her intellect, is the biggest social faux pas you could possibly make. If you sack her or she walks out, remember that Costa Rica's labor laws are also often loaded in favor of the employee and you might find yourself facing litigation. Your actions will probably also lose you the respect of the rest of your staff. C is most likely to achieve results. You are not offending the employee's honor, and are also trying to resolve a problem Tico-style through peaceable consensus.

SITUATION NINE

You have had a Tico friend for some time when it dawns on you that you have told him or her all of your most intimate secrets, problems and family issues. However, your friend has not revealed any comparable information about him or herself except in the most oblique terms. In fact, you're not even sure where he or she lives! Do you:

A   Think nothing of it. Your friend is witty, interesting and great fun to be around, and you realize that it can take some Ticos a long time to wear their hearts on their sleeves about personal stuff.

B   Stop seeing your friend so often. To you, opening up emotionally lies at the core of friendship.

C   Start probing your friend to open up more, telling him or her it is unhealthy to keep things bottled up.

Comments

A is the best solution. You come from a culture where people may immediately be very open. However, in Costa Rica one must often nurture friendships for some time until a person feels completely confident that he or she can really trust you to be discreet and supportive. It would be a shame to give up on what could become a very solid relationship (B), and C could make your friend feel embarrassed and awkward, possibly driving him or her away.

FURTHER READING

Many old books and theses about local culture are out of print and only available in libraries, which are always worth a visit. However, remember that in Tico libraries (except some university libraries) you cannot just browse among the shelves—you must look for what you want in the card files, fill out a form and give it to the librarian, who will find the publication. You cannot take books out of the library.

GENERAL

Amcham's Guide to Investing and Doing Business in Costa Rica. (AMCHAM, PO Box 4946, San José) Detailed run-down of the country's business and investment climate.

Beatrice Blake and Anne Becher. *The New Key to Costa Rica.* (Ulysses Press, USA, 2000, 15th edition) Great guide to the country, particularly for the eco-minded, with a 'sustainability rating' for resorts and businesses supporting the country's environmental, economic, and cultural balance.

Bill Blaker. *The Essential Road Guide for Costa Rica.* (International Marketing Partners, Inc., USA 1995)

Guy Brooks. *Costa Rica: A Kick-Start Guide for Business Travelers.* (Self Counsel Press, Canada, 1996)

Christopher Howard. *The New Golden Door to Retirement and Living in Costa Rica.* (Editora de Turismo Nacional, S.A., Costa Rica, 2000-2001) Chockful of contacts and tips, especially on visas, house-buying, investing, and setting up businesses both on and off-shore.

Judith Nobel and Jaime Lacasa. *The Hispanic Way: Aspects of Behaviour, Attitudes and Customs in the Spanish-Speaking World.* (Passport Books, Chicago, USA, 1991) Not specific to Costa Rica, but an excellent overview of how to understand and acclimatize to the idiosyncrasies of the Latin world in general.

Roger Peterson. *The Legal Guide to Costa Rica*. (Centro Legal, S.A., Costa Rica, 2002, 3rd edition) Available through http:www.costaricabooks.com

Raymond and Audrey Pritchard. *Driving the Pan-American Highway to Mexico and Central America* (Costa Rica Books, 1997) Crucial guide if you're planning on driving from the United States to Costa Rica. Also available through http:www.costaricabooks.com

LITERATURE

(For a list of Costa Rica's top authors to check out, see end of Culture section in Social Indicators chapter).

Jézer González Picado (ed.). *Antología del Relato Costarricense*. (Editorial de la Universidad de Costa Rica, San José, Costa Rica, 2000) Good selection of short stories by most of the country's top authors.

Enrique Jaramillo Levi (ed.). *When New Flowers Bloomed: Short Stories by Women Writers from Costa Rica and Panama*. (Latin American Literary Review Press, Pittsburgh, USA, 1991) Includes works by Rima de Vallbona, Carmen Naranjo, Carmen Lyra, Yolanda Oreamuno, and Emilia Macaya.

Tatiana Lobo *Negros y Blancos, Todos Mezclados* (Editorial de la Universidad de Costa Rica, San José, 1997) Chilean writer, long-time Costa Rican resident, focuses on Afro-Caribbean themes.

Barbara Ras. *Costa Rica: A Traveller's Literary Companion*. (Consortium Book Sales, St Paul, Minnesota, USA, 1994) Ideal introduction to Costa Rican literature.

Anacristina Rossi. *La Loca de Gandoca*. (San José EDUCA, Costa Rica, 2001) A thinly-veiled fictitious account of real events involving corruption, intrigue and illegal resort-building in the Manzanillo-Gandoca Reserve.

Yanina Rovinski. *En la Isla: Diario de un Viaje*. (Editorial Universidad Estatal a Distancia, Costa Rica) An account of a month's stay on the remote Isla del Coco, inspiration for Robert Louis Stevenson's *Treasure Island*.

Paul Theroux. *The Old Patagonian Express: By Train through the Americas.* (Houghton Mifflin, USA. Penguin, UK, reissue edition 1997) Includes some amusing descriptions of Costa Rica (circa 1979) by the relentlessly grumbly travel writer.

Thomas Youngholm. *In the Shadow of the Sphere: A Journey of Heart and Spirit* (Creative Imagination Concepts, San Diego, USA, 1999) Echoes of *The Celestine Prophecy* in this spiritual adventure book.

ANTHROPOLOGY

Mavis Hiltunen Biesanz, Richard Biesanz, and Karen Zubris Biesanz. *The Ticos: Culture and Social Change in Costa Rica.* (Lynne Rienner, Boulder, Colorado, USA, 1998) Easy to find, and very readable anthropological text. The authors have been almost half a century in the country, although many Ticos accuse them of seeing everything through rose-tinted spectacles.

May Brenes Marín and Mayra Zapparoli Zecca. *De que vuelan, vuelan!: Un análisis de la magia y la brujería en Costa ica.* (Editorial Costa Rica, San José. Out of print) Interesting account of the witchcraft and superstition that still persist beneath the country's modern skin.

Roberto Cabrera. *Santa Cruz Guanacaste: Una aproximación a la historia y la cultura popular* (Ediciones Guayacán, San José, 1989) Anthropological text on the customs of Guanacaste.

Tjabel Daling. *In Focus Costa Rica: A Guide to the People, Politics and Culture.* (Interlink, USA. Latin America Bureau, UK, 2001, 2nd edition) The most up-to-date book on the subject, well researched and illustrated.

Quince Duncan and Carlos Meléndez. *El Negro en Costa Rica.* (Editorial Costa Rica, 1989, 9th edition) Very interesting historical and current account of the situation and customs of black people in Costa Rica.

Marc Edelman and Joanne Kenen (eds.). *The Costa Rica Reader.* (Grove Atlantic, USA, 1989) Essays by Costa Rican historians and sociologists.

Martha Honey. *Hostile Acts—US Policy in Costa Rica.* (University of Florida Press, 1994) Minutely-detailed discussion of the US' policy of 'dual diplomacy' in Costa Rica during the 1980s as the Nicaraguan civil war raged to the north.

Constantino Lascaris. *El Costarricense* (Educa, San José, 1994) Though written many moons ago, it is humorous and still holds water. The book that Ticos say best describes them.

Ilse Abshagen Leitinger. *The Costa Rican Woman's Movement: A Reader.* (Pitt Latin American Series, University of Pittsburgh, USA, 1997) German feminist asks 41 women about their lives and changing conditions.

Paula Palmer. *What Happen?: A Folk History of Costa Rica's Talamanca Coast.* (Publications in English, San José, Costa Rica, 1993) Memories of older members of the Caribbean coast's black community.

Paula Palmer, Juanita Sánchez and Gloria Mayorga. *Taking Care of Sibö's Gifts.* (Editorama, San José, Costa Rica, 1993) Discussion of beliefs and practices of Bribri Indians in the KeköLdi indigenous reserve, and their often unhappy relationship with Tico neighbors.

Lara Ríos. *Mo.* (Farben, San José, 1993, 3rd edition) Description of the life and customs of Cabécar Indians told through the story of a young girl.

Rigoberto Stewart. *Limón Real* (Inlap, Alajuela, 1999) Controversial black academic's call for economic and political autonomy for Limón province.

Ivar Zapp and George Erikson. *Atlantis in America: Navigators of the Ancient World.* (Adventures Unlimited Press, Kempton, Illinois, USA, 1998) Esoteric theories about Costa Rica's mysterious stone spheres being used as a kind of sea chart for pre-historic navigators.

Elias Zeledón Cartín. *Leyendas Ticas de la Tierra, los Animales, las Cosas, la Religión y la Magia.* (Editorial Costa Rica, 2000) Selection of Tico legends still used to frighten children, such as *La Cegua* (a beautiful woman seduces unsuspecting men and then at the last minute develops the head of a horse), *La Carreta sin Bueyes* (the cart without oxen) and *La Llorona* (the weeping madwoman, who drowned her child in a river.)

NATURE AND SPORT

Mario A. Boza. *Costa Rica's National Parks.* (Editorial Heliconia, San José. Out of print) Great introduction to the national parks.

Philip J. De Vries. *The Butterflies of Costa Rica and their Natural History.* (Princeton University Press, USA, 1997) Beautifully illustrated, but quite scientific.

Daniel H. Janzen. *Costa Rican Natural History.* (University of Chicago Press, USA, 1983) Everything you could need to know about the country's species, natural history, and archaeology.

John Kricher. *A Neotropical Companion.* (Princeton University Press, USA, 1997) Must-read introduction to the American tropics and its ecosystems, plants, animals, and conservation.

Michael W. Mayfield and Raphael E. Gallow. *The Rivers of Costa Rica: A Canoeing, Kayaking and Rafting Guide.* (Menasha Ridge Press, USA, 1998)

Mike Parise. *The Surfer's Guide to Costa Rica.* (Surf Press Publishing, 1999) The definitive guide to the country's top surf spots, with details of more than 70 breaks on both coasts.

Donald Perry. *Life Above the Jungle Floor.* (Simon and Schuster, USA, 1998 reprint) Biologist Perry's story of designing and setting up his extraordinary Rainforest Aerial Tram in the Braulio Carrillo National Park.

F. Gary Stiles and Alexander F. Skutch. *A Guide to the Birds of Costa Rica.* (Cornell University Press, USA. Black Press, UK, 1990) Definitive bird guide.

DO'S AND DON'TS
APPENDIX

DO'S

- Learn to love eating black beans and rice three times a day.
- Expect lots of very up-front interest from the opposite sex if you're single and available (and even if not).
- Think twice about what people mean—Ticos may often not say what they actually mean in order to *quedar bien*, and avoid causing offence or embarrassing people.
- Shout *Upe!* when arriving at someone's house rather than knocking on the door.
- Expect people to be more conservative in both attitudes and dress than in many other Latino countries.
- Sound like a Tico by saying *pura vida* at every opportunity, and *con mucho gusto* every time that someone thanks you for something.
- Read up everything you can in the newspapers about what's going on in the country. This will impress Ticos no end. They love their country and will immediately draw you into conversation.
- Really make an effort to learn Spanish. Even though most Ticos can speak English, they will greatly appreciate your efforts, and you will have a much fuller experience of the country.
- Ask questions with specific answers. "Where is the *soda*?" is much better than "Is the *soda* around the corner?" If Ticos can answer a question with 'yes' or 'no' they may well do so even if they have no idea, simply to avoid looking silly.

- If you're male, you can expect to be gently teased for being insufficiently *macho*.
- Keep an open mind about traditional remedies and magic. You're bound to encounter at least one of these at some stage and a huge amount of Ticos swear by them.
- Remember that life doesn't begin and end in San José. To really know the country, you must also get to know its 'forgotten' people—the black population of the Caribbean coast and the indigenous peoples.
- Expect to hear *mi amor* (my love), *mi vida* (my life), *mi corazón* (my heart), and *te quiero* or *te amo* (I love you) a lot. Don't get freaked out—people use these terms a lot more glibly than they might where you are from.
- Expect to sit in huge lines in government offices, banks, and hospitals.
- Buy your fruit and vegetables at the local weekend *feria* rather than in the supermarket—much more fun!
- Resolve any conflict through consensus rather than confrontation.
- Drive carefully after weekend football matches—Tico driving gets even worse at this time, with plenty of drunks on the roads.
- Try out all of Costa Rica's amazing range of bizarre and delicious fruits, cakes, sweets, and home-made drinks.
- Err on the side of formality when meeting people, unless told otherwise. Use 'usted' rather than 'vos', and with older people use 'Señor', 'Señora', 'don', or 'doña'.
- Learn some 'Tiquismos' so you can pepper your language with local color and have a better understanding of your Tico friends and their humor.
- Get to know your cardinal points or even buy a compass so you can easily follow Tico directions.
- Learn to relax—things in Costa Rica can take ages, and raging against 'Tico Time' is pointless—you'll just end up with high blood pressure.

In business

- Be charming and make friends with everyone. The country is very small and everyone knows everyone else. A bad reputation travels fast and is not easily forgotten.
- Do plenty of market research before starting up any business in Costa Rica. The Tico consumer can be fickle, and a seemingly sure-fire bet may not be such a safe choice as you thought.
- Instead of wasting huge amounts of time and slowly going mad with frustration, pay a *gavilán* to sit in those interminable lines and wade through the seemingly infinite wreaths of red tape.
- Be on the lookout for con men, be aware of the differences between the legal systems of Costa Rica and your own country, and get a good lawyer.

DON'TS

- Expect Costa Rica to be as 'First World' as it may appear to be on the surface.
- Grumble about the state of the country, even if Ticos do so themselves. They're a very proud and nationalistic people, and may take offence.
- Refuse a shot of *guaro* or other hospitality from strangers. Such behavior might seem dubious at home, but it's natural in Costa Rica. Ticos are naturally warm and friendly and may be publicly embarrassed by your refusal.
- Get upset if your Tico friends rarely, if ever, invite you to their houses. Ticos are intensely private people at times, and the home is a sacred family haven.
- Eat turtle egg *bocas*—these are nearly always illegal, and are helping to drive the country's endangered sea turtles to extinction. The same goes for coral and turtle shell jewelry for sale on beaches, pinned exotic butterflies, and any other trinkets or foods made from endangered species.

- Shout at people or employees, no matter how frustrated you are, and especially not in public. Ticos take offence easily, and this will cause you more trouble than what the momentary relief was worth.
- Block a fan's view at a football match—social suicide in terms of soccer etiquette.
- Confuse Costa Rica and San José with Puerto Rico and San Juan —the mark of the most ignorant and unwelcome kind of tourist.
- Be flashy and ostentatious—Ticos hate such behavior, and much prefer people who are *humilde* (humble).
- Poke fun at people worse off than you. The concepts of class and snobbery are very understated in egalitarian Costa Rica— people are charitable towards the poor or those fallen on tough times, often calling them *pobrecitos* (poor little things).
- Expect to have the kind of 'modern' relationship you might have at home. Men in Costa Rica always pick up the tab, while women generally turn a blind eye to their mates' socially-acceptable infidelity.
- Miss out on a soccer game. Following a particular team is a defining feature of many Ticos' lives, regardless of sex.
- Get angry when men whisper *piropos* or hiss at you in the street—just ignore it, or try to see it as a compliment.
- Expect much of a social life in the countryside. Relaxing with an *Imperial* in a broken rocking chair at the local *pulpería* may be the sum total of a Saturday night's excitement.
- Wear shorts in the city. Away from the coast, such informality, as well as general scruffiness, is definitely looked down upon by the well-groomed Costa Rican fashion police. Forget innovation and wear what those around you are wearing if you want to blend in.
- Talk about Costa Rica on the same footing as the rest of Central America. Ticos still see themselves as important players on the world stage and won't thank you for lumping them together with their neighbors—especially Nicaraguans.

- Be surprised if Ticos think you strange for reading anything more taxing than beauty magazines. They may be the most literate people in the region, but they're much more interested in soap operas than the written word.
- Give alcohol as a gift when visiting a Tico's home. A family member may be a recovering alcoholic, or the family may be teetotal. Instead give a durable and unique gift, which can be enjoyed and shown-off indefinitely.
- Overstay your visa. You could be deported, and the Tico immigration police don't seem to share the famed friendliness of the general public.
- Expect any Tico to retain any of their niceties once behind the wheel of a car. A Costa Rican road is one of the most dangerous places you could find yourself this side of a war zone.

In business

- Pay bribes. It may or may not work out—but could easily end with your being deported.
- Use an overly-aggressive sales pitch. This will really turn potential Tico buyers off.
- Expect to get straight down to business. Personal contact is very important in Costa Rica—expect a fair amount of good-natured banter and chit-chat before the serious business begins.

GLOSSARY

These are some of the non-English words used in this book. Please refer to Chapter 8 on Languages for a list of basic Spanish phrases, local slang, and a pronounciation guide.

agua	water
amarillo	yellow
atún	tuna
baldazo	downpour
banano	banana
blanco	white
cabaneros	cowboys
cacique	chief
camarón	shrimp
campesinos	peasants
caseríos	hamlets
cédula	identity card
chapulines	grasshoppers
chorizos	literally sausages, meaning kickbacks/bribes
ciudadanos de oro	golden citizens
comehuevos	literally egg eaters—the Costa Rican equivalent of American 'white trash
corrientes	rip tides
corvina	sea bass
culto	cultured
curtido	pickled vegetables and chilies
fresa	strawberry
fútbol	football
gotera	hangover
guanábana	soursop

hidalgos	noblemen
humilde	humble
incumplidos	unreliable
langosta	lobster
leche	milk
limpiabotas	shoe shiners
mal de ojo	evil eye
marimba	a giant xylophone with gourd resonators
mestizos	people of mixed blood
mora	blackberry
mota	marijuana
muy calientes	very passionate
nuestros indígenas	indigenous people
pañas	Spaniards
pargo	snapper
pelo de gato	literally 'cat's fur', used to describe a drizzle
perico	cocaine
piña	pineapple
piratas	illegal taxi cabs
playos	homosexuals
plebeyos	commoners
pobrecito	poor little thing
pollo	chicken
pulperías	small stores
pulpo	octopus
salsa rosa	Thousand Island dressing
sandía	watermelon
sodas	cafés
telenovelas	soap operas
temporal	heavy rain falling without let-up over several days during the rainy season
tugurio	shanty town
vinear	to gossip

THE AUTHOR

 Claire Wallerstein's journalism career began nine years ago in London. A runner-up in the 1996 British Telecom Journalist of the Year Award, she later escaped the British climate to work as a freelance foreign correspondent for *The Guardian* and the BBC. Claire loves languages (she speaks English, Spanish, German, and French) and has also worked as a translator. She has lived in Germany, the Philippines, and Venezuela and traveled widely through Europe, East Africa, and Southeast Asia. During two years spent criss-crossing Latin America, she visited Angel Falls, Machu Picchu, and the Panama Canal—but left feeling more impressed by her experiences in tiny Costa Rica. She spent several months living among the Ticos to research this book, doing everything from participating in archaeological expeditions and crossing crocodile-infested rivers to spending time in indigenous communities and hanging out with the country's top surfers.

INDEX

A

accommodation 55, 222–23
agriculture 40–41, 47, 175, 191
AIDS 95, 225, 226
Alajuela 21, 23, 43, 62, 117,
    129, 155, 219
alcohol 75, 154, 161, 168,
    170–171, 185, 232
alcoholism 75, 169
army 26, 27, 31, 50, 90, 92,
    108, 112
artists 47, 142, 143, 144

B

bananas 27, 42, 46, 163, 164, 224
banks 31, 36, 92, 166, 187, 227,
    229
beaches 45–46, 49–50, 51, 55,
    58, 103, 123, 156
Bombas 84
books 70, 91–92, 94, 135,
    148–149
bribery 186–187
Bribris 73, 76, 78
Brunjkas 76
bullfights 80, 82, 129, 132, 170
buses 219–20
business 37, 135, 148, 171,
    174–79, 182–91, 206, 212,
    228

C

Calvo, Mínor 89, 93, 111
car 90, 111, 131, 189, 216,
    221–22
Cartago 20–21, 23, 43–44, 90, 94,
    112, 129, 131, 137, 154, 204,
    227
Catholics 133–35
cattle ranching 42, 50, 62
Central America 26, 32, 34, 39,
    50, 80, 87, 89, 95, 108,
    110–11, 125, 142, 150, 169,
    173, 189, 191, 211, 219, 226,
    229
cheese 47–48, 88, 160–61
children 22, 29, 66, 69–71, 75, 81,
    83, 89, 98–99, 103, 107–10,
    115, 123, 128, 132, 142,
    146–47, 154, 167, 170, 177,
    181, 204
Chorotegas 17, 20, 78, 83, 84
churches 21, 74, 94, 107, 216
civil war 23, 28, 30–32, 37,
    69–70, 79, 92
climate 24, 27, 39–40, 43, 47, 58,
    87, 144, 211, 223
coffee 24–28, 30–32, 39, 41–42,
    44, 66, 75, 86, 91, 94, 116,
    123, 126–27, 142–43, 146,
    152, 158–59, 165–68, 174,
    181, 183, 210, 220
coffee elite 25, 28, 31

Columbus, Christopher 16, 18
corruption 21, 34, 35, 60–61, 165,
    186–87
crime 86, 138–41, 150, 189
culture 26, 35, 37, 64, 67, 75,
    77–80, 87, 91, 93, 99, 104,
    107, 109, 111, 122, 129, 141,
    143, 147, 152, 184, 205, 222,
    232

D
dancing 68, 129–30, 170
Diquis Delta 17–19, 72
divorce 98, 109, 212
doctor 70, 113–14, 116, 138, 199,
    224, 226
dress sense 123
Drake, Francis 20

E
eco-tourism 56, 60, 62, 63, 78
education 28, 31, 36, 61, 74, 89,
    109–10, 140, 146–49, 173,
    186, 193
election 33–34
electricity 36–37, 63, 177, 229
English 28, 67–68, 70, 85, 88–89,
    150, 173, 177, 185, 190,
    192–94, 196–97, 203, 205–8,
    211, 221–22, 226, 231
environment 40, 53, 56, 60, 61, 80
environmentalists 37, 48, 177
Escazú 88, 136, 215, 222–23, 226

F
farmers 17, 29, 68, 88, 170, 204
Fernández, Juan Mora 26

festivals 70, 82
fiestas 81, 127–28
Figueres, José 30, 91, 95
fishing 28, 50, 58, 63, 68
flirting 104, 167
food 70, 74, 157–59, 161, 165,
    171, 176
free trade zones 191

G
gay 90, 110–11, 151, 225
González, Gil 18
gold 16–18, 20, 26, 43, 47, 50, 60,
    89, 123, 135, 142, 207
Golfito 20, 46, 55
Guaitil 46, 78, 83
Guanacaste 23, 26, 39, 42, 43, 45,
    49, 66, 79, 80–82, 129–31,
    159–60, 168–69, 182, 195,
    229
Guanacastecos 78–79
Guardia, Rafael Angel Calderón 29
Guardia, Tomás 27
Guatemala 20–21, 23, 32, 134,
    141
Guaymíes 73, 77

H
health 29–30, 61, 69, 73, 86, 114,
    135, 172, 224–26
Heredia 21, 23, 43–44, 65, 80,
    154–155
Honduras 20, 27, 32, 152, 154
hospital 94, 137, 172, 199, 226
hotel 80, 222
Huetares 74, 77

I

income tax 28, 191, 228
indigenous 16, 19–22, 52, 55,
    63–64, 67, 72–79, 83, 87, 92,
    113, 117, 125, 129, 134,
    136–37, 147, 164
Internet 37, 107, 175, 231

J

Jamaica 27, 68–69, 71, 92, 165

K

Keith, Minor 27

L

Le Lacheur, William 24
Limón 66, 69, 71–72, 92, 165
literacy 31, 73, 146, 148
lottery 120–21, 134, 136

M

machismo 81, 106–7, 109, 111,
    218
mail 229
Malekus 76, 78
marriage 74, 78, 107, 212
Meseta Central 19, 39, 43, 44, 60,
    65–67, 70, 74, 79, 155, 160,
    167, 171, 195, 223, 227
Mexico 17, 19, 21, 23, 80, 86–87,
    94, 96, 141, 143
Monge, Luis Alberto 34
Mora, Juan Rafael 26
Mora, Manuel 29
music 70, 82, 84, 87, 91, 119, 124,
    131–132, 231

N

Náhuatl 79
national park 40, 45, 47, 51, 53,
    60, 62–63, 80
newspapers 96, 109, 148, 153, 223
Ngabës 76, 77
Nicaragua 20, 21, 23, 26, 31–32,
    39, 56, 58, 63, 68, 73, 78–80,
    85–86, 89, 95, 141, 152, 158,
    195, 203–4, 214, 220
nicknames 117, 118
Nicoya 18, 45, 78, 94, 132
Nobel Peace Prize 33, 95

P

Panama 18, 55, 67, 68, 73, 77,
    131, 139, 146, 152, 211, 214,
    220, 230
pobrecito 114, 115, 180
police 34, 86, 89, 110, 111, 125,
    138, 140–41, 154, 191, 209,
    214, 218
politics 33, 144, 173
pollution 51, 61
population 16–17, 19–21, 23, 29,
    39, 41, 43–44, 48, 50, 56,
    63–68, 72–73, 75, 85, 87,
    119, 129, 141, 150, 169,
    173–74, 186
poverty 21, 29, 41, 62–63, 67, 69,
    85, 146
pulpería 76, 94, 118, 119, 168
Puntarenas 24, 25, 43, 45, 47, 103,
    130, 217, 229

R

radio 30, 90, 93, 112, 120, 123,
    151, 231

263

railway 27–28, 64, 68, 76, 142
Romero, Sor María 94, 138

S
San José 21, 23, 26, 34, 38–39,
    43–45, 47–48, 51, 60–62,
    64–66, 68, 70, 73–74, 88, 90,
    94–95, 100, 102–4, 107–8,
    111, 114, 120, 123–24, 126,
    128–29, 132, 136, 140–41,
    143–44, 149, 154–55,
    158–59, 175, 179, 185,
    204, 206, 215–17, 219–20,
    222–23, 226, 229
Sánchez, Oscar Arias 32, 95
Santamaría, Juan 26, 95, 117, 129,
    182, 219
schools 66, 73, 74, 110, 112, 147,
    193
Sibö 17, 75, 76
slaves 16, 18, 20, 22, 26, 67,
    70–71, 79, 145
soccer 125, 151–54
Spain 18–20, 23, 72, 79, 143, 161,
    193, 203, 207
Spaniards 17, 19, 22, 69, 132
Spanish 16–18, 20, 22, 25, 62,
    65–67, 70, 73–74, 77, 79,
    83, 88–89, 92, 103, 106,
    108, 112, 113, 115, 118,
    137, 148, 151, 159, 165,
    185, 190, 192–97, 203–4,
    210–12, 225, 231
stock exchange 191
swimming 49, 123, 222

T
tax 24, 28, 37, 60, 61, 87, 142,
    179, 186, 191, 221, 228, 232
taxi 111, 149, 207, 220, 221
telephones 229
television 100, 112, 119, 122, 141,
    144, 150, 154, 231
Teribes 77
Theroux, Paul 34, 44
Tico time 103
Tinoco, Frederico 29, 30
tipping 232
tourism 46–48, 56, 60, 62, 80,
    108, 111, 174–75, 185, 191
translation 84, 190
transportation 16
turtles 49, 54, 57–58

U
Ulate, Otilio 30–31
unemployment 72, 80, 85
United States 26, 30, 32–35, 40,
    52, 63, 67, 85–87, 95–96,
    98–99, 109, 111, 117, 122,
    124, 126, 139–140, 145, 164,
    181, 184–85, 187–88, 210,
    212–14, 218–19, 222–23,
    228, 231

V
Vesco, Robert 87, 95, 188
visas 177, 214, 220
volcanoes 38, 50, 53, 171

W
Walker, William 26, 30, 50, 90, 95
World Cup 153–54